RICHARD HOGGART: CULTURE AND CRITIQUE

Edited by
Michael Bailey and Mary Eagleton

CCCP

Critical, Cultural and Communications Press
London
2011

Richard Hoggart: Culture and Critique
edited by Michael Bailey and Mary Eagleton

The rights of Michael Bailey and Mary Eagleton to be identified as editors of this work have been asserted by them in accordance with the Copyright, Designs and Patents Act, 1988.

First published in Great Britain by Critical, Cultural and Communications Press, 2011.

Repinted 2017. Reprinted with corrections, 2023.

Cover photograph courtesy of the University of Sheffield Library. Reproduced by permission.

Cover design by Andrew Dawson.

CONTENTS

ACKNOWLEDGEMENTS

Parts of Nick Stevenson's paper are reprinted from an earlier article, 'European Democratic Socialism, Multiculturalism and the "third way"', *Cultural Studies* 23 (1), 2009, pp. 48-69, by kind permission of the Taylor and Francis Group.

In memory of Michael Green (1942-2010)

PREFACE
Stuart Hall

This is a thought-provoking, inquiring collection of new essays, which opens up a rich matrix of themes, many not hitherto explored. It is another welcome sign of a long-overdue revival of interest and scholarship in Richard Hoggart's work. The scholarship boy experience, working-class culture, media studies, literature and value, the 'Angry Young Man' syndrome, the Pilkington Report and its commercial advertising critics, Democratic Education, The Beatles, autobiography, the Scottish Folk Song Revival, even the 'Baroque' — these themes, analysed in a wide variety of different places and kinds of writing, touch so many sensitive points in the cultural debates of the post-war world that his seminal contribution cannot be in doubt.

Amidst such variety in the play of mind he brought to the critical task, *The Uses of Literacy* remains a foundational text — in part because it has been so influential, is still so widely read and referenced and had such a profound impact on personal lives; perhaps also because, finally, the precise meaning of its title remains tantalisingly ambiguous. It evokes the rich working-class culture of his childhood. It brilliantly deploys the skills of 'close reading' — of life rather than just of texts - and imaginative reconstruction to conjure up the complex meanings, the dense moral texture, of a whole way of life and of seeing the world, which, because it is not always 'articulate' in the traditional sense, has been patronised or ignored by many academics.

This world was changing before our eyes, and the question behind his inventory was, how, in what direction and with what consequences. Was post-war affluence and mass culture, with America now as their paradigm instance, 'unbending the springs of action'? This was a political as well as a hugely-significant cultural question, though Hoggart did not address it in political terms. He was determined to return a measured answer to the questions about change. But the tone sharpens unmistakably in the later sections of the book.

It was his method and its underpinning values, not the content of the answer, which left its impact. And this is what this exploration of his work in cultural criticism brings sharply into focus. The critical movement known as Cultural Studies was only one of the many influences which flowed from it. I was privileged to work with him in that enterprise and, though we had very different formations, treasure his moral seriousness, his warm friendship and unfailing kindness.

London, May 2011

FOREWORD
Peter Bailey

I first read Richard Hoggart's *The Uses of Literacy* on a train journey leaving Oxford in 1961 shortly after taking final exams. This had been a disturbing experience. Confronted with the paper on Modern English history I had at first failed to recognise a single question that fell within my forecast of likely topics. After further anxious scrutiny I did however find one that spoke to my slender repertoire. It read: '"The opposition to the Henrician reformation was exiguous." Discuss.' Well, I knew about the Henrician reformation alright, having been to his school, King Henry VIII Grammar School in Coventry, and I knew something of the opposition, the Pilgrimage of Grace, mounted by disgruntled northerners, as you might expect. But I didn't know what 'exiguous' meant. So, I bunged down everything I knew about the Henrician reformation, then everything I knew about the opposition, and moved to a conclusion. 'Was the opposition to the Henrician reformation exiguous?' I asked. Answer: 'The evidence clearly speaks for itself!'

Reading Hoggart's semi-autobiographical *The Uses of Literacy* on the trials and tribulations of the scholarship boy and the anxieties of cultural displacement provided some post-exam comfort. The world he described rang true and appealing. And it offered an invitation to examine one's own world and its particular 'culture', an intriguing word in such a new context (though pretty soon there seemed to be a lot of it about). I've returned to Hoggart's work many times in teaching and writing social and cultural history. Though I've found him inspirational in many ways, my first exposure to *The Uses of Literacy* occasioned considerable personal angst. Together with E. P. Thompson and Raymond Williams, Hoggart licensed the academic study of popular culture to which I was an eager recruit. At the same time he laid claim to a model of life experience and practice as a prerequisite for such work, measured against which I was to be found woefully, glaringly in default … a class traitor, a quisling, a cultural *collaborateur*.

Hoggart wrote of his childhood and adolescence in the 1920s and 1930s as a struggle against the odds. Orphaned at eight, he overcame poverty, an early speech defect, shortness of height, failing the equivalent of the 11 plus and a nervous breakdown to win himself a proper education, his working-class origins a source of strength as well as deprivation. He championed the warmth and integrity of working-class culture, an invaluable historic resource to be defended against the toxic seductions of a new mass culture. Though he warned against sentimentality, his picture of 'the full rich life' of a working-class neighbourhood community with its 'certain gripping wholeness' was compelling, not least in its gritty but nurturing location in the backstreets of Leeds, a great city in the industrial North, itself awarded heroic status by its native son (Hoggart 1957: 59, 110-137).

Though I came from a working-class family I was a stranger to the Sturm und Drang of struggle and adversity. I lived in Coventry, a boom town of the 1950s so they said, but a suburban boom town rather than a frontier boom town, peopled with immigrant workers on high wages, a city of inward looking strangers savouring their own relative good fortune. Nothing heroic here, no 'gripping wholeness' or distinct cultural identity in what Hoggart came to characterise as 'the mild Midlands' (Hoggart 1992: 27-46). A beneficiary of the 1944 Education Act I was safely installed on the social escalator of the new state system, the local grammar school — King Henry VIII — a more open and supportive vehicle than that of Hoggart's day. Here I was being fed a diet of elite or genteel culture. Patrician exponents of the real thing would come down from Oxford to encourage us, opening with the inevitable Latin tag: 'You'll remember it was Virgil who said "Timeo Danaos et dona ferentes"...' Our teachers would nod in self-congratulatory acknowledgment. I was uncertain of the wisdom but impressed by the style: snobbery by allusion as the way up.

Unlike the solitary scholarship boy that was Hoggart, scholarship boys like myself were now in a majority. There were none of the severely traumatic discrepancies between the worlds of home and school recorded in several accounts of the period. In any case I was less disturbed by any difference in codes because of a no doubt despicable readiness to assimilate the manners of my elders and betters as necessary competence rather than defensive colouring. In this I gave a passable enough impersonation to secure the approval of the headmaster, who began his letter of reference for my application to Oxford: 'Bailey is a gentleman', thereby conferring both an accolade and a curse that have proved difficult either to live up to or to live down (Bailey, 1999: 22-40).

More cultural schizophrenia lay ahead at Oxford. Intimidated yet seduced by its general *savoir faire* I pursued the authentic self in two opposite directions at once. On the one hand I strove for ever more plausible imitations of the true *bourgeois gentilhomme*, sporting my cavalry twills, learning to tie a bow tie and correcting my muddy and unglamorous midlands accent. On the other hand I essayed a faux populism, a prolier than thou approach, rather like George Orwell in the BBC canteen noisily slurping his tea out of the saucer in what he thought was typical working-class behaviour. With other victims of privileged alienation I flaunted a similar form of inverted snobbery that failed to impress the opposition.

10

'What a dull life,' observed a Wykhamist, 'drinking beer, throwing darts and saying fuck'. Political revenge for the agony of bipolar identity was exacted in symbolic fashion — a yobbish campaign to disestablish the college beagle pack, throwing up on an old Etonian — in Gramscian terms a war of position rather than a war of movement. Perplexed rather than angry and guilty for not having been truly oppressed, I assumed an heroic class alias in history, a safely distanced role reinforced by geography as I left England for Canada, the Coventry of the Commonwealth, less the organic intellectual than the petty bourgeois place seeker. At the University of Manitoba in Winnipeg, another flat midlands city, I salved my class conscience by teaching a no doubt highly tendentious course on the history of the common people with extensive borrowings from Hoggart.

I continued to learn from Hoggart and the new field of cultural studies. Culture was ordinary, we were told, pulsing away under our noses in the most banal and everyday forms, right down to beer mats and bus tickets. I now conceived of culture as some vast amniotic fluid in which we all swam, except somebody had pissed in the pool. According to Hoggart, such contamination came from the agents and artefacts of a new mass culture, full of what he deplored as a 'corrupt brightness', peddling among other suspect wares 'sex in shiny packets' (Hoggart 1957: 202, 277). The trouble was I rather liked 'sex in shiny packets'; it was the illicit clandestine soft porn I'd read by flashlight under the bedclothes as a teenager in the repressed fifties. But then Hoggart allowed that he tended to the puritanical, confessing in the first volume of his autobiography 'playfulness still eludes me' (Hoggart, 1988: 177). After all he was a child of Primitive Methodism. Nonetheless he had some interesting things to say about the popular song of the traditional working class, an element in the 'full rich life' he celebrated. So I could sense him looking benevolently over my shoulder as I worked on deconstructing the Victorian music hall, albeit with the help of theoretical models promoted by his successors at the Birmingham Centre for Contemporary Cultural Studies complete with their earnest injunction 'Keep It Complex!' (Bailey, 1998).

'Know thyself' is an ancient Delphic injunction with which most of us would concur, while adding the hasty rider 'but keep it to thyself'. Though not the only one to do so Hoggart encouraged what we have come to know as reflexivity in the scholar enquirer, putting oneself and one's identity on the literary sociological couch, and I thank him for that. Thus I learned that not all selves or cultures are a given, as in Hoggart's account. They may have to be constructed, invented, performed, and that's no bad thing. How else would I have realised that although a petty bourgeois poseur I was an *authentic* petty bourgeois poseur, as fruitfully hooked on the kaleidoscope of language as he was.

And even if he didn't practice it himself, Hoggart left room for playfulness in others. You'll remember it was Virgil who said, 'Timeo Danaos et dona ferentes ... I fear the Greeks when they bring doughnuts'. Exiguously speaking, that is.

Bibliography

Bailey, P. (1998) *Popular Culture and Performance in the Victorian City* (Cambridge: Cambridge University Press).

——— (1999) 'Jazz at the Spirella: Coming of Age in 1950s Coventry'. In B. Conekin, F. Mort and C. Waters (eds.), *Moments of Modernity: Reconstructing Britain 1945-1964* (London: Rivers Oram), pp. 22-40.

Hoggart, R. (1957) *The Uses of Literacy: Aspects of Working-Class Life* (London: Chatto and Windus).

——— (1988) *A Local Habitation: Life and Times 1918-1940* (London: Chatto and Windus).

——— (1992) *An Imagined Life: Life and Times 1959-1991* (London: Chatto and Windus).

INTRODUCTION:
THE LIFE AND TIMES OF RICHARD HOGGART
Michael Bailey and Mary Eagleton

Since the publication of *The Uses of Literacy* in 1957, Richard Hoggart has been one of Britain's foremost public intellectuals and cultural commentators. Though a literary critic by training, his work has repeatedly challenged entrenched disciplinary and social boundaries, addressing a wide range of subjects including literature, popular culture and the development of public policy. His reputation for being both a critical and practical intellectual is evident in the way that he worked tirelessly within and without the world of academe for much of his career, working as an extra-mural lecturer at the University of Hull (1946-1959), Senior Lecturer in English at the University of Leicester (1959-1962), Professor of English and founding Director for the Centre for Contemporary Cultural Studies at the University of Birmingham (1962-1973), Assistant Director-General of UNESCO (1971-1975) and Warden of Goldsmiths College, University of London (1976-1984). He has also been a key member of numerous other public bodies and committees, including the Albemarle Committee on Youth Services (1958-1960), the Pilkington Committee on Broadcasting (1960-1962), the Arts Council of Great Britain (1976-1981), the Royal Shakespeare Theatre (1962-1988), the Advisory Council for Adult and Continuing Education (1977-1983) and the Broadcasting Research Unit (1981-1991). During this time he has published over thirty books and contributed to numerous policy documents, the sum of which represents an extensive and entirely consistent engagement with normative questions and public discourses that continue to inform contemporary debates about, among other things, culture, literacy, educated citizenship and social democracy.

A local habitation: 'no place like home'

Born in Leeds in 1918, Herbert Richard Hoggart was orphaned at the age of eight and subsequently raised as an only child by five adult relatives — his grandmother, two aunts, an uncle and an older cousin — in a terraced back-to-back in Hunslet. Once a thriving working-class neighbourhood located just south of the city-centre, the local habitation of Hunslet was to profoundly influence Hoggart's later interest in working-class life, not least working people's cultural habits, social rituals and changing attitudes. Hoggart's working-class childhood was also to shape his enduring attachment to cultural ideals and social practices with an emphasis on communal values, particularly working-class neighbourliness. Like many working-class people who grew up in the urban North of England during the inter-war period, Hoggart's childhood was characterised by economic hardship and 'having to make do', an austere way of life that often depended on unofficial acts of charity, goodwill and fellowship. As Hoggart himself has noted more than once in his writings, 'you had to stick together'. To not help one's neighbours in times of need could result in additional suffering and public humiliation, a misfortune that could all too easily become one's own family, as Hoggart knew only too well from his own childhood legacy. Hence Hoggart's oft cited admiration for the friendly societies tradition, a nineteenth-century, working-class institution built upon common need, public trust, mutual honesty and social responsibility, in short, an individual and collective willingness to 'improve each other's lot' (Hoggart 1957: 82).

Hoggart's boyhood experience also explains his liking for 'the sense of family attachment'. Nearly every human being is born into a family, has ancestors, parents, brothers and sisters, kindred, and, will quite probably, in later life, form new familial relationships — to wife or husband, to children, even grandchildren. This multifariousness of familial relations was especially pertinent for Hoggart, whose family history was complex as a result of Hoggart and his two siblings being orphaned at an early age, and having to live with different relatives. In spite of the emotional upheaval and the isolation from his older brother and younger sister, Hoggart distinctly remembers the relief he felt when it was decided that he and his siblings would be cared for by the extended family rather than being sent to an orphanage: 'We were "family" and we stayed family' (Hoggart 2001: 223). Not surprisingly, this sense of 'belonging to somebody' resonates strongly in Hoggart's writings. Time again, we hear him eulogising the family as a place in which we learn to love others, and not just to love ourselves. A family 'can give us unique access to our own emotions, can constantly open the heart; if we will let it' (Hoggart 1999: 178). In other words, like neighbourliness, family life teaches us to be empathetic; in so doing, it broadens and enriches our social being and interpersonal connectedness.

This said, Hoggart is also aware of the conservativism that often underpins neighbourliness and family life, not least the preference for daily routine and orderliness, both of which provide a kind of security in an otherwise complex and uncertain world, a bulwark against outside threats. Consequently, neighbourliness can sometimes manifest itself as a deep-rooted suspicion of anything or anyone that deviates from the ordinary and everyday; like club memberships, there are rules and regulations to observe, some of which are unspoken and can be used to deliberately exclude new-comers. In extreme cases, neighbourliness can take the form of malice, best seen in the use of unkind gossip — often exaggerated and unfounded — aimed at causing trouble for the unsuspecting target (see, for example, Hoggart 2003: 75-83).

In spite of these reservations, many of which are borne out of a genuine self-reflexivity, Hoggart has been repeatedly accused of idealising working-class life and sentimental patronage; for being too emotionally involved and nostalgic in his reminiscences. More crucially, Hoggart's descriptions of family and neighbourhood have been criticised precisely because they tend to focus on the domestic sphere and neglect the political. For some critics, though incredibly rich in their attention to ethnographic detail, Hoggart's writings render working-class people as apolitical: for example, working-class women as domestic angels and frivolous; or working-class men as downtrodden and defeatist. Hoggart's counterattack — and it is an entirely credible one — has been to argue that such criticisms 'overrate the place of political activity in working-class life, that they do not always have an adequate sense of the grass-roots of that life' (Hoggart 1957: 16). This was certainly the case when Hoggart was writing in the 1950s, a time when much academic literature, even literature that sought to explain the socio-historical dimensions to working-class life, had little to say about the everyday lived experiences of working-class people in their local habitations.

Between two worlds: 'anxious' and 'uprooted'

If 'hearth and home' was instrumental in shaping Hoggart's deep-rooted sense of *communis*, the world of 'education and learning' was to prove equally important in terms of his future commitment to critical discrimination in matters social and cultural. In spite of failing the eleven plus examination, he was fortunate to be educated at the local grammar school, thanks to a Headmaster who thought Hoggart had 'talent' and insisted the LEA admit him to Cockburn High. Financial assistance from the local Board of Guardians provided him with the opportunity to continue studying for his Higher School Certificate, a prerequisite qualification for entrance into university. Further financial assistance in the form of a LEA scholarship enabled him to take up a place in the English Department at Leeds University, where he was taught by Bonamy Dobrée.[1]

It was under the tutelage of Dobrée that Hoggart developed and finessed his literary and analytical skills. Dobrée also exposed Hoggart to different forms of social conduct and manners, ones that were mostly alien to a person from a working-class background. Indeed, the combination of cultural improvement and changing social *habitus* was to fill Hoggart with a deep ambivalence and uncertainty. On the one hand, education — meant

---

[1] For a fuller account of Dobrée and the influence he had upon Hoggart, see Hoggart (1970a: 189-204).

here in the broadest possible sense — provided him with unimagined opportunities for learning and upward social mobility. On the other hand, education exacerbated his class self-consciousness, not least his self-confessed obsession with his own cultural proficiency compared to that of his peers, many of whom were solidly middle-class.

The experience of being betwixt and between two social classes, the consequent 'sense of loss' and 'self-doubt', and the earnest pursuit of 'sweetness and light', was to cause Hoggart to feel extremely 'anxious' and 'uprooted'. And though this sense of 'unease' and 'dissatisfaction' was present throughout Hoggart's childhood — a result of being 'marked out' among his peers from an early age — it was accentuated as he became progressively detached from the vitality of his working-class past. Not unlike one of Matthew Arnold's 'aliens', he was no longer one of 'us', but nor did he feel himself to be one of 'them', something he was to reflect upon when writing about his childhood experience of being a 'scholarship boy':

> Almost every working-class boy [*sic*] who goes through the process of further education by scholarships finds himself chafing against his environment during adolescence. He is at the friction-point of two cultures ... As childhood gives way to adolescence and that to manhood this kind of boy tends to be progressively cut off from the ordinary life of his group ... He has left his class, at least in spirit, by being in certain ways unusual; and he is still unusual in another class, too tense and over-wound ... He is sad and also solitary; he finds it difficult to establish contact even with others in his condition. (Hoggart 1957: 292-303)

It was quite probably because of this deep-rooted sense of alienation that resulted in Hoggart transcending some of the more rarefied ideas, customs and habits of the class to which he nominally belonged as a child, and the professional class he was to later join as an adult; he chose, instead, Arnold's example — to be led 'by a general humane spirit, by the love of human perfection', to perfect one's 'best self' not only for oneself, but also for the greater good. It also explains Hoggart's refusal to follow a one-size-fits-all Marxist doctrinaire, in spite of his obvious socialist leanings. That is to say, though driven by a profound sense of belonging to and a responsibility for others, Hoggart was nevertheless suspicious of communitarianism, which he always thought 'levelling' and 'centralising'. Hence his insistence that 'We should feel members one of another, but also retain all we have of sparky, spikey individuality' (Hoggart 1990: 78).

The common pursuit: 'culture is ordinary'

After completing his undergraduate studies — and a rushed MA thesis on Jonathan Swift — Hoggart embarked on five years active service in wartime North Africa and Italy. Towards the end of the war, Hoggart became involved in adult education, which also served as an opportunity to rekindle his three main intellectual interests: politics, documentary and literature. His initial exposure to the world of adult learning was through the Army Education Corps and the Army Bureau of Current Affairs. It was here that Hoggart first witnessed the liberating experience of uneducated adults giving meaning to their lives in and through the pursuit of knowledge (see Hoggart 1990: 48-147). Like many of his contemporaries who had a strong moral sense of social purpose bordering upon the puritanical (e.g. Raymond Williams, E. P. Thompson, Roy Shaw, S. G. Raybould, Asa Briggs, to name but a few), the 'Great Tradition' was as much 'a calling' as it was a career. This was especially so in the late-1940s when non-vocational education for adult learners, especially returning servicemen, was widely promoted as an essential part of the post-war reconstruction effort to foster an 'educated democracy', a political rationality that was already evident in The Beveridge Report (1942), Butler's Education Act (1944), and the concomitant growth in university extra-mural departments up and down the county, including the University College of Hull, where Hoggart worked as an extra-mural lecturer for much of the 1950s.

Not surprisingly, much of Hoggart's writing during this period was for adult education journals, such as *Adult Education, The Tutor's Bulletin* and *The Highway*. Many of the articles were simply about 'aims', 'first principles' and 'methods of teaching' (Hoggart, 1990: 126). However, literature — in particular poetry — remained his 'main love' (Hoggart, 1988: 195). Apart from the writings of William Shakespeare, William Blake, Matthew Arnold, Thomas Hardy, Henry James, Herbert Spencer, George Orwell, Ezra Pound, D. H. Lawrence, Graham Greene, J. B. Priestley and such like, Hoggart was greatly influenced by a handful of living poets, among them T. S. Eliot, Dylan Thomas, Cecil Day Lewis, Stephen Spender and Louis MacNeice. Foremost amongst these was W. H. Auden, whose work Hoggart had first come across in the 1930s. And, in spite of Auden's waning reputation by the late-1940s, his poetry continued to captivate Hoggart, so much so that he started to write a critical study, which soon became a book manuscript that was eventually published by Chatto and Windus in 1951.

As well as it being his first full-length book, what was most striking about *Auden: An Introductory Essay* was that it was the first full-length study of the poet's work. It was also the beginning of Hoggart's career as a public intellectual. Following a handful of good reviews within literary-type journals and the popular press, Hoggart started to receive invitations to contribute to edited publications and to speak at conferences. He was even asked to broadcast a programme about Auden for the BBC. Moreover, Hoggart had made a formal contribution to that long and noble tradition that F. R. Leavis once referred to as the 'common pursuit of true judgement', which is to say, literary criticism. In so doing, he now belonged to that 'small minority' so valued and entrusted by the cultural elite.

In spite of the accolades and widely acclaimed success of his first serious venture into literary criticism, Hoggart's approach to his subject was to change radically over the next few years. Partly as a result of his own intellectual restlessness and isolation from mainstream academe, but also because of his experience of teaching adult learners who readily challenged received wisdoms and pedagogic conventions, Hoggart began to rethink the importance of literature — or literacy, to be more precise — particularly in relation to the rapidly changing milieu of popular culture — or what he was to famously call 'the newer mass art' — in what is undoubtedly his most celebrated and important publication, *The Uses of Literacy*.

Originally entitled *The Abuses of Literacy*, the book started out as a series of related essays and lectures about changes in working-class culture, especially in relation to mass publications (e.g. newspapers, magazines, sex and violence paperbacks, etc). Unlike many of his academic colleagues who dismissed all forms of popular literature and art as vulgar and corrupting, Hoggart argued that it was important for literary critics and educationalists to base their judgements about the likely effects of such cultural forms on a more detailed understanding about 'what people might make of that material' (Hoggart 1990: 135). Even those colleagues whom Hoggart admired and had written extensively on popular art — the Leavises for example — failed to understand the changing relationship between literature and society because of their elitist judgements and a misplaced nostalgia for an 'organic' pre-industrial culture.

On the other hand, Hoggart was genuinely concerned that, though the overall quality of working-class life had advanced over the course of the early-twentieth century (e.g. better living and working conditions, better health provision, greater educational opportunities, and so on), there had occurred a simultaneous and paradoxical decline in traditional working-class attitudes and social practices; in short, not an improvement but a worsening of a certain 'way of life'. Hoggart much preferred what he famously referred to as an urban culture 'of the people', as opposed to the 'culturally classless society' that he describes from the 1940s onwards. Notwithstanding these concerns, Hoggart refrained from lamenting the complete decline or disappearance of an older 'working class'. He always maintained that working-class people 'still possess some of the older and inner resistances'.

> My argument is not that there was ... an urban culture still very much "of the people" and that now there is only a mass urban culture. It is rather that the appeals made by the mass publicists are for a great number of reasons made more insistently, effectively, and in a more comprehensive and centralised form today than they were earlier; that we are moving towards the creation of a mass culture; that the remnants of what was at least in parts an urban culture "of the people" are being destroyed; and that the new mass culture is in some easy less healthy than the often crude culture it is replacing. (Hoggart 1957: 24)

In other words, whilst Hoggart believed that 'the methods of literary criticism and analysis' ought to be made 'relevant to the better understanding of all levels of writing and much else in popular culture, and of the way people responded to them', he also upheld the Arnoldian belief that people ought to have access to the 'best' (Hoggart 1990: 129-30). Thus *Uses* was not the clarion call for cultural populism — much less relativism — that some of his critics would have us believe. Nor was it a nostalgic retreat to a golden age. Rather, it was part of an emerging educational argument that popular cultural forms could be understood both as a lived experience and as literary texts that could be analysed and evaluated using literary critical skills, an argument that finally came to fruition with the eventual formation and subsequent development of cultural studies as an academic discipline.

Indeed, after a brief spell at Leicester University, Hoggart was offered a chair at the University of Birmingham. It was here that he established the Centre for Contemporary Cultural Studies (CCCS) in 1964, a postgraduate interdisciplinary research centre that sought to synthesise literary studies with sociological ideas and analytical methods. Though Hoggart's personal instinct was to teach students a literary approach to understanding popular cultural texts — written and visual — the Centre soon established a reputation as a hotbed for critical theory, a volatile synthesis of Marxism, feminism, structuralism, and other politically motivated methods of analysis. The work of Stuart Hall was exemplary in this respect, and though he and Hoggart's different approaches to popular culture complemented one another, Hall's influence on the Centre was to take it in a very different direction to that originally envisaged by Hoggart, who, by the 1970s had in any case become increasingly occupied with cultural policy, administration and matters of public importance. Hence, Hoggart's eventual departure from the Centre and the resignation of his Birmingham chair in 1970 to enable him to concentrate more fully on the post of

Assistant Director General of UNESCO, an appointment that was to remove Hoggart from the world of academe for five years.

Educationalist-cum-public intellectual: speaking truth to power

In between publishing *Uses*, the setting up CCCS and his eventual departure, Hoggart was engaged in various public duties. One of the earliest examples of his meteoric rise to fame as a public intellectual was the *Lady Chatterley's Lover* trial in 1960, during which Hoggart appeared on several occasions as an expert witness for the defence, the publisher, Penguin Books. When asked if he thought the book 'vicious', Hoggart replied by famously declaring the book — and its author D. H. Lawrence — as 'virtuous', 'if not puritanical' (Hoggart 1992: 52-9; see also, Hoggart 2001: 85-100). Flummoxed by this paradoxical description, the prosecution soon collapsed and Hoggart was widely celebrated as the person that had turned the case around in favour of the defence, resulting in admiration and critical acclaim from literary figures. Furthermore, it was his first of many run-ins with that body of people — the clergy, social do-gooders, columnists, moralists — he was to call the 'Guardians' (see Hoggart 1970b: 201-4).

Though Hoggart's appearance in the trial had made him a hero among the liberal intelligentsia, the defining moment in his career was arguably the part he played in debating and influencing the recommendations of the Pilkington Committee. This was set up in 1960 under the chairmanship of British industrialist, Sir Harry Pilkington in order to consider the future of broadcasting in light of the introduction of independent television in 1956. The report was to recommend 'whether additional [televisual] services should be provided', and to 'propose what financial and other conditions should apply to the conduct of ... these services' (Hoggart 1992: 59-72; 1970b: 182-96). Not surprisingly, it severely criticised Independent Television for being too commercial and trivial in its programming; and it was largely because of this that the BBC was awarded a second channel.

More crucially, whilst the report was unanimous in its recommendation, it was widely felt that Hoggart had exercised an undue influence during the course of the committee, prompting the press to dub the report the 'Hoggart Report'. Indeed, in an essay written shortly after the report was published, and writing in his autobiography some forty years later, Hoggart noted that the committee 'were engaged to the best of our ability in a study in social philosophy. We were asking about the nature of good broadcasting in a democracy. We could not enforce our judgements scientifically; we could only say at the end, in Leavis' formulation: This is so, is it not?' (Hoggart 1992: 62). Furthermore, in spite of Pilkington's best efforts to assure the public that the report's findings were based 'on facts', the report was rounded upon by the national popular press, which thought the report 'nannying … elitist … patronising … grundyish … do-gooding … superior … schoolmarmish' (Hoggart 1992: 60-61). The one sentence that all critics seized upon without fail was the statement that reminded broadcasters that they were 'in a constant and sensitive relationship with the moral condition of society', which many took to epitomise the moralising tone of the report. However, Hoggart defended this particular clause on the grounds that it was intended to give broadcasters a 'responsibility difficult to define but not easy to shrug off'. It was also a reference to the not unreasonable claim that, again quoting Hoggart, 'the quality of the life of a society as expressed in its texture — its assumptions and values as bodied out in its habits and ways of life … will be reflected and to some extent affected by broadcasting as by other forms of mass communication'. What Hoggart and others were not saying was that 'broadcasters had a responsibility for the direct propagation of the Ten Commandments', or 'that broadcasting has a duty to promote ethical precepts'. Instead, Pilkington was 'an argument about freedom and responsibility in a democracy' (Hoggart 1970b: 193-95). This is an argument that Hoggart has pursued ever since, not least whilst chair of the independent, plurally funded Broadcasting Research Unit (later renamed the Broadcasting Research Institute) throughout the 1980s, by which point Hoggart was a minority voice in his efforts to ensure that democratic broadcasting remained at the forefront of public and academic debate.

'Taking stock: and soldiering on'
Though officially retired from academic and public life for some twenty-odd years now — his final place of employment was as Warden of Goldsmiths College which he left in 1984 — Hoggart continues to write and publish books from his home in Farnham, Surrey. During this time he has written several books, including a three-volume autobiography (collectively entitled *Life and Times*), which has been widely celebrated as an incredibly rich social history of English working-class life in the twentieth century. In it, he takes stock of the Arts and the English temperament as expressed in its culture (literature in particular), indeed, the ideas and aspirations of a whole generation — a good many now dead — that witnessed unprecedented politico-economic turmoil and socio-cultural change. Read in this way, the three volumes have established Hoggart's reputation as both an autobiographer and social chronicler *par excellence*.

His other recent publications can be read more broadly as a critical commentary on the condition of England generally. Though increasingly preoccupied with the uncertainties of old age and thoughts of death, Hoggart continues to write on the social importance of the need for maintaining cultural standards both as an *a posteriori* principle and as a bulwark against creeping commercialism and the decline in authority. And though his general argument may seem a little dated, sometimes patronising, and occasionally contemptuous, his criticisms against, *inter alia* 'dumbing down', 'levelling', 'relativism' and 'popularism', represent an increasingly important engagement with the idea of public culture as a primary facilitator of democracy; this is particularly evident in light of the current political climate where the governmental usage of financial markets and private corporations would seem to be the preferred technique for regulating socio-cultural relations, processes and institutional practices.

Such convictions are premised upon Hoggart's firmly-held belief in well-meaning paternalism, critical judgement, progress and social democracy. The alternative is a world dominated by private and superficial interests, completely lacking in any communal values whatsoever. Hence his clarion call that we should 'never join the big battalions', but 'try to think for ourselves', and 'try to act like free citizens, not subjects or dupes' (Hoggart 2004: 81). Anything less would be a betrayal of all the democratic gains that have been hard fought for and won over the past two hundred years or so.

The uses of Richard Hoggart

This collection covers the range of Hoggart's writings: for instance Bill Hughes on *The Way We Live Now* (1996) and the two volumes of essays, *Speaking to Each Other* (1970); Yudishthir Raj Iser on *An Idea and Its Servants: UNESCO from Within* (1978); Macdonald Daly on *Mass Media in a Mass Market: Myth and Reality* (2004); Sue Owen on *Only Connect* (1972). Yet, inevitably, *The Uses of Literacy* looms large over the collection. It is a sign not only of its cultural significance but of its affective power that readers frequently remember their first encounter. For example, Peter Bailey found through *The Uses of Literacy* a way of understanding his own biography, the 'cultural schizophrenia' both he and Hoggart negotiated and he believes the study offered an entrée into a new understanding of culture — an idea explored in diverse ways across the papers. Less tolerant, Rosalind Brunt annotated her first copy of the text with indignant marginalia: 'overdone! sentimental! evidence?'. The first encounter takes contributors into autobiography — what was I doing then? — but also raises the issue of the retrospective mode. This is evident, of course, in Hoggart's own analysis of an earlier period but also in how *we* now look back at his work to make sense of it for the audience of the twenty-first century. Hence, Jeremy Seabrook commends the retrospective in Hoggart, the struggle to hold onto and value what is being lost, while himself taking a retrospective stance to contextualise a social history of change. There is an 'illusory durability', which is a source of poignancy in Hoggart's work, but Seabrook also finds legacies, continuities, real durabilities, particularly through considering immigrant experience. On the other hand, in discussing the place of *The Uses of Literacy* within media studies, Brunt notes how, for students, the retrospective can reduce the text to being simply a period piece with scant relevance for the contemporary audience.

Brunt is considering education in terms of her own teaching practice while Nick Stevenson focuses on Hoggart's contribution to a more philosophical understanding of a democratic education and both have interesting strategies for supporting the relevance of Hoggart. In her teaching, Brunt makes Hoggart speak to the present in part by placing him in a critical tradition, the very tradition which Hoggart himself has often rejected, cautioned against or qualified — phenomenology and theories of social construction, Gramsci and Foucault. Brunt shows how problematic for her are the stoppages where Hoggart offers a fascinating argument or position but fails to pursue or interrogate it but, equally, she sees how productive for students is a sensitive reading of the detail of Hoggart's work. Stevenson situates Hoggart's views on education within the current moment of the end of New Labour and the start of a Conservative-Liberal alliance. Tracing the recent neo-liberal ethic in education — one of market-driven values, vocationalism, spurious notions of 'choice' and 'opportunity' — Stevenson asks how we might 'reimagine' a democratic education and a democratic socialism and turns to Hoggart for answers. Stevenson recognises that our moment is different from Hoggart's but believes that Hoggart's notion of a 'common culture' with all its egalitarian and cultural associations has much to offer. Like Hoggart's own project, the future of education must link politics, morality and culture.

Brunt's reference to Hoggart's love of the specific and concrete and the analytical demands that mode of writing makes reminds us of the kind of literary practical criticism in which Hoggart was trained as a student and which remained a key approach throughout his career. For example, Yudhishthir Raj Isar shows how a literary practice imbued Hoggart's time at UNESCO in his acute ear for language and his shrewd awareness of the fictions that institutions create for themselves. Particular essays more directly relate to the literary in associating Hoggart with specific texts and movements. Both Alice Ferrebe and Tracy Hargreaves link the year of publication of *The Uses of Literacy*, 1957, with other texts of that year as a way to read between Hoggart and a wider culture of the 1950s. Ferrebe finds a surprising number of connections between Elizabeth Taylor's *Angel*, a novel about a writer of romantic fiction, and Hoggart's critique of precisely that kind of writing: both texts betray anxieties about romance as a genre; both explore the experience of social dislocation; both invite strategies of 'double reading'. Ferrebe claims that a reassessment of feminine middlebrow fiction, such as Taylor's, can produce a questioning of class difference and uprootedness which is as significant as that of the so-called 'Angry Young Man' (AYM) of the time and bears relation to Hoggart's own questioning. It is one of these AYMs, John Braine, who is the focus of Hargreaves's essay. Moving between Hoggart, Braine's *Room at the Top*, and its film adaptation, Hargreaves finds, as so many of our contributors do, what Hoggart calls one of those 'new little cultural patterns' that can have a much wider resonance. In two main ways, Hargreaves explores the common concern in these texts with cultural value and cultural loss: first, in the preoccupation with mass-market publications — to the extent that Joe Lampton's narrative voice can become a 'collage' of slogans, catch-phrases, jingles — and, second, through the issue of embodiment, particularly the figure of the woman, and the desire to recuperate the parental figure. As Hargreaves suggests, the deployment of the gaze in the film version of *Room at the Top* foregrounds a *discontented* female figure, a harbinger of a more radical sexual politics that was just on the horizon.

Hoggart's applicability to music as much as literature is evident in the two papers by James McGrath and Corey Gibson. Both use *The Uses of Literacy* as their key text to understand the cultural and social significance of, respectively, The Beatles and the Scottish folk-song revival. One of Ferrebe's further links between Elizabeth Taylor's *Angel* and Hoggart's *The Uses of Literacy* is in the concept of the 'baroque' as an escape from daily meanness. This concept is more fully explored in McGrath's contribution where he locates the baroque in The Beatles' interest in the Indian musical tradition and in the grotesque. In this essay, McGrath weaves together four conceptual strands he finds in *The Uses of Literacy* and in the output of The Beatles: 'uprooting', 'personalisation', 'working-class "baroque"' and 'primary religion'. In so doing, The Beatles are repositioned from 'youth culture', as Hoggart would designate, to 'working-class culture'. Noting always the differences as much as the similarities between Lennon, McCartney and Harrison, McGrath sees The Beatles as ambiguously placed in class terms — with respect to aspirations as much as origins — but with continuing representations of working-class life in their work alongside gestures to inclusiveness. In Gibson's paper, '"mass culture" in the North of England' meets '"traditional culture" in Scotland'. Gibson reads Hoggart with respect to Hamish Henderson and Hugh MacDiarmid and the 'flytings' or public exchanges that took place between Henderson and MacDiarmid between 1959 and 1960. Though the links between Hoggart and Henderson — methodological, theoretical, structural — might, at first, seem to predominate, Gibson finds shared concerns between Hoggart and MacDiarmid as well, particularly when considering the second half of *The Uses of Literacy*.

Discussing literature or music inevitably puts questions of value, affect and hierarchy at the centre of the debate. In analysing Hoggart's Reith lectures of 1971, Sue Owen finds an interconnection between Hoggart's valuing of the literary and his valuing of the ordinary. The unique 'tone' and, as Hoggart sees it, the disinterestedness of the literary work can enable, not a precious elitism, but a way of knowing the self and a way of communicating with others. Owen is interested in Hoggart's view of literature as empowering rather than imposing and, equally, in his view of the working class as discriminating, capable of appreciating the aesthetic and understanding the difference between 'quality' and 'highbrow'. Through literature, Hoggart finds both a deep sense of self and a common humanity. This is not mere essentialism or universalism, believes Owen, but a political, moral — even spiritual — endeavour. Ben Clarke would endorse this view. In a move away from scientism, Clarke believes that Hoggart — deliberately and creatively — brings into the analytical the revelatory moment or the intuitive insight of literature.

John Corner's exploration of Hoggart and value is carefully situated with respect to three framing discourses — on cultural improvement, political improvement and the 'politics of inequality'. He considers four ways in which cultural value features in Hoggart's writings: the relation between culture as a way of life and culture as an aesthetic product; between value and cultural difference; between culture, morality and politics; and between cultural value and change, and problems of economics and market relations. Corner shows how Hoggart may be constrained by limitations in the relation between and development of these framing discourses but how he still struggles to move beyond them. He is aided in this by the complexity of his own class experience and, as Owen has noted, his concern for the 'inner life'. Corner further comments on the importance of Hoggart's close observation in helping him to resist easy generalisations. As we have seen, this is a quality remarked upon by Brunt; it is there as well in the Geertzian 'thick description' that Ferrebe commends.

For Bill Hughes, this attention to detail in Hoggart's work is of major importance. He wants to rescue Hoggart from the disdain that has been directed towards empiricism in recent decades. Where Brunt sees a 'wilful binarism' in Hoggart, Hughes finds an over-looked sophistication and a distinctive 'dialectical cast of thought' in Hoggart's dialogue between sociology and literature, or between the particular and the macro or conceptual. Hughes recognises the methodological importance of concrete detail in understanding working-class life but, more than that, he sees such attentiveness as vitalising and sustaining that life. Moreover, the concept of the dialectical is worked in several ways throughout this collection. Gibson uses the concept in what he sees as the 'common dialectical tensions' in Hoggart and Henderson and the 'dialogical opposition' between Henderson and MacDiarmid. Clarke also describes Hoggart's approach as 'dialectical' and quotes Hoggart's own words about a practice which explores 'generalization and its relations to particular things'. In this context, Clarke especially sees the significance of Hoggart's use of autobiography: it can bring to academic discourse an excluded group as a legitimate focus of study; it can offer a qualitative analysis of that group in all its variety and complexity; and it necessarily problematises the position of the author as both inside and outside the scene he describes.

Several essays engage with Hoggart as the public man. Though Michael Green warmly remembers the personal qualities and kindnesses, one can discern other attributes, strategic and organisational, in his account of Hoggart's time at the University of Birmingham — as Chair of English, member of University committees and, especially, as founder of the Centre for Contemporary Cultural Studies. This represented the creation of a new discourse and new modes of working within a difficult institutional politics. Isar, reflecting on Hoggart's time at UNESCO, discusses his contribution to debates on cultural policy — 'cultural democratisation v. cultural democracy', the problem of relativism, the elasticity of the concept of culture. Sean Nixon remarks briefly on Hoggart's role as a defence witness for Penguin books in the *Lady Chatterley's Lover* trial but considers more extensively Hoggart's work for the Pilkington Committee on broadcasting. Nixon traces the narrative whereby Hoggart's critique of advertising and its emotive power was countered within the industry precisely by an appeal to the 'emotional and symbolic dimension of goods', the pleasures and desires advertising might express. Many discussions of Hoggart betray unease around the terms 'moral', 'morality', 'moralism'. Nixon is alert to the distinctions while embracing 'moralism' as both Hoggart's greatest strength and his greatest weakness.

Unsurprisingly, the dominant mode of this collection is one of critical engagement with Hoggart. The breadth of his experience, and the quantity and range of his output lead contributors into social history, culture and the arts, the media, education, policy and politics. The over-riding question is: How does Hoggart speak to us now? Occasionally there is a sharper tone. Daly is indignant upon first reading *Mass Media in a Mass Market: Myth and Reality* and bemoans, as he sees it, the lack of argument and — shades of the youthful Brunt — the lack of evidence. But in subsequent readings, Daly acknowledges an indomitable spirit. At the age of 86 when the book was first published, Hoggart is still insisting that we recognise the importance of a moral and aesthetic sensibility. Some contributions to this collection come from a personal knowledge of and collegial friendship with Hoggart and help us to know more about particular aspects of his biography — at the University of Birmingham (Green) or at UNESCO (Isar). In both there is appreciation of the regard in which Hoggart was held. Both also note the quiet, undemonstrative virtues — a 'responsible civic humanism' (Green), 'sober idealism' (Isar) — which could lead the casual observer to miss the significant contributions Hoggart made. Jean-Claude Passeron has no doubts about the importance of Hoggart's contribution. Introducing the French translation of *The Uses of Literacy*, he comments on the 'extreme originality of the work' and the 'rather overwhelming richness of the book'. Elsewhere in this collection, contributors have sought to fit Hoggart within a British tradition from Matthew Arnold, through F. R. Leavis to E. P. Thompson and Raymond Williams. Passeron, though, views Hoggart as the stimulus to a new tradition. Like Clarke, Passeron approves of Hoggart's resistance to 'a certain methodological imperialism'; like Clarke too he admires Hoggart's reflexivity about his own position. In Passeron's view, Hoggart's combination of autobiography and ethnography, his particular balance of distance and participation produce theory without 'theoretical fanfares' and a new model for the committed intellectual.

Postscript

Though Hoggart's early work played a pivotal part in what is now described as 'the cultural turn', his influence began to wane with the arrival of continental critical theory and its many 'isms' in the late 1960s. Just as Hoggart and his contemporaries had reacted against the elitism of their forbearers — Arnold, Eliot, Leavis — Hoggart's successors reacted against his analytical methods, producing work that was more theoretical and politically orientated. The names of the game since the 1970s have been predominantly French, whilst Hoggart and many of his British counter-parts have become increasingly marginalised, widely seen as being too empirically focused, morally judgmental and backward looking. Whilst some of theses criticisms are no doubt justified, a new generation of readers are beginning to reappraise his work, taking inspiration from older colleagues who have remained faithful to Hoggart's cultural politics. That this reappraisal has coincided with a revival in ideas commonly associated with liberal humanism and social democracy — widely vilified by cultural theorists in the 1970/80s as ruling-class ideologies and betrayals of 1960s radicalism — has been a blessing for Hoggartian type of scholarship.

This renaissance is evident in the recent and forthcoming flurry of academic activity that seeks to rethink the continuing usefulness of Hoggart. For example, *The Uses of Richard Hoggart* conference, hosted by the Department of English Literature at the University of Sheffield, 3-5 April 2006, was instrumental in bringing together scholars from across disciplinary boundaries to explore the ideas and analytical methods that underpin Hoggart's writings from his early critical study of Auden to his autobiographical later writing and engagement with public bodies and institutions. The conference also marked the inauguration of a special collection of Hoggart's papers held by Sheffield University Library, an invaluable resource for anybody wanting to gain new insights into Hoggart's life and work.

Recent collections of essays include the March 2007 issue of the *International Journal of Cultural Studies*, *Re-reading Richard Hoggart* (Cambridge Scholars, 2007) and *Richard Hoggart and Cultural Studies* (Palgrave, 2008), all edited by Sue Owen (who also organised the aforementioned conference). Forthcoming publications include *The Uses of Richard Hoggart: A Pedagogy of Hope* by Michael Bailey, Ben Clarke and John Walton (Wiley-Blackwell, forthcoming 2011) and a special issue of the Chinese journal *Differences* edited by Michael Bailey and Huimin Jin (forthcoming 2011). All of the publications seek to refresh and renew Hoggart's approach to popular culture by applying his method to both historical and contemporary cultural issues. Several colleagues and ourselves also organised an international conference at Leeds Metropolitan University, 10-11 July 2009. The following essays are just a small sample of the papers presented by colleagues at that conference.

In sum, the uses of Hoggart are considerable and his work continues to inform our understanding of a variety of historical and contemporary lived cultures, literary forms and institutional practices. Whereas other cultural commentators have long since given up on the idea of 'a culture for democracy', Hoggart's writings 'go on going on' to provide, in the words of Raymond Williams, a 'resource for hope', for new and old readers alike. They appeal to the best in each of us and remind us of that which we 'do not yet know, and might not like, but should know for its sake and ours' (Hoggart 2004: 131-32). Above all, not unlike the example of Hector in Alan Bennett's *The History Boys*, Hoggart's gift is to teach us that culture and education are best understood as social, dialogical processes to which we all contribute, no matter how fleetingly. Hoggart's own legacy is nothing but exemplary. 'Take it, feel it and pass it on.'

Bibliography

Hoggart, Richard (1957) The *Uses of Literacy: Aspects of Working-Class Life* (London: Chatto and Windus).

———— (1970a) *Speaking to Each Other, Volume 2: About Literature* (London: Chatto and Windus).

———— (1970b) *Speaking to Each Other, Volume 1: About Society* (London: Chatto and Windus).

———— (1988) *A Local Habitation: 1918-40* (London: Chatto and

Windus).

———— (1990) *A Sort of Clowning. Life and Times, Volume 2: 1940-59* (London: Chatto and Windus).

———— (1992) *An Imagined Life, Volume 3: 1959-91* (London: Chatto and Windus).

———— (1999) *First and Last Things: The Uses of Old Age* (London: Aurum Press).

———— (2001) *Between Two Worlds: Essays, 1978-1999* (London: Aurum Press).

———— (2003) *Everyday Language and Everyday Life* (New Jersey: Transaction Publishers).

———— (2004) *Mass Media in a Mass Society: Myth and Reality* (London: Continuum).

RICHARD HOGGART IN A WORKING CONTEXT: BIRMINGHAM ENGLISH IN THE SIXTIES
Michael Green

What follows is a brief sketch of knowing Richard Hoggart as a colleague, within the very distinctive environment of Birmingham University's English Department in the mid-1960s. This is the university and the department in which the Centre for Contemporary Cultural Studies was born (to die later, just under 40 years on, without any reference to or perhaps even awareness of its founder).

Richard, his wife Mary and young family, had arrived from Leicester University in 1963 in order for him to take up a Chair in English and to found the Centre. At school in Leicester my brother had known his elder son, Simon. It was partly through this connection that I also arrived at Birmingham a year later, sumptuously appointed to be an Assistant Lecturer (Temporary) in English Language and Literature. I was privileged to work with Richard, to see something of the first years of the Centre, and to glimpse something of his life and character as an academic in what was very clearly regarded as a redbrick, and also provincial, institution.

Both city and university were then extraordinarily unlike their present, more stylish, gleaming and brand-conscious incarnations. Birmingham itself had just gone though one of its recurrent and exceedingly major reconstructions. This had been a city with outstanding Victorian architecture and a commitment to civic reform. Now much was changing, finely caught in Roy Fisher's long poem *The City*:

> The new city is bred out of a hard will, but as it appears, it shows itself a little ingratiating, a place of arcades, passages, easy ascents, good light ...

> The whale-back hill assumes its concrete city:
> The white-flanked towers, the stillborn monuments;
> The thousand golden offices, untenanted ...

> (*Collected Poems*, 1969)

Writers on urban design saw its dedication to roads and to wholesale demolition as among the greatest planning disasters ever to befall a major English city. Away from the already dated 'new' Bull Ring shopping malls (where a campaigning Harold Wilson held a crowd and its hecklers for over an hour almost without notes, punch lines timed precisely to be live on the 9 o'clock news), gloomy canals were scarcely approachable, even by gaslight.

Other observers were positive. A feature writer (David Kemp) discussing Hoggart's new venture in, perhaps surprisingly, *The Scotsman* (18 December 1965), noted the 'uncompromisingly New Brutalist' architecture, 'acres of glass ... great concrete slabs and neon-capped towers ... reflecting the aggressive philistinism of Britain's second city'. But beyond this 'brash and opulent core' of a city traditionally reliant on heavy industry, now 'the flashpoint for confrontations on immigration and contraception', were pubs and clubs, beat groups, striptease and football teams which 'flourish in the affluent Midlands conurbation and provide the obvious locale for the first scientific studies of mass culture'.

Far from all this in many senses, Arts and allied Departments in Birmingham University had not long before decamped from city centre terracotta to an extremely spacious campus in Edgbaston. The city's oldest suburb was in mood a long distance from Enoch Powell to the north, and from areas such as Handsworth and Balsall Heath (earlier dubbed 'little Africa' and 'little Asia'), though it did contain a controversial clinic attracting anti-abortion protests. Here on the campus new radial buildings spread out from the allegedly Siennese high clock tower (from which, with the aid of binoculars, Edgbaston cricket scores could be relayed to the Vice-Chancellor). Medics, scientists, and according to rumour, Freemasonry, dominated. Uniformed porters were available to assist dons and undergraduates, while many hours could be spent searching the file card index catalogue to the extensive main library.

Yet this was an institution commissioning a series of modernist buildings outwith its magisterial turn of the century Court and Great Hall. It was a university named in the Commons for sheltering a left discussion group perceived as a Communist cell. Its compulsory programme of general studies, undergraduates from all disciplines taking options together, and a huge Arts scheme of Combined Honours, were something of a break-out from the tyranny of single subjects. Shortly the campus was to become the locus for a very major sit-in, generating a long report on wide-ranging university reform. As for Birmingham's Arts Faculty, it already contained, at the time of Richard's arrival, extremely eminent scholars across all disciplines, with something of a 'progressive' consensus.

The large English Department itself was split into rather competitive syllabii and staff groupings: Anglo-Saxon and Medieval, Renaissance and Modern literature, each with distinguished academics and particular attitudes, though united in opposition to the scientistic, value-free pretensions of the upstart linguistics and perhaps envious of its earning power. Richard presided over the Modern grouping, including the already celebrated young writers Malcolm Bradbury (his jovial manner concealing a certain melancholia) and David Lodge (of whom the converse may have been true).

The Department's own culture, certainly as remembered from the glacial realms of the next century's academe, was remarkable. 'In loco parentis' was taken most seriously by staff, with advice on diet given by one colleague in first year lectures, and alarmingly frank discussions during exam boards of the personal problems of named students. The mutual concern extended to new and younger colleagues, one of them arriving at New St station to be met by the Head of Department's wife. There were also very regular parties, Mary and Richard among the various hosts, welcoming people into their family life — with three children — in a large and rambling detached Victorian house near campus.

Despite many calls on his energies from outside the university, and his role as a husband and father, Richard's commitments on campus were extensive. As a Professor, he took serious part in lengthy debates on Faculty Board and in Senate, before new managerialism did away with such democratic and collegiate niceties. In the Department, while chairing the Modernist camp, he played many and full teaching roles. Though lecturing and leading seminars, he also took tutorials with groups of two (or even three!) undergraduates, was a personal tutor to many, and produced a flow of literary and social criticism. At the same time he was happy to attend the Department's 'away' reading parties for students, and to engage inside and outside the Common Room in debates gathering force about universities' role and purposes.

Within the new Centre, Richard had recruited (in a fashion typical of his open-mindedness about people quite unlike himself) Stuart Hall. This important relationship was not easily understood from the outside, while of Stuart it was typically muttered in the Senior Common Room 'say what you like about him, but he's very *clever*'. Their work in developing CCCS itself, then strictly a postgraduate research unit within English and far from its later autonomy, was undertaken in difficult, under-nourished circumstances: these were (and always remained later) far from straightforward times for the new Centre. There was a marked disparity between the reputation of its founder (and soon of the Centre's publications) and a distinct lack of resource, symbolised by early location in a slightly ramshackle hut. At the same time, and not least among academics on the left, there was open distrust of the fledgling enterprise.

The Uses of Literacy (which back in the sixth form I had read with excitement in its hardback Chatto edition, to be followed rapidly by successive paperback reprints and ever-changing covers in Penguin) though praised by general reviewers had been suspected academically of being not quite literary criticism, not quite sociology, not quite autobiography, not quite political in any way which might be readily grasped. In short, this was always a potential cuckoo in the academic nest, attracting doubts, and projections of what CCCS was up to, with which all those actually involved had to cope, and in response evolve appropriate survival strategies. Even now it seems better not to record many a prospective PhD topic submitted to a funding body, which then swerved in another direction over time. If Richard had his own uncertainties about the Centre's trajectory and future (concerned with issues which, as letters requesting applicants' references indicated, lay in a 'new and relatively uncharted area') then these were steadfastly concealed.

Richard's own account of these times is typically measured and amused, thoughtful and perceptive in his treatment of what he calls the 'wrongly styled' label of 'permissiveness' for the times. Yet this period became for him difficult, and must have assisted his decision to leave for work in UNESCO. Student protest in Birmingham concerned not the Situationists' 'beneath the pavement, the beach', but an earnest and responsible concern with representation and governance. Authoritarian responses prompted a sit-in, then a major occupation of administration offices. As always, Richard was concerned to listen and to reason, where possible trying to put 'speaking to each other' into practice. But the developing situation, and the aggressive and threatened response by the authorities, soon made any middle ground uncomfortable. Challenges were made, sides were taken. Richard found himself mistrusted by some students and by many entrenched professors. Perhaps this had become a limit case for liberal dialogue. His card, and in the gossip and collective memory of the institution that of CCCS also, was now marked.

A very significant omission in the autobiography for this time concerns the role of his wife Mary, reading and sharing in his work alongside being a parent. Motherly, sympathetic and supportive in manner, solicitous in asking after families and friends, Mary was also (even at parties) an acute questioner, at times mildly sardonic, not inclined to let things go. The fantasy of 'faculty wives' grossly misleads about such roles and personalities. This was not someone standing in her husband's shadow but a force — kindly, shrewd, sharp — in her own right.

Of Richard himself four impressions dominate, decades on. First, this was someone of immense purposeful energy with much to do and not enough time to do it in. He could be seen along Arts Faculty corridors in his academic gown, probably a little late, perhaps slightly limping, striding forward urgently to give a lecture. Giving invariably a 'sleeves up, hands on' impression he was clearly someone eager to get on with his many aims and tasks without much patience with formalities.

Second, of his great kindness we catch only brief glimpse in his autobiography recording help given to students (*An Imagined Life*, Vol. III, p. 135 : 'caring and not caring ... at the deepest level uninvolved ... above that ... very concerned'). I find it flabbergasting to remember of myself that he could make time to visit (complete, of course, with soup) a young colleague down with flu. If there was a hint of the paterfamilias, even of the patriarch, it flowed partly from responsibilities taken seriously in this branch of 1960s academe, and partly very much from his own consistent generosity.

Third, this was a seeker of knowledge and information, clearly short of time to read all he wanted, making use of people, listening with head cocked, asking questions, taking it all in. Finding out about people and things, attentive, listening with an occasional sardonic chuckle, he embodied at all times and in all circumstances the far from universal scholarly enquiring mind.

But, last and more puzzling, it seemed that Richard was perpetually worrying away to establish not so much an opinion as a judgment: measuring, balancing, testing, evaluating, weighing the odds, at the last pronouncing a view. The sources of this drive were not clearly in view, neither were the bases for judgments always explicit, unless perhaps they lay in the responsible civic humanism characterising all of his work. The phrase sounds dull in impatient times. Richard, remarkably tolerant but consistently challenging, was not.

RICHARD HOGGART AND WORKING-CLASS VIRTUES
Jeremy Seabrook

I

It has often been the fate of books about the working class to appear at a remove from the historic moment they address. This was certainly true of Marx's great work, which was published in 1867 in Germany, but appeared in English only in the 1880s. Much of the work on the conditions of the working classes was gathered by Engels some twenty years before and this itself was based upon an experience earlier in the nineteenth century. By the time *Kapital* appeared, it had, to some degree, already been overtaken by events. The power of its analysis notwithstanding, its capacity for prediction was based upon scenes of misery that were already passing away. It is a curious paradox that, while Marx was constantly aware of the mobility and creative-destructive force of capitalism, his followers embalmed what he saw as fluid and protean in dogma that froze as swiftly as the snow falling on the plains of Russia.

A different archaism is detectable in the wonderful work of E. P. Thompson, whose *Making of the English Working Class* appeared in the 1960s. This book of retrospective admiration and tenderness for victims who were also actors in the drama of transformation, actually appeared just as the unmaking of the working classes was under way, as a consequence of what later came to be called global economic integration.

A similar time-lag occurred with *The Uses of Literacy*, although Richard Hoggart was well aware of the danger at the time of writing. He was concerned not to present a backward-looking sense of regret at the passing of cultural values, which were common, but not unique to, the working classes of Britain. He remained cautious in his judgments on the capacity of a wisdom acquired in great pain and grief to withstand the onslaught of commercial culture. But the fact remains that he had assembled his account of working-class philosophy during his childhood in the 1920s and 1930s; and at the time of its publication, these were already fast being superseded. It was this tension that gave it such vibrancy and originality; and it spoke to us with the force of revelation.

It seems that only when cultures are on the verge of dissolution can they convey to those who bear them a sense of their relative nature: while they are lived, they exist unreflectingly. 'The sommer's flowre is to the summer sweet; tho to itselfe it onely live and die.' The poignancy of values and beliefs passing into obsolescence can be perceived only by posterity and those who no longer share them. In this respect, Hoggart had already outgrown what he lovingly chronicled. It is a work of valediction, a sorrowful farewell, in spite of his optimistic disposition and a desire to see the best in changes he knew were inevitable.

The Uses of Literacy is, therefore, the work of a kind of prescient obituarist; like those eulogies stacked up in newspaper offices waiting in advance for the death of the luminaries whose lives they celebrate. Of course, the history of the working class over the past fifty years could not have been foretold but there are enough inklings and foreshadowings in Hoggart's cautious but regretful words. He carefully notes the fraying of the 'settled' working-class culture. But he observes the precise ways in which the loosening solidarities are eroded, how appeals to abandon them are couched in terms that appeal to collective popular wisdom, how the very virtues of the working class become the conduit for an attack upon them. Hoggart is chronicling the vulnerabilities of the 'cultural' identity of the working-class, ways in which it was open to manipulation, to alteration and finally to dissolution.

In the mid-fifties, the disintegration of the industrial base of Britain in the interests of globalisation was just beginning. Of course, old industries and trades had always become obsolete and had been succeeded by new ones - no more dramatic example exists than in the changeover from horsepower to motorised transport. What a vast range of old competences were wiped out within a couple of decades, the work of farriers, blacksmiths, stable personnel, veterinary experts, saddlers and harness-makers, carters, dray-men. But they were replaced by the even greater numbers employed by the rise of the internal combustion engine. However, the last three or four decades of the twentieth century saw a comprehensive demolition of the basis of manufacturing industry in Britain, the circumstances in which 'working-class life' had grown and flourished.

It should not be thought that this way of life was of particular antiquity. It was not. Eric Hobsbawm placed the moment of stability from around the 1870s to the beginning of the Second World War. In a mere three generations, working-class life rooted itself in the brick streets, factories, friendly societies, working-men's clubs, burial societies, trades unions, pubs, pawnbrokers, corner shops, clothing clubs - the institutions, collective and private, through which the business of a majority of working-class people was conducted. Yet how permanent the aspects of life delineated by Richard Hoggart seemed! How readily its values were seen as expressing something essential or basic about the British working class! It all lasted such a short time — three quarters of a century — but that was long enough for observers and chroniclers of working-class life to see in them an illusory durability and an uneasy awareness of this gives

Hoggart's work an apprehensive poignancy. All this, he seems to say, the insight and tolerant wisdom, gained in such hardship and sorrow, surely cannot be easily swept away. As indeed it was not, even though that particular embodiment of those values *was* destined to be swept away.

II

The story of the fragmentation of the working class is well known: the recruitment of workers from the Caribbean and South Asia in the early fifties to keep public services and the textile industry from collapse; new stratifications by age in the emergence of teenagers, whose function turned out to be pioneers of consumerism; the entry of increasing numbers of women into the labour market; the explosion of employment in retail, travel and services; expansion of higher education, public services and administration - all this seemed to remove more and more people from the spaces in which a never-homogeneous working class had existed in its brief moment of apparent stability.

The absorption of a new generation into new forms of labour and the decline of the old industries left behind what were at first seen as the laggards of development, the 'left behind', the unskilled, the vulnerable and the old, who could not adapt to the altered circumstances of the times, or respond to expanding opportunities. By the 1980s, these were, for a time at least, dismissed as being part of an 'underclass', a particularly ugly description, since it suggested the skeleton of a working class which had moved on and out, and had achieved the growing rank of a decidedly global middle class. Such members of society became objects of public scorn: they had earlier been sheltered in the wider working-class community, corrected and disciplined at times perhaps, victims of values which could be puritanical and repressive, but which also shielded them from the police and the poor law, the asylum and the workhouse, unless their transgressions were exceptional. It is significant also that they have even more recently been 're-discovered' by the intrepid explorers of the media, and to some degree rehabilitated as 'the white working class' — a category about which we heard a great deal in the USA before the election of President Obama. They still represent a significant minority who, as the Labour Party discovered to its cost, could no longer be taken for granted, but did indeed have 'somewhere else to go', to fringe racist parties or to the state of alienation sometimes called apathy. The concern with which these issues are now treated is in inverse proportion to their earlier dismissal as the expendables of progress, or more dismissively still, as white trash. It goes without saying that the psyche and sensibility of this group have been changed beyond all recognition from the archetypes who figure in Hoggart's work.

Richard Hoggart's admonitions on the emergence of a consumerism which has since grown more florid and individualistic than anything he chronicled in that strangely innocent time the 1950s now appears to have been vindicated. For instance, working-class wisdom that time is short and you should enjoy yourself while you can, has readily mutated into the contemporary culture of bingeing, getting rat-arsed, wasted, legless, out of your skull, and all the other graphic terms of escape from realities to which an earlier working class was also no stranger. The shortest way out of Wigan or Scunthorpe was through the pub door, it used to be said. The only difference is that the way of life formerly associated with the rough, non-respectable working class, has become a wider norm. Further, when Hoggart looked at the influence of commerce upon a working class which had largely lived a life apart and had been only a modest participant in the consumer market, he looked primarily at its cultural and ideological impact on the people. Cradle-to-grave entertainment has had a rather different long-term effect from that described by Hoggart. He was, after all, focussing on literacy, the reading matter of the people. He wrote before the audio-visual age, the siege of the eyes and ears, the proliferation of aural and visual stimuli, which are such potent inhibitors of the subtlety of ideas. It is perhaps no accident that these senses have become the primary mode of cultural experience in the last half-century.

One consequence of this socio-cultural change has been that the attack on the old values or virtues has been less ideological and political than psychological and emotional. The question Hoggart would ask if he were beginning his work today, would surely be: 'What is the effect upon the affective lives of the people, especially children, exposed to such hyper-intensive emotional experiences? What happens to poor human lives and loves in the presence of epic passions, murder, lust, jealousy and ecstatic coupling which is the staple fare of the contemporary entertainment industry?' He might have wondered whether mere flesh and blood can cope with this excess; and whether at the root of the breaking of human bonds might not be influenced by the reductive calculus of the psychic economics which govern societal relationships.

Of course, the shift from known roles in the old working class to relationships in contemporary culture is a deeply ambiguous process. Known patterns of behaviour in the streets were as clear as the patterned lino, the parlour furniture, the freezing functional bedrooms. Everyone knew then what it meant to be a good son or daughter, a good wife or husband — a good man tipped up his wages to his wife, didn't drink too much, didn't mistreat her or the children; a good wife knew her limited place, put food on the table and occupied the house as though she were tethered to it. A good son or daughter looked after their parents, didn't marry too far away, maintained almost daily contact. People entered marriage as they might have entered a neighbour's house, expecting to find everything in its place, from the antimacassars to the rag-rug, the clock on the mantelpiece and the blackleaded grate. The replacement of roles by relationships, in which feelings have to be constantly negotiated, and people make demands upon each other which are intensely personal and unpredictable, has created a world of exciting possibilities, but also of bewildering strangeness. That individual relationships have overtaken ascribed roles is a symptom of the profound shift that has taken place in our consciousness of ourselves; and it is in this context that we should consider the impact of popular media upon the affective, psychic and sexual lives of people, as well as the fracturing of shared cultural values.

III

So what became of the values, the tolerant wisdom, the common destiny of Hoggart's people, whose sensibility appears to us now so remote and archaic? To be sure, the ideology of individualism has undermined the basis for the consolation that we were all in the same boat, the shared assumptions that made it safe to talk to strangers, the common experience in which people recognised one another as members of a vast extended family and called each other, in consequence, 'love' or 'duck' or 'hin', not as sexist put-downs, but in acknowledgement of a collective predicament. However, it would be inaccurate to say that these values have entirely disappeared. It is a profound irony that many of the principles identified by Hoggart live on in newcomers, migrants who came to occupy the central areas of the old towns and cities. It is a grievous omission, that the leaders and rulers of Britain, both nationally and locally, did not perceive how those who inherited the back-to-back housing, also assumed many of the virtues left behind by the former working class, just as these had abandoned old pieces of furniture as they moved on to a private life in exurbia — ornaments, broken horsehair sofas, rusting cutlery and abandoned dishes, family albums with sepia photographs of children dying of consumption and soldiers smiling before they perished in war.

In other words, it should not be thought that the griefs and joys experienced by people in the nineteenth-century industrial towns disappeared when they departed for a better future inscribed in new estates, both public and private. The sorrows and pleasures, cares and anxieties of the old inhabitants lingered in dusty cupboards and cellars, attics and dark recesses, waiting, as it were, to reclaim the next generation of occupants, wherever they might come from. Thus the world-view of communities from Pakistan, Bangladesh and elsewhere, strikingly resembles that of a white working class which, only the day before yesterday, lived in the crowded terraces in the shadow of the mill. Echoes of ways of life that, superficially, could scarcely appear more different, create a powerful sense of history revisited in the dwindling streets and reconstructed row-houses of the inner city. It is not the differences between people that cause friction, resentment and a sense of displacement, but the samenesses. It is the continuities that tug at the heart and the memory, and which also set up pathologies that made people view incomers and migrants as usurpers, when in fact, they are merely fulfilling roles and functions which, until the recent past, were the life-blood of a white working class.

Of course, poor people are always poor in the same way. Insufficiency and insecurity do not distinguish between forms of worship (or absence of them); the exploitation of flesh and blood is common to people of all skin colours. Inadequate income and the pooling of resources (including human resources), contriving and combining to make ends meet — all this was not so long ago second nature to working communities all over Britain. The phenomenon of the 'labouring poor' has never gone away; people who, no matter how hard they work, can still barely provide for the needs of themselves and those who depend on them. It is simply that different populations come to fulfil the particular role with the passing of time. Whatever the impulse that brought them to occupy the memory-charged streets of Blackburn, Keighley, Bolton or Leeds, it is not only a question of the economic position of migrants. The social arrangements by which they survive offer a resonant echo of forms of survival common in these same streets only two generations ago.

The people of the early industrial era were also migrants, as Richard Hoggart records in his account of how it took two or three generations for them to become truly urban. With what trepidation people left the enclosed commons and impoverished villages of the late eighteenth and early nineteenth centuries for the bare bleak towns arising on the fields and meadows of Lancashire! Who can imagine now the wounds to the psyche of country people, as they learned to abandon the rural cycle of sowing and harvest, and adapt to the accelerated rhythms of industrial life? How similar was that disturbance of two centuries ago to the hopeful anxiety of people coming from rural Punjab or Sylhet in the 1960s and 1970s to the soft drizzle of Lancashire and the lowering skies of Yorkshire. The upheaval of that first group of migrants, arriving from a mere twenty miles away, on foot with their meagre belongings piled on a handcart, was not less than that of people flying for the first time, with battered suitcases tied up with string, ancient trunks and jute sacks from an East Pakistan soon to become Bangladesh.

These are not casual comparisons. For if the economic and social conditions which gave rise to movements of people in both the early and late industrial age were identical, the patterns of family roles and relationships faithfully replicate the structures of feeling of those who lived in the now wasting streets when these were new, thrown up speculatively to accommodate waves of migrants, refugees from a depleted countryside. We are all economic migrants in one way or another; but instead of seeing a common heritage, we too often look upon others with incomprehension and animosity. Hence, beyond the otherness of appearance, women have the same protective role, desperately trying to keep body and soul — and the family itself — together. The same mothers look anxiously upon their sons, wondering at the company they keep, the people they mix with, and how to preserve them from a life of petty — or serious — crime. They regard with apprehension the boys their daughters might come into contact with, the Pashtun or the boy from Kashmir, or even from the English suburbs, who cannot be expected to fit in with the customs and practices of home. The same anxieties clouded the eyes of mothers two or three generations ago, when their young formed relationships with boys and girls who were not chapel, or who came from the rough, rather than the respectable, part of town. The men, too, privileged patriarchs, whose word is no longer law, seek in vain to compel their refractory children, sometimes using canes and fists, just as fathers in these same houses readily taught their children right from wrong with the buckle-end of a belt.

The differences are nuances, shades of colour, the similarities stark and conspicuous. How sad it is, to live in a society so seduced by surfaces that we observe in the colour of skin, the sounds of language or the inflections of prayer, insurmountable barriers, rather than perceiving in them our own gestures of love, ties of affection and kinship and the bonds of neighbourhood — everything that represents our readily forgotten past. It is not to the unrelatedness of experience that the source of smouldering resentments are to be traced, but to what we recognise too well as the ruin of belonging.

IV

In 2007, a friend and I had an extensive conversation with young Muslims in Blackburn, sixth-formers who are third-generation British. Their grandparents had migrated, mostly from Gujarat or Punjab in Pakistan, while two came via East Africa. These worked in the textile mills in the late 1960s, long shifts, often nights, in order to keep the Lancashire industry viable. Within less than two decades most of the mills had closed, leaving them stranded, just as their white counterparts had been. A few of the original migrants have returned to Gujarat or Pakistan; some have died, but most survivors still live with, or close to, the families of the teenagers. The next generation grew up to be bilingual, but there has been a falling away of language in the third generation. Parents try to inculcate a knowledge of Urdu or Gujarati, while grandparents are still more at ease with the language of home, and their grandchildren make an effort — not always successfully — to communicate with them.

The story the young people tell might have come from the pages of *The Uses of Literacy*. The family remains the centre of social life. Extended families are still common, with uncles and aunts and cousins next door, in the same street or just round the corner. Some have relatives in other towns in Lancashire. The small rivalries of siblings cover a deeper commitment, and older children accept their role in looking after the younger ones. When they spoke of the coming and going between households, it sounded deeply familiar. The story of their grandparents was also reminiscent of the migration of British country-people into the fast-growing mill towns in the 1830s and 1840s. The story ought to be recognised by the old working class; but it has been forgotten, overlaid by a history of war, unemployment, and above all, the coming of a hitherto unknown prosperity; so that when they confronted the newcomers of the mid-twentieth century, they did so with a look of estrangement, not only from people of a different ethnicity or religion, but equally, from their former selves, selves delineated with such warmth and compassion by Richard Hoggart.

The young Muslims speak of their elders with respect. If they chafe at some of the disciplines, they know that these are necessary if they want to get on. Among their fathers is a tyre-fitter, a taxi-driver, one unemployed, one working in a family business, a social worker, a carpet-weaver, a community worker, while some mothers work as teaching assistants and nurses. All parents see the value of education as the surest guarantor of social mobility; and nearly all of the young people we spoke to expect to go to university; and in this, they are characteristic of Hoggart's scholarship boys and girls. They have a clear idea of their future, and aim to become clinical psychologist, optometrist, dentist, barrister, teacher. Many are doing four A-levels: Psychology is popular, as are Law, Chemistry, Physics, Biology, Maths and English. Several say they wish to give back to society something in return for the privileges they have enjoyed. The world is open to these new pioneers of a Muslim middle class. My companion and I were able to read into their experience the same relationship we had with our parents fifty years ago — the exasperated love, the fretful chafing at authority, the pain of people united by flesh and blood but divided by temperament and the education they wished us to have.

The family is also the focus for wider religious celebrations and observances — Eid ul Fitr, Eid ul Azha, the iftar breaking of the fast on each day of Ramzan. While the secular aspects of the inherited tradition decay — language and folk-memory — religious commitment seems to intensify, although their sensibility could not be further removed from bigotry or extremism. The most searching debate was sparked by the question of whether they see themselves as British Muslims or Muslim British.

V

It is in this context that new forms of 'us' and 'them' have been formulated, especially among the remnant of the old working class. In many poorer white areas, older complicities of class have been transformed into a complicity of race. When people defer to the altered circumstances of the time and declare they have not a racist bone in their body, it sounds strangely like the lower orders of the Victorian era, anxious not to show themselves up in front of their betters, minding their manners and p's and q's. 'I'm not a racist but ...' usually serves as a moral disclaimer to complaint or abuse, although this may not be uttered with the same uninhibited vigour of forty years ago. A new, but distinctly recognisable 'them' and 'us' replicates the defensive solidarity formed in the old industrial areas by the workers against millowner, magistrate, parson and all the social apparatus that sustained the power of privilege against them. Old patterns of feeling remain; only the players are different.

A complex code has evolved of nods and winks, often wordless, to signal that 'our' views have been denied, our voices muted, our right to free speech forbidden. The semaphore is 'political correctness gone mad'. This euphemism means we may no longer speak our mind, a particularly grievous imposition upon people in the North, whose proudest boast was that they spoke as they found, and called things by their proper name. The bush of anti-racism must now be beaten about by the sometime fearless speakers of truth. This sets up bitterness and hard feeling, which may remain sullenly dormant for years, until periodic outbursts of dissent articulate them, as the intermittent popularity of racist and xenophobic parties suggest.

In public at least the code is cautious. But apparently anodyne observations such as 'It used to be lovely round here' contain profound reproachful comment on a whole history of social change. 'Blackburn — or Burnley or Halifax or Dewsbury — isn't Blackburn any more.' And once the terms of the discourse have been recognised by both parties, the path is clear to a more open sharing of grievances.

This should not be exaggerated. A majority of people lead their lives in a state of fairly benign indifference towards each other. And who can complain about that? After all, the rich don't mix with the poor or the young with the old. What is so special about ethnicity, that people must 'integrate?' 'You just get on with your lives' is the dominant opinion.

One of the most persistent complaints against 'Asians' or 'Pakis' or 'Muslims' (often pronounced so as to be almost indistinguishable from 'muslin') is that 'they' keep themselves to themselves, are clannish and self-contained. 'They' live close together in extended families, are always in and out of each other's houses. Everybody is somebody's cousin. They have too many children. They put themselves first. They are thick as thieves. However, the most striking thing about these vices is that they were, until recently, the most prized virtues of the white working class. Only the day before yesterday 'we' looked out for one another. We knew everybody in the street. If help was needed, people didn't wait to be asked. Our doors always stood open. Children called neighbours auntie and uncle.

This reversal provides the key to many of the unresolved issues of 'parallel lives' in Britain. There is a powerful sense that 'they' have taken over, not only the inner-city streets, but also social and moral attributes we claimed as our own most cherished characteristics until about two generations ago. This remains the long lament in many working-class towns, pit villages and manufacturing districts.

Nor does the feeling that 'our' values have been appropriated end there. Many young Muslims in particular, who do not take part in the alcohol culture, say that their social lives are exciting enough without the assistance of stimulants. 'We get high on air' one young woman said; we create our own sense of enjoyment from within an ample store of internal resources. 'We make our own fun' uncannily parodies an older working-class generation, who prided themselves on how much they could do with little money, and how they enjoyed themselves simply by being together, walking on the moors, taking a picnic in the countryside, blackberrying, bluebelling or gathering nuts in autumn.

Religious commitment tugs at the strings of memory, as the very old recall chapel outings, temperance meetings, the Band of Hope and the Brethren, church teas and summer camps in the hills. 'They' still know who they are, and have a sense of rootedness in spite of their status as recent migrants. These were also 'our' qualities, while we knew our purpose and function in a division of labour, where a majority of people were spinners, weavers, miners or makers of useful goods.

Hostility often focuses on the belief that more money is pumped into 'Asian' areas than into poor white estates, which fall into neglect, prey to all the villainies of contemporary life. But as well as the sense of injustice is a deeper feeling, not so much of enmity as of sadness, puzzlement and almost envy. Why have things changed in ways that we never willed? Why has the better world for which so many hoped and struggled been accompanied by so much that is socially, morally, psychologically worse? These unanswered questions have been scorned by politicians and all the experts who insist that everything that has happened has been pure gain, that the advantages showered upon us are a reward for past privations, poverty and suffering.

But suppose the abandonment of the consolations of solidarity, neighbourliness and kinship can never be fully compensated by material improvements? Rancour and vexation at what 'they' have has nothing to do with the outlandishness of dress, religion, colour or speech, but because 'they' embody things we have mislaid, or perhaps, squandered. It is not difference that taunts us, but the sameness of what was ours, but has mysteriously slipped through our fingers, even as we grasped them ever more tightly over the purchases we made each day in the hypermarkets of plenty.

No wonder the word 'cohesion' has such vibrant meaning to those who have forfeited it, partly as the result of a bargain struck — unwittingly — long ago between the leaders of labour and the forces of capital. Untold sacrifices have been demanded by a version of progress, which sometimes now looks tawdry and less substantial, since it has also, like a thief in the night, purloined purpose and meaning from human lives.

VI

This is, of course, to look at one form taken by what Richard Hoggart had identified as working-class virtues. If many recent migrants and their descendants retain a sense of existential vulnerability, this does not mean they are the sole repository of values of neighbourliness, decency and a tragi-comic view of a shared predicament. Like so much in our society that is of value and beauty, the capacity for mutuality and self-recognition in the fate of others, values forged in a long experience of loss and sorrow, these have also been taken over by the middle class. Like many of the former Victorian villas and terraces in industrial towns and cities, neighbourliness and solidarity have also been substantially gentrified. These things were simply too good to be permitted to lapse, and accordingly, have been appropriated by those who recognise a good thing when they see it. This assumption of moral attributes has its counterpart in the material world: browsers in antique and curiosity shops have rescued artefacts which they have been restored and rendered chic. How many well-to-do homes now contain refurbished Windsor chairs, deal tables, chenille tablecloths, grandfather clocks, dressers and craft objects that had been abandoned by a working class seeking refuge in new flats and houses, who simply abandoned the possessions associated with poverty in anticipation of a better world?

We can speak only of what we know. In the modestly affluent places where I have lived in London for the past twenty years, the elderly and the sick are not neglected; the bereaved and the unhappy are comforted by neighbours. There are unspoken rotas for hospital visiting, shopping, sitting with the lonely, the woman with the broken hip and the man who has lost his wife, the anorexic and the widow who has survived her husband by more than forty years. What was embodied in a working-class life recorded by Hoggart is certainly not lost; and indeed, in many ways, it never 'belonged' to the working class, but was a common human response to the certain woes and misfortunes of existence, the fleeting joys and lasting grief, the pleasure and pain of being. It was simply that in those particular circumstances of the smoke-filled sooty streets, between the factory siren and the pub piano, the allotment and the beer-stained working men's club, the premature death and the constant childbirth, social and economic burdens were added to known and predictable wrongs. This did not itself create the culture of caring and mutuality, which has been present in most human societies through recorded time; but it did intensify that culture, made it inescapable, as existential evils were compounded by alterable and human-made afflictions. These are basic human responses, and they arise as a matter of course wherever people live together, and if they survive, it is in defiance of all those who would cozen or cheat us out of our birthright, persuade us that life is about something else, the merchants and hucksters of perpetual feasting and fun, the brewers who were the doughty champions of the working-man's right to his glass of ale, even though his children were cold and hungry at home; and in more recent times, those who distract us from life and entertain us to death. But human values are not the property of one class or one particular society; even though they will certainly be inflected by the conditions of the local and particular.

VII

If the working class, absconding from poverty in the streets and tenements of the inner city, neglected to take with them many of the artefacts that served their austere lives, they did not wholly forget the virtues of kindliness, tolerance and compassion. Whatever bizarre tales of the lives of the poorest emerge from the squalid estates and the inner-city ghettoes, the stabbing in the stairwell, the gunfire in the streets, the brutalisation of the elderly, the torment of Victoria Climbié or Baby Peter, the core of society retains much of the heritage of mutual care and solidaristic ideas - for these were also embodied in the welfare state, the health service and provision for the weak and old. Despite the vast social and economic changes, the intensification of commercial processes which were only beginning when Hoggart was working, his insights remain. Yes, there is a continuous assault, and some do succumb, but the lived experience of flesh and blood is more powerful than the flickering of shadows on the screens of fantasy — no matter how potent the technology — and we continue to recognise our hopes and frailties, our joys and sorrows more readily in one another across social classes than some would have us believe.

There has been greater polarisation in the past half century; the poor have been left more exposed as the strong have become empowered. The gulf between rich and poor, the comfortably off and the most wretched has widened. This is directly related to a differential surrender and resistance to the forces which see in the weaknesses of humanity yet another business opportunity. Despite the convulsive changes that have transformed the landscapes, both material and psychic, of Britain, a transformation Hoggart could not have foreseen, it seems to me his optimism is vindicated and his worst fears have not quite been realised. That says a great deal about the resilience of humanity; although, of course, it isn't over yet; and societies themselves are always only provisional, poised between decency and indifference, and always threatened by the sombre temptations of barbarism.

Bibliography

Hoggart, Richard (1957) *The Uses of Literacy: Aspects of Working-Class Life* (London: Chatto and Windus).

Thompson, E. P. (1963) *The Making of the English Working Class* (London: Victor Gollancz).

CONSIDERING RICHARD HOGGART'S RELEVANCE FOR TEACHING CONTEMPORARY MEDIA STUDIES
Rosalind Brunt

What I want to offer here are some reflections on teaching media studies with or through Richard Hoggart's work. As a teacher of media studies myself I have always referenced it (*The Uses of Literacy* in particular) as highly relevant to students' analytical practice. But re-reading it recently I have more doubts, more ambivalences than previously. This essay voices some of them, highlighting the ways I think Richard Hoggart has quite unnecessarily limited the theoretical scope and general applicability of his work. It concludes, however, by suggesting a positive re-assessment of his original innovative project for cultural studies.

So what to make of Richard Hoggart in teaching practice today? As an external examiner in media and cultural studies I have come across several study guide exhortations to read him, particularly in relation to popular representations of working-class life. 'Believe it or not,' runs one media studies course handbook, 'Hoggart's *Uses of Literacy* was a major influence on the thinking behind the British soap opera, *Coronation St.*.' The guide goes on to outline a seminar linking discussion of a recent serial episode with the required course reading from 'The Newer Mass Art' chapter. This sounded like an engaging approach to *The Uses of Literacy* so I asked the lively young lecturer how the seminar went. Feeling she had put a lot of preparation into the session she was very dispirited. Not only had students taken a strong dislike to the extract, seeing it as snobby and elitist, they also disliked, and claimed 'never' to watch *Coronation St.*oth the serial and Richard Hoggart were just uncool and old-fashioned.

Around a decade after its first publication, my own first reading of *The Uses of Literacy* as a student was not actually dissimilar. My copy of a late sixties edition of the book is riddled with pencilled exclamation marks and marginal comments: overdone! sentimental! evidence? Admittedly this was in the light of being overly impressed with the more fashionable works of Marshall McLuhan. But such student responses do raise an initial question about teaching Richard Hoggart. *The Uses of Literacy* is directly and concretely tied to two specific eras of English life: between the first and second world war and the first decade after the second. So an immediate question arises about whether it is only realistic and possible now to teach the book as something of a period piece. That is, to regard Part One as mainly an historically significant documentation of the lived values of a particular regional and corporate class fraction. Then to treat Part Two from the perspective of a 'symptomatic reading', seeing it as offering a critique of perceived post-war Americanisation and mass commercial debasement from within a particular English culture-and-society formation and a tradition of cultural pessimism.

In considering whether *The Uses of Literacy* has only 'of its time' significance, I have revised my views of both McLuhan and Hoggart since my own time as a student. Indeed, I regard them more clearly now as *both* the inheritors of the culture-and-society tradition, particularly given the indelible impression the notion of some kind of organic community has made upon the thinking of each writer. But while McLuhan has become newly relevant for a media studies concerned with globalisation and new technology, Hoggart has remained stubbornly unfashionable, a much harder sell to students. Yet whereas I can now clearly discern the showier superficialities of McLuhan's work which Hoggart unerringly homed in on in his review of *Understanding Media* at the time of its publication (Hoggart 1970a: 114), I have also, since becoming a teacher of media studies, gained a more respectful awareness of the contribution to 'understanding media' that *The Uses of Literacy* can offer.

When I first started teaching various media-based components of Communication and Cultural Studies degrees in the late seventies I always referred to the relevance of Part One of the book. In particular I stressed how Hoggart looks at language here, particularly the everyday idioms and axioms that people get by on and how that work of densely detailed ethnography provides an entry point for reflecting how the popular media may relate to lived experience. Highlighting the chapters on '"Them" and "Us"' and 'The "Real" World of People', I attempted to encourage students away from the stark top-down propagandist model of the media that they tend to prefer.

I still find that these early chapters of *The Uses of Literacy* serve as a useful corrective in encouraging students to think how the media work with the grain of everyday cultural values. Even into the nineties, when media studies was being established as a single honours undergraduate degree in its own right, I have set students seminar exercises based on *The Uses of Literacy*: Do they recognise the speech idioms Hoggart describes? Could they provide a similar account of current idioms; the values they embody and how they might be represented in the media?

While very conscious of media studies' insistence on up-dated references, I have nevertheless continued to relate these chapters to classic work on phenomenology and theories of social construction, such as Berger and Luckmann's (1971) analyses of sedimentation and legitimation and Parkin's *Class Inequality and Social Order* (1972). Indeed, Parkin's discussion of how value-systems are based on class explicitly draws on Hoggart for his arguments around 'subordinate' value-systems and the notion of 'reward' and was itself influential in establishing the 'cultural turn' in media audience studies (for example, Brunsdon and Morley 1978). Then I might also refer to the continuing significance of Gramsci's (1971) work on common sense, hegemony and consent. And with postgraduate students I will throw into the mix Foucauldian analyses of discourse and genealogies and the perspectives on language and power developed by critical linguistics.

This indicative list suggests that, far from a period piece, there remains a substantial relevance to 'Richard Hoggart, Our Contemporary'. But it also shows how I have always taught *The Uses of Literacy* by stressing its links to some other work. The book's Part One provides for students the vivid concrete instance and the telling anecdote worked on with the experiential and imaginative insights that Hoggart bases on close textual and linguistic interpretation. As this is mainly done so aptly and immediately, it could sound invidious to expect more. But there is also a way in which *The Uses of Literacy* offers itself as unique and original, an innovatory one-off text to which you can only give assent - as if to the Leavisite rhetorical question, 'This is so, is it not?' Hence I have always felt it requires another, different sort of text to provide the sort of classroom discussion and argument that derives from an analytical overview.

But another reason why I offer theoretical texts to supplement and complement *The Uses of Literacy* is because of the almost wilful binarism of the book: as if it has got to be *either* the generalisable overview *or* the lived particularity. Richard Hoggart's insistence on the latter, the experiential, the autobiographical telling detail, almost by definition appears to exclude the larger conceptual framework that generates theory. Repeatedly he represents the theoretical in the shape of some forced imposition, a conformist straightjacket restricting the graphic, sensuous and the processual, whether the theory derives from the merely fashionable western European sphere or, more threateningly, has some collectivist provenance which makes it the product of some authoritarian groupthink.

I do not think this is an exaggeration. The autobiographical writing demonstrates a profound Cold War formation that shapes both the sort of social democratic trajectory Hoggart follows and contributes to his repeated assertion of the value of non-conforming individual action. His approach to theory is expressed, however, in a typically self-deprecating tone, as here after one of his descriptions of the development of British cultural studies:

I have put it in my own, largely untheoretical, terms. I admire and sometimes use a language of theory which captures concepts irreplaceably. I mistrust the way some people use abstractions as props or crutches, substitutes for thought, ways of showing others and assuring themselves that they belong to an inner group. I suspect anyone who peppers his papers with 'heuristic', 'hegemony', 'hierarchy', 'paradigm', 'problematic', 'reification', 'homology' and the like. One can sometimes work through almost intelligible and certainly reparative papers only to realise at the end that, though what they say is sensible and in some ways perceptive, it could have been said almost entirely without that apparatus of in-group theoretical language. (Hoggart 1992: 95)

Well, this is indeed so, is it not? Any cultural researcher could easily give their own examples of what is being referred to. Yet there is an element of an attack on straw people here and an important distinction to be made between the obscure and pedantic theoreticism that Hoggart is evoking and the theory that he concedes he finds 'captures concepts irreplaceably' but for which he provides no list of examples. The list of concepts he deprecates are indeed many of the selfsame theoretical notions from sociology, Marxism and post-structuralism that I have linked to his own work in teaching it. But this is not a connection Hoggart himself is willing to make. There is a defensiveness that the next passage implies:

One English critic, friendly but slightly regretful, described my way of going on as 'deceptively descriptive to the point of casualness'. I expect he wished to find an explicit pattern of hypotheses, a set of linked generalisations which the individual descriptions supported (as one commonly finds in French writings). But it was a French sociologist, J-C Passeron, who, in the introduction to the French edition of *The Uses of Literacy*, suggested - to my surprise - that his countrymen look again at their predilection for theoretical structures and learn something from this English commitment to 'phenomenological' detail. He did not think my procedure 'casual' but, rather, 'extraordinarily precise'. (Hoggart 1992: 95)

Again this is modestly and lightly conveyed. But just as Passeron (2007/1971) uses his celebration of Hoggart to criticise a French intelligentsia for their 'outsider' view of working-class values, so Hoggart finds in Passeron a rather too convenient alibi covering his defensive attitude to the theoretical.

Why I described this attitude as 'wilful' is that I think Hoggart repeatedly and unnecessarily boxes himself in. For instance, looking through the essays on the media collected in *Speaking to Each Other: About Society* (Hoggart 1970a) I am forcibly struck by wise, acute perceptions about, say, the BBC and broadcasters' 'self-defining tendency'; McLuhan himself and the problems associated with his 'coolness'; or the smugness of the *Daily Mirror*. Undoubtedly these have intrinsic historical merit and would be well worth putting on a media studies booklist if only to demonstrate how Hoggart's thinking about the media could be ahead of its time. But repeatedly, a vein of productive thought is opened up only to be closed down just as it promises to develop from empirical description to carefully nuanced evaluation and analysis. So the thought remains sometimes little more than a throwaway remark, frequently and unnecessarily leading into some socially conservative polemic or self-justificatory defence of say, individualism, earnestness or unfashionability. Even one of the most perceptive of these essays, 'The Argument about Effects', first delivered as a Cambridge University lecture in 1966, shuts down at its key moments. Challenging then-dominant media research paradigms derived from behaviourism and 'uses-and-gratifications' theory, Hoggart insists on the importance of taking account of value and emotion in audience responses and the need to produce new 'hypotheses about change'. But the theoretical point cannot be sustained. It gets lost in the move to an easy stereotyping of a familiar group: 'Too many of "the intelligentsia" hate serious analysis of the mass media. They prefer them to be kept in a compartment labelled "For Fun Only"; and they dismiss attempts to discuss them as "puritan", "over-earnest", "old-fashioned moralizing..."' (Hoggart 1970a: 226). Some of the limitations of these essays obviously relate to the exigencies of Richard Hoggart's career, from the late fifties onwards, as a public intellectual, and his involvement in broadcasting and the arts, particularly in extensive committee-work. So that while he remains a prolific writer into the new millenium, his later writing on the media and culture is primarily confined to the lecture, the review and the short article.

But as David Lodge suggested in his paper to the *Uses of Hoggart* conference at Sheffield University in 2006 (Owen, 2008), it was also 'no accident' that Richard Hoggart left the Birmingham Centre for Contemporary Cultural Studies after being invited by the British Ministry for Overseas Development to apply for one of the five Assistant Director-General posts at UNESCO. Hoggart had created the Centre in 1964, only a year after his appointment as Professor of English. As Lodge pointed out, it was 1970 when Hoggart made the move from academia to administration, just as the tide of Marxist theory came pouring in to European and American cultural studies as one of the aftermaths of 1968. But by then Hoggart's suspicions both of any form of collectivism and of theoretical generalisation were to be, far from shifted, merely more strongly reinforced. This is evidenced by the brief, oblique, but very pointed remarks about the development of the Centre after his departure that Hoggart (1993: 76) makes in the autobiographical chapter, 'Great Hopes from Birmingham'.

However, while I think theoretical follow-through remains the lacuna of all Hoggart's writing my continuing engagement with *The Uses of Literacy* in media studies teaching also extends to referencing Part Two of the book, entitled, 'Yielding Place to New', which provides a post-war context that relates more directly to the workings of modern media. Its first chapter, 'Unbending the Springs of Action', is the one I think has most to offer media studies. It helps to counter students' hard-to-shift notions of the media as primarily based on conspiracies or lies, such as the long-prevailing adherence to some version of the Herman-Chomsky propaganda model (1988). What I value about the 'Unbending the Springs' chapter is the nuanced subtlety of its recognition of how the popular press relates to its audience. Following on from Part One's discussion of everyday language as kinds of coping strategy, this chapter indicates how the popular press adapts those idiomatic maxims based on a long class experience of living out subordination and expressing resilience, tolerance and sometimes resistance. Ventriloquising these sayings back to their audiences in the different context of tabloid news values, their capacity for expressing what we might now call 'empowerment' is diminished in the process.

As usual, Hoggart is making a moral rather than political point here about 'regrettable aspects of change'. His notion of 'action' is related to the moral and cultural values that encourage a corporate class-in-itself to maintain what Hoggart summed up as the product of his own upbringing: 'a capacity, now and again, to say "come off it" and an ability to go on going on' (Hoggart 1970a: 27). This is a very different conception from any political transformation that might be wrought by a class-*for*-itself - and many critics have pointed to the downplaying of traditions of working-class activism in Hoggart's work (Mulhern 2000: 63). Nevertheless, I think the specific practices and strategies he identifies can, again, be read in the light of theoretical texts, Gramsci or Althusser, say, as concrete examples of how the media invite subordinate groups to 'freely' consent to live out their continued subordination. Again, with the close attention paid to language, right down to the detail of adjectives and phrases, Hoggart charts precisely how facile media appeals to tolerance and egalitarianism are effectively turned into their opposites inviting their audiences into an anything-goes mentality or an apparent anti-elitism that neither informs anyone or invites any substantive questioning, let alone challenge, of authority figures.

In this chapter, and the following ones on 'Invitations to a Candyfloss World' and 'Unbent Springs: A note on scepticism' where Hoggart's publisher required that he made up examples from the media and popular fiction rather than used direct quotations, his illustrations still resonate with a striking prescience. When I was writing about the tabloid response to Archbishop Rowan Williams' lecture on the applicability of sharia law in the British legal context as summed up in the *Sun*'s 8 February 2008 headline, 'What a Burkha', (Brunt 2010: 152), I noted the similarity with one of Hoggart's fictitious popular press articles. The pastiche extract he invents describes the '60-year-old bachelor Archprelate of Pontyholoth' giving a talk mildly critical of 'passive' recreations such as doing the weekly pools. This is headlined and introduced: 'IT BEATS ME. Here we go again, chums! Who is it *this time*?' And goes on to attack the cleric for intolerance, smugness and hypocrisy: 'Perhaps we got it wrong, because we also thought that Christian leaders were on the side of FREEDOM and EQUALITY. But maybe these ideas are only alright for the Archprelate and his pals...' (Hoggart 1958: 241).

Although obviously the slang is now outdated, Hoggart's demonstration of the appeal to common sense through a colloquial address to the figure of what the chapter subsequently describes as the mythical 'common man', highlights precisely how mass circulation media position themselves as on the side of 'us' while effectively acting for 'them' against our interests, our right to be informed of what is happening in this situation. Hoggart then continues to tease out and illustrate a number of facets of 'Unbending the Springs of Action' in tabloid news reporting, such as the aggressive plain man's stance; the band-wagon mentality; personalisation; progressivism and fragmentation. As I suggest to students, all these perspectives have contemporary relevance for media studies in helping us reflect on the many ways in which newspapers invite identification: indeed, *pace* Hoggart, how they 'interpellate' us as Althusserian subjects.

But while I continue to find 'unbending the springs' a very productive metaphor for teaching media studies, at the same time, any re-reading of Part Two cannot fail to note how this resonant idea is repeatedly left just *as* resonant, stopped in the tracks of the thought by overwrought assertions that actually risk undermining the very subtlety of the notion. These purple passages detract from careful evaluation because they make polemically simple references to audience passivity and also represent the media as undifferentiated propaganda machines - without even the saving grace of the sort of detailed political economy and a clear analysis of power relations that Herman and Chomsky (1988) provide. There is a further frustration for teacher and student that, just at places where Richard Hoggart could be expanding a particular *aperçu* and developing discussion about it, other voices take over and are left to make the point. This is the irritating and unnecessary move to the many literary and moral quotations that Mulhern (2000: 59) describes as providing 'an entire chorus of wisdom and insight' for *The Uses of Literacy* and ultimately what its 'true authority' rests on.

Throughout the book, quotations that draw primarily on an English culture-and-society tradition from Bunyan to Lawrence and T. S. Eliot feature as epigraphs to chapters or are juxtaposed to examples of modern mass culture. I would describe them as *touchstones* because they act in the Arnoldian sense of 'the best that has been thought and said'. They function in two main ways. In the first place they are used for the purposes of comparison, always to the detriment of the mass commercialised medium or artefact under discussion. For instance, to take one of Hoggart's more egregious examples, his pastiche extract of 'a typical gangster-novelette' is followed with the comment, 'There comes to mind the ending, a century and a half ago, of *Sense and Sensibility*'. The final paragraph of this novel is then introduced without comment as the conclusion to 'The Newer Mass Art' chapter (Hoggart 1958: 272). The tone is magisterial: no argument is necessary for the very comparison, gangster fiction v. Jane Austen, is taken to contain its own obvious justification.

This comparative style reaches its apogee in *The Way We Live Now* (Hoggart 1996) when it becomes sufficient to juxtapose the admired name or title against the lesser or debased one: whatever their genre or period context they stand or fall by some indefinable intrinsic qualities. Hence it is Milton versus Bob Dylan or Elizabeth Gaskell's *North and South* against Robert Tressell's *Ragged Trousered Philanthropists*: enough said. The second type of touchstone is the one that functions as an epigraph and acts as a framing device to a chapter or section. This may similarly have the effect of pre-empting argument, as if the very stating of a quotation would make any further discussion or commentary superfluous.

There are many difficulties with this approach. Despite the large-hearted generosity and honesty of *The Uses of Literacy* that has made it undoubtedly the beloved book that has changed lives, I think any contemporary reckoning of Richard Hoggart cannot ignore how frequently a kind of literary sensibility is evoked and assumed which is both ineffable and only 'proved on the pulses' of those already in the know. I disagree with those who point to sections like 'The Juke Box Boys' as embarrassing aberrations; the touchstone tendency of an implied moral and aesthetic capacity to act as cultural arbiter in ways that do not require spelling out is written into the very fabric of the book.

Hence the touchstones come across as abstract and timeless generalities, removed from their historical, or any, context and presented as assertions as if the reader is being invited to assent to them without demur. For all

Richard Hoggart's diffident disclaimers in the Conclusion of *The Uses of Literacy*: this is only one person's opinion, this is just the start of the debate; for all the apparently open-minded qualifications scattered through the text, 'for good or ill', there are really no options, no scope for discussion.

However, there are occasions where the touchstones work effectively. These are when, irrespective of context, Hoggart adapts them, inhabits them as his own and seizes on the germ of an idea to develop for his purposes. I think this is the case with the key figure of 'unbending the springs'. The metaphor comes, not from the English culture and society tradition, but from a text Hoggart much respects, refers to throughout his long writing career and quotes six times in *The Uses of Literacy*: Alexis de Tocqueville's *Democracy in America*, written between 1835-40 (1965). De Tocqueville's epigraph opens the first chapter of Part Two thus: 'By this means, a kind of virtuous materialism may ultimately be established in the world, which would not corrupt, but enervate the soul, and noiselessly unbend its springs of action' (Hoggart 1958:168). But while the use Hoggart makes of 'unbending the springs' becomes a central and resonant motif for the whole of the second part of the book and, as I have indicated, a highly productive metaphor for considering one of the dominant types of media-audience relationship, I think there is also a problem with the use of the de Tocqueville touchstones that is quite symptomatic of what can be troubling about Hoggart's writing and hence limit its usefulness for media studies teaching.

For instance, if you attempted to collect most of the epigraphs and quotations from de Tocqueville in Hoggart's texts, admittedly a rather pedantic exercise, you would get an impression of some old aristocrat bemoaning the modern in the counter-revolutionary way that conforms only too well to the stereotype of him summed up in his most famous maxim about 'the tyranny of the majority' (Commager 1993: 18). You would not get any glimpse of a de Tocqueville that modern historians have seen as, say, a precursor of Marx, whose project is to analyse and compare the success, as he sees it, of democracy in America, with the post-revolutionary history of France, and who is full of praise for the energy of the settlers, the way their townships work, and so on. Indeed, *Democracy in America* with its meticulous attention to specifics and wide scope offers something akin to a modern SWOT analysis of strengths and weaknesses, opportunities and threats within an emerging social formation. What Hoggart takes from de Tocqueville are, unfailingly, all the more negative questions he raises about the weaknesses of new democracy. Authors are, of course, entitled to select anything from another text to make their points. But my concern is not about some 'bias' or a lack of 'balance' on Hoggart's part. What I find dispiriting about the way de Tocqueville, like many of the other authors abstracted from their context, is used to make a point in *The Uses of Literacy* is that the 'springs' of his own work are thereby unbent. In other words, de Tocqueville is a more interesting figure than Hoggart allows, precisely because he, unlike Hoggart himself for the most part, demonstrates a grasp of complexity and contradiction. The source of my disappointment with Hoggart's writing is that, along with the tendency to back away from sustained argument and his reliance on assumed common ground with the reader, there is this repeated preference for the vague binaries, the contrapuntal schema of the 'older' versus the 'newer' cultural values where ultimately a universalist choice of either/or must be made. This is not the both-and arena of complexity and contradiction.

Hence the 'newer mass art' of Part Two inevitably comes to be seen, despite all the caveats and hesitancies that Hoggart inserts, as 'anti-life'. The polemical final pages of the Conclusion are unequivocal: 'Most mass entertainments are in the end what D. H. Lawrence described as "anti-life". They are full of a corrupt brightness, of improper appeals and moral evasions … These productions belong to a vicarious, spectators' world; they offer nothing which can really grip the brain or heart' (Hoggart 1958: 340).

However, the limitations of this dichotomous thinking and the pervasive pessimism about the post-war 'new' mass media are themselves highlighted by Hoggart's own more complex interpretations of interwar media in Part One. These also contain the awareness, mainly denied in Part Two, of the possibility of contradiction. To take just two examples. First, the discussion of popular song which comes at the very end of Part One in the chapter, 'The Full Rich Life'. In a powerfully evocative reading, Hoggart addresses the criticism that these songs are sentimental. He concurs but goes on to consider how they are both taken very seriously by singers and audiences while at the same time understood by them to be excessive. He then introduces a third term, 'the feeling heart', and concludes:

A feeling heart can often be soft and sentimental, but it is not to be derided. Most of these songs express … the 'feeling heart'. They touch old chords … Life outside, life on a Monday morning, can be a dour affair … and no doubt their sentiments remain somewhere in the memory through all the unsentimental ordinariness of the working week. (Hoggart 1958: 165-166)

The awareness of both-and works together here with a moving recognition of the real material conditions which the songs not only reflect but also offer an escape from. The same sense of complexity is also apparent in Hoggart's consideration of women's magazine stories in 'The "Real" World of People' chapter. 'I shall refer to them as the "older magazines",' he says, thinking again of the interwar period and the popularity of the *Peg's Paper* tradition. Picking up on one of the central features of I. A. Richards' seminal approach to practical criticism, Hoggart concedes that the *Peg's Paper* stories are full of cliché and 'stock responses'. However:

> the strongest impression ... is of their extraordinary fidelity to the detail of their readers' lives ... If we regard them as faithful but dramatized presentations of a life whose form and values are known, we might find it more useful to ask what are the values they embody ... [W]e need to appreciate ... that they may in all their triteness speak for a solid and relevant way of life ... The world these stories present is a limited and simple one ... It is often a childish and garish world and the springs of the emotions work in great gushings. But they do work: it is not a corrupt or a pretentious world. (Hoggart 1958: 126;129)

This passage again demonstrates the patient teasing out of a complex and contradictory reading of a medium. But it is not one to be afforded to 'the newer kind of magazines': the chapter ends by anticipating Part Two's negative assessments of post-war media with a polemic against 'the smartness of the newer magazines' which can degenerate into 'a slickness ... a kittenish domesticity and a manner predominantly arch or whimsical' (Hoggart 1958: 131).

I am suggesting, then, that the polemical exigencies of an almost automatically negative response to the 'now' and the 'new' unnecessarily inhibits the analysis of post-war media and cultural artefacts as against the richness of interpretation provided for those of the interwar period. In the dichotomous world of *The Uses of Literacy* it is as if Part One as a whole acts as the touchstone against which all that is examined in Part Two must inevitably be judged and ultimately fail in the comparison. Hence, with the particular exception of the 'unbending the spring' metaphor, I think Hoggart has more to offer the teaching of media studies when the touchstones, the moral binaries and the accompanying overheated polemic, can be put to one side and the observational and specifically experiential come to the fore: as with the detailed linguistic interpretations of 'common sense' from both Parts One and Two, that can still offer constructive insights into the kind of legitimations that any contract between the media and its audiences requires.

Returning to the specifics also offers, I suggest, one further reason for media studies looking to Richard Hoggart's writing and teaching. It relates to my current concern that students of media often struggle with representing their object of study. Despite or because of their very familiarity with the variety of forms and artefacts that constitute 'the media', students are often less comfortable with exploring that variety and plurality than with designating 'the media' as a singular system, a homogenous 'it'. Hence it might be worth re-visiting and re-working Hoggart's original project for developing cultural studies as a way of encouraging students to reconnect with their own experience of the media and then reflect on its specificity. In his 1963 inaugural professorial lecture at Birmingham, 'Schools of English and Contemporary Society', Hoggart (1970b: 255) outlined 'the field for possible work in contemporary cultural studies' which he divided into three parts: one broadly historical; a second, broadly sociological; while 'the third - which will be the most important, is the literary critical'.

When the Birmingham Centre for Contemporary Cultural Studies was established a year later the priority given to the literary-critical reflected not only Hoggart's disciplinary background but that of the original staff and research fellows. And when it began taking postgraduate students from 1967, the weekly seminar run by Richard Hoggart was based on practical criticism of a poem or an extract from a novel or magazine. The emphasis was on 'close reading' and 'reading for tone' with students repeatedly enjoined to respond to the concrete in the text. The problem was that these sessions were such virtuoso riffs that it was hard to see how others could join in. Nevertheless, the insights gained always justified the method - one which some of its originators, such as I. A. Richards, always insisted involved techniques that researchers could be trained in. It might therefore be useful for cultural studies to re-acquaint itself with some of its English literature origins. The methods of literary practical criticism, paying close attention to the empirical detail of the text could certainly offer a corrective to a flatly essentialist view of 'the media'.

Finally, at its most generous and open-minded, Richard Hoggart's cultural studies project proposes, not simply the prioritising of literary criticism, but an equitable interdisciplinary enterprise. He outlines its dimensions in his 1967 talk to the sociology section of the British Association, 'The Literary Imagination and the Sociological Imagination' (Hoggart 1970b: 260). Although C. Wright Mills (1970/1959) had already explored many dimensions of 'the sociological imagination', it is Hoggart who addresses here what both disciplines may have in common: 'Sustained imaginative perception only looks like a sudden gift; it takes off from saturation in experience' (Hoggart 1970b: 268). He also enquires into their different but possibly complementary approaches suggesting that the literary offers a 'sense of pattern-and-lack-of-pattern', while the best social theory demands a critical stance and 'intellectual discipline' based on constantly questioning research (Hoggart 1970b: 236) and he cites hospitably a wide range of social theorists from Myrdal to Adorno to Levi-Strauss.

This is not the self-dramatising and thin-skinned persona that appears in the volumes of autobiographical memoirs or sections of *The Uses of Literacy*, clinging defensively to the touchstones of the canon with the sometimes glib value-judgement. It is the confident voice of the cultural researcher who wants, not just to defend the empirical, the experiential and the concrete, but to analyse it by drawing on a wide variety of disciplinary contexts. Who is prepared to move from assertions of value to the detailed analysis of specific values and meanings - to discover the *value-orientation* of the text and how it actually 'works'. Hoggart's own career took a different trajectory into educational administration and he did not go on to explore and develop his original vision. Nevertheless, media studies would still do well to pick up on the promise of a project that contains both interpretative rigour and the dynamic notion of interdisciplinary 'imaginations'.

Bibliography

Berger, P. and Luckmann, T. (1971) *The Social Construction of Reality* (Harmondsworth: Penguin).

Brunsdon, C. and Morley, D. (1978) *Everyday Television 'Nationwide'* (London: British Film Institute).

Brunt, R. (2010) '"What a Burkha": reflections on the UK media coverage of the sharia law controversy'. In R. Brunt and R Cere (eds.), *Postcolonial Media Culture in Britain* (London: Palgrave).

Commager, H. (1993) *On Tocqueville* (Columbia: University of Missouri Press).

Gramsci, A. (1971) *Selections from Prison Notebooks* (London: Lawrence and Wishart).

Herman, E., and Chomsky, N. (1988) *Manufacturing Consent* (New York: Pantheon).

Hoggart, R. (1958) *The Uses of Literacy* (Harmondsworth: Pelican Books).

———— (1970a) *Speaking to Each Other, Volume 1: About Society* (London: Chatto and Windus).

———— (1970b) *Speaking to Each Other, Volume 2: About Literature* (London: Chatto and Windus).

———— (1993) *An Imagined Life* (Oxford: Oxford University Press).

———— (1996) *The Way We Live Now* (London: Pimlico).

Lodge, D. (2008) 'Richard Hoggart: a personal appreciation'. In S. Owen (ed.), *Re-reading Richard Hoggart: life, literature, language, education* (Newcastle:

Cambridge Scholars Publishing).

Mulhern, F. (2000) *Culture/Metaculture* (London: Routledge).

Parkin, F. (1972) *Class, Inequality and Political Order* (London: Paladin).

Passeron, J-C. (2007) 'Introduction to the French edition of *The Uses of Literacy*', (trans. R. Dyer). In A.Gray, J. Campbell, M. Erickson, S. Hanson, and H. Wood (eds.), *CCCS selected working papers* (London: Routledge).

Tocqueville, A. de (1965) *Democracy in America*, (ed. H Steele Commager) (Oxford: World Classics, Oxford University Press).

Wright Mills, F. (1970/1959) *The Sociological Imagination* (Harmondsworth: Penguin).

CONFRONTING VALUE: A NOTE
John Corner

In this short essay I want to explore some aspects of Richard Hoggart's work by focusing on an agenda of questions concerning his 'reading' of cultural value and cultural change.[1] I am aware that a sizeable literature of critical commentary has developed around the key writings, particularly in recent years, but my aim is to present a brief, focused and, I hope, provocative agenda of critical points and in doing this I shall restrict myself to referencing this wider literature sparingly. Hoggart's descriptions and assessments, particularly in *The Uses of Literacy* (1957, but page references below are to 1958 edition), have been seen as a point of necessary orientation in any serious address to cultural change in post-war Britain, particularly to changes in working-class culture, although references to his work in current research are perhaps less frequent than they were, despite arguments about his particular perspective and approach 'coming back' into stronger visibility after successive waves of often conceptually elaborate bodies of cultural theory. It is important to note how, in cultural studies, the response to Hoggart has mostly taken the form of a critical dialogue, particularly with his view of the cultural changes of the 1950s, rather than a straightforward affirmation and development. There have also been assessments of a more markedly negative kind (see, for instance, Sparks, 1974 on questions of class and Owen, 2008 for a review of feminist critiques).

It is impossible to address Hoggart's work properly without recognising the broader difficulties and awkwardness of engaging academically with 'popular culture'. These follow from the tensions and sometimes contradictions — ethical and political but also aesthetic — which derive in turn from the complex interconnections and diverse normative perspectives that the notion of popular culture throws up. The phrase combines, as Stuart Hall has observed (Hall 1981), the problems of two historically complex and contested terms, reverberating with the different arguments that have employed them as central points of reference and of orientation. The difficulties and the awkwardness continue in much cultural analysis today, their presence sometimes admitted but more often disguised by a vocabulary more specialised and self-consciously impersonal than Hoggart's own. They are to be found lying behind what I see as the distinctive 'double dynamics' of cultural studies, both that

---

[1] The idea of 'reading' is, of course, particularly applicable to Hoggart's work, given his interest in extending the analytic methods of literary criticism in order to interpret social values.

towards affirmation and even celebration and that towards the identification of deficits and the articulation of critique. This gives to the whole area of study a degree of instability in aims and approaches, however much masked by confident assertions of intent. The underlying tensions are unlikely to disappear whatever the achievements by way of empirical work and theoretical development. Indeed, there are grounds for seeing them as so deeply entailed in the project of engaging evaluatively with 'popular culture' as to have become a necessary element of serious inquiry and discussion in this area.

Hoggart organised *The Uses of Literacy*, both its autobiographical ethnography and its analytic reading of contemporary cultural tendencies, around a sense of 'crisis', of impending 'danger' to which the working class were particularly, although not exclusively, exposed as a result of forms of cultural exploitation with potentially 'debilitating' outcomes for lived values. This sense of change comes through at several points, most sharply in its final chapter. I want in what follows to suggest that we can identify three different 'frames' within which Hoggart's descriptive and evaluative work is carried out, and that the relationship between these frames is significant for the character of the overall cultural judgment that emerges. This is a judgement that, whilst it shares something with the work, for instance, of Stuart Hall, Raymond Williams and Pierre Bourdieu, displays quite distinctive features in its engagement with matters of value. In a subsequent section, I shall then try to make four related points about how issues of value are 'confronted' in Hoggart's work and how a critical review of his approach is the best way of continuing to employ this work in our thinking about the current and future, as well as historical, conditions of culture.

Three Frames

The first frame I am interested in is the frame of 'cultural improvement'. This is the dominant frame in much of Hoggart's work and it is closely related to his sense of the need for a much greater extension of educational opportunity together with the wider and improved range of cultural choice that would follow from this. 'Cultural improvement' partly involves a greater number of people being able to enjoy a wider array of cultural artefacts and productions, including those that require some degree of acquired competence through steady familiarity. There is a prophylactic character to this 'improvement' too, insofar as Hoggart implies that a consequence of the opportunities it entails would mean a reduced audience and readership for those aspects of the currently 'popular' that he finds aesthetically, socially and spiritually questionable (as features of 'the candy floss world', Hoggart 1958: 206-245). A strong new educational policy would not bring about cultural transformation on its own, but it would be the centrepiece of a broader set of policy shifts introduced into the areas of arts and media. The aim is explicitly not the impractical one of making everyone 'highbrow'. It is that of giving support for a range of different kinds of cultural experience and of cultural 'tastes' so as to find better conditions for achieving integrity and critical independence, thereby bringing about improved circumstances of personal and social fulfilment.

The second frame at work is that of 'political improvement'. This looks towards greater democratic participation, a more alert questioning of current political values and language and, therefore, a strengthened sense of the 'public' and the 'civic' in national life. The aspirations here are placed against a sense of a growing 'uniformity' being imposed upon ordinary people, in part by increasingly 'centralised' forms of social management, a uniformity in which significant freedoms, including the space for a proper degree of democratic self-determination, may be lost. Part of the broader changes has involved a significant shift in the composition and the character of the working class, with some of its more intellectually able members, among them those that constituted the 'earnest minority' of the class (Hoggart 1958: 318-323), now being recruited into the professional middle class through educational change. There is a sense of a new 'classless class' in the making as a result of technological and economic shifts in the shaping of material and cultural life. Hoggart, fully recognising both the benefits of education and the limiting aspects of class identities, wants nevertheless to emphasise the reduction in the critical resilience of working-class culture as a result of these shifts and the consequent weakening, essentially *political* in character, of its internal resources and self-identity.

However, whereas, for instance, in the work of Raymond Williams and certainly of Stuart Hall, the political is the primary frame, with change here being seen as a necessary context for significant cultural transformation (allowing for continuing interaction between the political and the cultural), in Hoggart it is essentially a secondary frame, although one which appears more strongly at the end of *Uses* than perhaps anywhere else in his major writings. 'Cultural improvement' against the growing tendency towards cultural impoverishment and exploitation, is the dominant theme. It is related explicitly to the political at many points, its grounds are primarily ethical and sometimes spiritual; it is about greater fairness in the way people live and greater equality in the kinds of things they can enjoy and that can improve the non-material quality of their lives.

This brings us to a third frame, which I will call here the 'frame of the politics of inequality'. This differs from that of 'political improvement' because it is essentially about the diagnosis of deficits rather than the aspiration to reduce these deficits. We can see it as a broad theoretico-analytic frame in which ideas of cultural improvement and of political improvement can be variously situated. In this sense, it is a frame of a different order from the two others. Whilst in Williams (e.g Williams 1961), in Hall (e.g Hall 1981) and perhaps most explicitly in the work of E. P. Thompson (classically, Thompson 1963), this third frame is strongly evidenced and articulated with economic and political history, particularly the history of social class relations, in Hoggart it is far more muted in expression. In his work, it can take on something of a 'folksy' character (as in discussion of the trope of 'them and us', Hoggart 1958: 72-101). This approach, while it may show a keener ear for the actual vocabulary of class tension and be illuminating about the nature of popular perceptions, is not fully adequate to the deep historical and economic divisions and relations of power that are involved. Hoggart sometimes alludes to these divisions with a sharp sense of their scale and over-arching importance, without ever giving them sustained address. The relatively modest attention that his analysis gives to the role of work and of work-based organisations in shaping the broader patterns of leisure and of lived culture, including the forms of engagement with mediated popular culture, is fully consonant with this perspective.

On the basis of such a rough typology, I would want to claim that the weak relation of ideas of cultural improvement to political improvement and the lack of a developed frame for addressing 'the politics of inequality', in particular the absence of any serious engagement with the history of capitalist relations, limits the cogency of Hoggart's cultural criticism. Too often, despite the subtlety of the local analysis and the overall generosity of engagement, normative ideas like that of 'spiritual dry rot' (Hoggart 1958: 248) gain prominence at the expense of a more focused and materialist account of the dominant cultural dynamics at work and of just what might be required effectively to oppose them and introduce new options. I shall return to this point later but now, in what is essentially an attempt at further development of parts of the preceding discussion, I want to look at four aspects of the way in which matters of cultural value appear in the writings, giving what I think is a justified prominence to *The Uses of Literacy*.

Four Points about 'Value'

I

First of all, I think it is productive when considering Hoggart's work to note how that longstanding duality in uses of the idea of 'culture' - culture as both 'way of life' and as 'expressive artefacts' (sometimes as 'art') - appears within it. In discussion of this duality, it is regularly pointed out that the relationship between these two dimensions of the cultural is so close that differentiation may be difficult and even at times distortive. However, whilst recognising this interplay, I would want to emphasise the continuing gap between the two senses of the word, a gap which I think is still frequently under-recognised in cultural studies research in a way that leads to an unfortunate merging of what are essentially sociological ideas with what are essentially aesthetic-critical ones. It is certainly true that, across a wide area of arts and expressive practice, the connections outwards to broader values and meanings and to the contexts of lived experience within which expressive work is encountered need to be recognised and often made an integral part of critical assessment. It is also true that any account of ways of living that leaves out attention to the diverse forms of the aesthetic and of creative expressivity in circulation will be greatly reduced in its scope. However, the kind of analytic approach that is most directly appropriate to each side of the duality may differ considerably and so may the kind of evaluative scheme that can most productively be applied.

If due notice is not taken of this differentiation, it has a tendency to produce tensions and even contradictions in the arguments subsequently developed. Hoggart sees a 'corrupt brightness' (Hoggart 1958: 340) in much of the contemporary popular culture that he discusses. Some of this he regards as 'dangerous'. In making these judgements about what is primarily *the social and political risk* that the cultural products carry, he often uses terms of judgment drawn from a literary-ethical vocabulary. A good example would be the idea of an artefact being in certain respects 'anti-life' (Hoggart 1958: 340), an assessment that draws on the language of D. H. Lawrence in a way quite close to some of the judgements made both by F. R. Leavis and Q.D. Leavis in their own, more directly literary, appraisal of art-life relations.[2] However, as well as warning of the risks to social values, to ways of living, posed by forms of 'bad' popular culture, Hoggart wishes to keep some disjunction between the world of this culture and the everyday world of ordinary people. He does not wish to see the 'badness' of popular culture at the level of many commercially produced artefacts and modes of cultural consumption as simply an indicator (or indeed a reflector) of 'badness' at the level of ordinary values. In the final chapter of *The Uses of Literacy*, he notes the various ways in which ordinary people are 'resilient' although he then wants to warn against the risk of slipping too easily into assuming from this that there is

---

[2] F. R. Leavis is stronger than Q.D. Leavis on 'life values', taking his cue from Lawrence, but Q.D. Leavis's work on popular literature (Leavis, 1932) is an important forerunner of *The Uses of Literacy* and Hoggart has noted that he was a 'great admirer' of her work, with reservations about her evaluative attitude (see, for instance, Corner 1992).

no threat from the cultural tendencies he has discussed. One of the reasons he does not want to align popular output too tightly with popular consciousness is that he has too much respect for (and a sense of protectiveness towards) ordinary people to allow him to identify a deficit here. This is not, of course, a problem for many of the 'mass culture' critics who preceded him or for some who have offered cultural commentary since. Another, related, reason for holding back on such an alignment is that doing so provides a continuing 'space for hope', a sense of ordinary living not yet irredeemably contaminated by the cultural materials in general circulation (which nevertheless have consequences both 'widespread and uniform' ref 264) and it therefore also provides some grounding for the development of a public for new, better and wider cultural provision within the terms of revised policies and institutional practices. There is instability here, in an assessment that wishes to warn of the negative impact of much of the cultural material currently 'popular' and yet also wishes to affirm a sense of ordinary values having a degree of independence and integrity. It is a type of instability also occasionally present, albeit in rather different ways, in the work of Raymond Williams and Stuart Hall and it is one that is finally grounded in the dynamics of the democratic imagination and democratic hope. This does not, however, reduce the limitations it places on coherent and consistent argument about cultural value and the character of cultural change.[3]

II

A second, significant dimension of the engagement with 'value' is the form of address to questions of cultural difference. Cultural commentators vary in the extent to which they relate 'difference' to 'inequality'. To bring inequality strongly into the picture is to introduce a negative, critical perspective on 'difference' whereas, by contrast, to give emphasis to 'diversity' is often to present difference as positive. Clearly, some recognition of inequality is present, if implicit, in most writing on contemporary culture but it differs quite widely in the form in takes within the overall analysis and argument. In the influential work of Pierre Bourdieu, (notably Bourdieu 1984) cultural inequality is seen as part of the

---

[3] This instability can also be seen in many areas of media studies, including the debate about the values of 'reality television' and the long-running discussion from the 1980s onwards about the degree to which popular audiences interpret media texts in ways which include strong elements of independence and resistance, thereby weakening claims about the role of such texts in ideological control.

unequal distribution of cultural capital within the economic and social order. This might seem to provide the basis for an argument in favour of 'cultural improvement' of the kind that lies behind a good deal of Hoggart's writing, an improvement that has a strong basis in education as well as in changes to media and arts policy. However, Bourdieu regards cultural differentiation, as it shows itself for instance in the appreciation of the higher art forms, as primarily a *positional* variation within a cultural system clearly stratified by social class rather than as an unequal chance to enjoy the *intrinsic values* of specific forms of cultural product and performance. Within this perspective, any direct idea of a 'cultural improvement' achieved by bringing to the disadvantaged the benefits of enjoying superior cultural works, with the enhancement of their quality of life that will follow, is made extremely difficult to advance. Hoggart would clearly want to argue both for the benefits of personal satisfaction which the opportunity to engage with work of quality in the arts offer and also the benefits of personal 'improvement' (e.g. of heightened awareness of other ways of living and perhaps, to move in a more Leavisite direction, of expanded moral sensibility) that are related to this. He would probably give short shrift to the kind of relativism that is a recurrent (and problematic) aspect of Bourdieu's assessment of cultural value.[4] However, Bourdieu's firmly sociological recognition of social class relations and of cultural inequality, not only as formed by the traditional hierarchic social order but as imperatives of the transformed economic order within capitalism, gives to his account a robustness that Hoggart's own diagnosis of cultural ills cannot really match.

Those recommending cultural improvement have often insufficiently pursued the question of the economic roots of cultural inequality and of the historical formation of differences in 'taste'. This has often left recommendations conveying what is finally a more gestural and impractical sense of the options for change and reform than might otherwise be the case.[5] Despite the thoughtful depth of his analysis, an analysis that is registered as part of a personal as well as a scholarly project, Hoggart shows himself to be disinclined to work too far outside established and dominant ideas of cultural value and, with moments of exception, outside of established ideas about the 'scope for change' within the economic, social and political order.

---

[4] On this, see among other commentaries, Frow (1987).
[5] Examples might include the Report of the Pilkington Committee on Broadcasting (Home Office, 1962), of which Hoggart was a co-author, and the Arts Council Report *The Glory of the Garden*, together with elements of many reports on education over the last 30 years.

III

Connecting with many of the points discussed above, there is the question of the relationship between culture, morality and politics. Another way of putting some of the comments I have already made is to observe that Hoggart's work does not make strong connections between culture and *power*. In the later work of the Birmingham CCCS this perspective would be exchanged for one in which the political relations of popular culture (in particular its role in the reproduction of ideology) would become the primary point of reference (see, for instance, the contributions to CCCS, 1977). It could be argued that the later position seriously displaced, at least for a time, questions of aesthetics and of cultural experience (including the experience of pleasure) from the frame of inquiry. In that context, the more recent 'rediscovery' of Hoggart as continuingly suggestive on these questions is understandable. Nevertheless, a more comprehensive recognition of the profound ways in which many aspects of culture are connected to the 'power system' would have strengthened Hoggart's analysis and the force both of his critique and his recommendations for change. If there are dangers in seeing the cultural too directly in terms of structures of power (and I think that there are), then there is also a price to be paid for addressing cultural change at the general, national level and not making the terms of its positioning within the spaces of power an explicit and important part of the assessment. It is not as if (unlike some Liberal commentators) Hoggart did not identify any problem at the level of the political system. At the end of *The Uses of Literacy* he refers to the 'false lights' (Hoggart 1958: 345) that are now appearing in respect of political direction. In a move towards balancing his concern here, he observes that these may be partly inevitable during a period of disruption and change. He notes the possibility that important freedoms might be lost within the dynamics of a centralising uniformity which is seen as close to features of totalitarianism in some of its effects and which is bringing about a move from 'class to mass' (Hoggart 1958: 343). Such loss, he speculates, might not be recognised widely given repeated official assurances that people are 'free'. This is a line of thinking running quite close to a Marxian sense of 'false consciousness' as well as to the realms of Orwellian dystopia. However, all this is never developed as fully as it could be as a firm background for making more specific observations about cultural tendencies and the possibilities for taking 'other routes'. Just as he has a sense of the existing popular potential for cultural improvement, Hoggart sees the popular potential for democratic development too. However, both are perceived against a marked risk of bad circumstances becoming even worse. Any clearer sense of the play-off between the need for anxiety and the basis for hope is made difficult by the relative lack of a structural framework for locating 'historically and sociologically' what he has found wanting in the current cultural conditions of the working classes and in the media and entertainment industries which occupy a significant proportion of their leisure time.

IV

My fourth point is essentially one that frames many aspects of the other three. It concerns the ways in which cultural value and change are related to questions of cultural economics and to cultural market relations. Hoggart was clear that 'commercialisation' (sometimes identified in the form of 'Americanisation') was part of the new, negative dynamics he saw at work in British popular culture. Nevertheless, as I noted earlier, it is interesting that in his most pessimistic judgements towards the end of *The Uses of Literacy* it is 'uniformity' that is identified as the main risk, thus connecting his argument directly with the negative or at least nervous evaluations of previous 'mass society' theorists such as McDonald (1953). Despite the empathetic character of most of his writing, in *The Uses of Literacy* he perhaps failed to understand fully *why* so many aspects of the new 'shiny' commercial culture appealed so strongly, particularly to an emerging generation of teenagers who had experienced their childhood within the more restricted popular cultural tonalities of the 1940s and early 1950s. Nevertheless, he was writing at a time when it was possible to believe that a firm redirection of public policy and regulation might remedy some of the more negative consequences of the newly released commercial energies at work in the reshaping of British popular culture. It is worth remembering that *The Uses of Literacy* was published only two years after commercial television began broadcasting in Britain in 1955 and that Hoggart had started it several years earlier, even before the Parliamentary decision to go ahead with this major change in national cultural life. This was a change that, of course, Hoggart would later reflect on with a largely negative appraisal as a member of the Pilkington Committee on Broadcasting and an influential contributor to its Report of 1962 (see Milland 2004 for a discussion of his involvement here).

The extent to which popular culture space is an economic space, a space for the competitive achievement of profits across different market segments, has become much clearer since Hoggart's major writing and it is reflected in some of his later commentary. It is now impossible to engage with questions of national cultural direction of the kind which so concerned Hoggart without seeing how much these questions are in large part about the restructuring of the economy and the rise of new forms of domestic consumption, connecting directly to the shifting character of the international system. For all, or nearly all, areas of media and cultural research, the impact of markets upon quality and choice and upon the perception and experience of 'the cultural' has become a central point of critical debate. How far is it possible to work outside the dominant market frame? How far is that frame itself varied enough in its conditions and possibilities to allow for work that extends and expands the 'public good' in culture, granted that there will be a continuing argument about definitions and criteria here, rather than seeming to deplete and debilitate it? While the cultural dynamics to which Hoggart attended so perceptively — of individual, familial and social class pleasures and fulfilments, of a variety of 'tastes' within an unequal spread of opportunities — still require our attention, these now need to be seen more sharply in relation to the massive structuring power of the cultural industries and the forms of consumption that they encourage and resource (Corner 2009).

I want to conclude by making just a few summary comments about Hoggart and value, comments which will doubtless connect with what is said elsewhere in this volume, probably from different points of judgment. What seems to me to be important first of all is recognising the extent to which Hoggart's writing, certainly in *The Uses of Literacy,* works within the established frame of 'mass society' and 'mass culture' diagnosis and then the extent to which it pushes beyond this. There is no doubt that the 'mass culture' perspective with its fears of centralisation and standardisation, its suspicion of the commercial popular and its intimations of decline, is an influential one for the account of change that Hoggart develops. What allows his writing to transcend this framework is the strength of his autobiographical engagement combined with the complexity of his class allegiance and the closely observed subtleties of his local instances and interpretations. Although, on occasion, a movement towards 'easy' generalisation can be seen and some of the formulations are over-asserted and under-argued, Hoggart is too caught up personally in what I earlier described as the awkwardness of making firm assessments in this area to fall deeply into the passing of unreflexive, 'received' verdicts.

As many commentators have noted, *The Uses of Literacy* is a book which we now see as remarkable for the way in which it address a general, educated readership. It engages them without condescension in the serious discussion of matters felt to be of 'common' concern. The articulation of 'feeling' is also quietly central in different ways to most of Hoggart's writing, further strengthening the bond with the reader. It is essentially projected as a 'public' rather than 'academic' project. In that sense it is an achievement predicated on relationships of writing and reading that no longer flourish and are unlikely to return with quite the same confident combination of scholarly and civic values.

Hoggart's engagement with questions of cultural value, informed by his background, his social commitments and his training as a literary critic, takes him into the centre of issues whose defining contours finally lie beyond the frames he employs. However, the rich detail of his descriptions of changing forms of living and of sensibility (we can think here of Williams' still suggestive idea of 'structures of feeling',[6] the honesty of his concerns for the 'inner life' and for the ethical within the social), will ensure that his writing remains a necessary, and often inspiring, point of reference for any understanding of class, culture and the media in Britain.

Bibliography

Arts Council of Great Britain, (1984). *The Glory of the Garden* (London: Arts Council).

CCCS (1977) Birmingham: Centre for Contemporary Cultural Studies: *Cultural Studies 10,* Special Issue *On Ideology.*

Bourdieu, P. (1984) *Distinction: A Social Critique of the Judgement of Taste.* (London: Routledge).

Corner, J. (1992) 'An Interview with Richard Hoggart', added item to reprint of Hoggart, R. *The Uses of Literacy* (Harmondsworth: Penguin), pp. 379-399.

Corner, J. (2009) 'Public Knowledge and Popular Culture', *Media, Culture and Society* 31 (1), pp. 141-149

Frow, J. (1987) 'Accounting for Tastes: Some Problems with Bourdieu's Sociology of Culture', *Cultural Studies* 1 (1), pp. 59-73.

Hall. S. (1981) 'Notes on Deconstructing the Popular'. In Raphael Samuel (ed.) *People's History and Socialist Theory* (London: Routledge), pp. 227-240.

Home Office (1962) Report of the Committee on Broadcasting 1960 (Pilkington Report – Cmnd 1753) (London: HMSO).

Hoggart, R. (1958) *The Uses of Literacy* (Harmondsworth. Pelican Books).

Thompson, E. P. (1963) *The Making of the English Working Class* (London: Victor Gollancz).

Leavis, Q. D. (1932) *Fiction and the Reading Public* (London: Chatto and Windus).

McDonald, D. (1953) 'A Theory of Mass Culture', *Diogenes* 1 (3), pp. 1-17.

Milland, J. (2004) 'Courting Malvolio: The Background to the Pilkington Committee on Broadcasting, 1960-62', *Contemporary British History*, 18 (2), pp.76-102.

Owen, S. 'Hoggart and Women'. In Sue Owen (ed.) *Richard Hoggart and*

---

[6] See, for instance, Williams (1961). The term has received regular critical attention in relation to its combination of structural and experiential elements but precisely this mix has led to it being regularly employed by writers on culture since Williams' first use of it.

Cultural Studies (Houndsmills: Palgrave Macmillan), pp. 227-242.

Sparks C. (1974) 'The Abuses of Literacy', *Working Papers in Cultural Studies* 6. Reprinted as Chapter 7 in Gray, A., Hanson., S. Wood., H. Campbell, J. and Erikson, M. (eds) (2006) *CCCS Selected Working Papers*, 2, 2nd ed. (London: Routledge), pp. 111-122.

Williams, R. (1961) *The Long Revolution* (London: Chatto and Windus).

WHY LITERATURE MATTERS
Sue Owen

Literature is central to Richard Hoggart's thinking, whether he is writing about broadcasting, culture, the working class or growing up in Leeds. Hoggart is known as the author of important works on culture and class, notably *The Uses of Literacy* (1957), as a key figure in the rise of cultural studies and founder of the Birmingham Centre for Contemporary Cultural Studies. Yet he began as a literary critic and retained a love of good literature. In his Inaugural Lecture he argues that Schools of English should pay attention to contemporary culture, but that they must also remain grounded within literary tradition. This is for similar reasons to his argument in *The Uses of Literacy*: good literature is important because it arms the working class against the 'popular persuaders', admen, tabloids and other purveyors of self-interested or manipulative language. I do not want to repeat what I have said elsewhere about Hoggart's argument in *The Uses of Literacy*, his Inaugural Lecture and the various essays in *Speaking to Each Other* (Owen 2005, 2007, 2008b, 2008c). In this essay I want to take as my starting point what Hoggart says about literature in his Reith Lectures on Culture and Communication in 1971, published as *Only Connect* in 1972.

These lectures on broadcasting were given at a time when Hoggart was working at UNESCO, having left the Centre for Contemporary Cultural Studies in the charge of the more theoretically-oriented Stuart Hall. Hoggart was therefore geographically and to some extent intellectually marginalised; and yet the invitation to give the lectures shows the respect for him within wider society. It is to this wider society that Hoggart often speaks. He had become known as a broadcaster and writer on broadcasting since publishing his influential 'The Uses of Television' in *Encounter* in 1960. Here Hoggart questioned facile assumptions about TV's advantages but also conveyed a sense of excitement at the medium's new possibilities and a plea to ask bolder questions. In the Reith lecture series he works up ideas about broadcasting through what seem like very simple ideas about communication at its most basic levels. I will try to show that there is a subtlety and a value in these simple ideas. Literary awareness imbues the whole framework of the Reith lectures and I will show how, for Hoggart, literature epitomises good communication. My wider purpose is to suggest that literature is still important in culture today and that literary criticism has a place within cultural studies.

The subject of the first lecture 'Taking for Granted' is communication without words. Literary allusions permeate a significant passage about suburban life:

It [suburban life] can be small-minded, keeping-itself-to-itself, fearful about status to a depressing extent. It can be claustrophobically turned in upon itself; as at moments during a grammar-school speech day when you can look around at all the carefully groomed mothers and fathers and feel the heavy weight of socio-academic anxiety bearing down on that platform. How can we be so totally engrossed in this particular bit of Western Hemisphere ritualism? How lacking in perspective can we get? You recall Auden's unpleasant line about 'The clerk going "oompah, oompah" to his minor grave'.

But Auden also wrote a poem called 'In Praise of Limestone' which can be seen as a tribute to aspects of suburban life, to the lives of people who are, in Auden's phrase: 'adjusted to the local needs of valleys'. In some ways, he is saying, people who settle for a domestic scale among others who have done the same, who have no great urge towards power or asceticism, may be in touch with important and neglected parts of our being. Their lives may not be full of striking contours; but they can now and again reveal some things about *not* going places, about one sort of harmony ... If we looked more closely at suburban life we would see that it can at times achieve a domesticity and neighbourliness which are a kind of quiet triumph. (Hoggart 1972: 24-5)

Two things are immediately striking here: first, the unfashionable defence of suburban living. I think this can be related to ideas about the importance of ordinariness for Hoggart which critics have already noticed. John Hartley (1999: 16) has argued that *The Uses of Literacy* made ordinariness 'a positive civic goal'. Melissa Gregg (2006: 35) has written extensively on the way 'his chosen mode of address shifts investigative attention to the realm of the unspectacular everyday, the ordinary — one of the key interventions for which cultural studies would become known' (cf Gregg 2007). Sean Matthews (2008) has shown the slipperiness of the idea of ordinariness in the Lady Chatterley trial and the importance of Hoggart's own representatively ordinary, working-class, origins.

The second striking feature of this passage is the way literature imbues all Hoggart's ways of making sense of the world and all his own efforts at communication. Even in an essay about communication without words, Auden gives him a framework within which to express his instinctive understanding and a vocabulary to talk with. Hoggart assumes his audience will be as familiar with Auden as he is. But it would be somewhat banal and not quite right simply to say that Hoggart loves literature and that literature helps him make sense of the world and articulate his experience. It goes deeper than this. Hoggart's message in the Reith lectures is about the primacy of personal creativity. His message is an empowering one 'about the strength of the readings offered by our cultures and about the need to reinterpret those readings for ourselves' (Hoggart 1972: 25). There is a link between the importance of literature and the celebration of ordinary life at the level of empowering ordinary individuals.

The second lecture, 'Talking to Yourself', exemplifies the paradoxical simplicity and depth of this theme. Literature is important because it exemplifies the necessary reaching down inside the self to find a tone to talk with. And it is important as an expression of an individual author:

I am going to talk now mainly about getting in touch through words; or more accurately through tone, tone in writing. Getting in touch not only with other people but also, and first of all, with oneself. If we are writing about anything important to us we are both trying to speak to others and developing a relationship with ourselves. Finding a tone to talk with begins with finding one that seems right to and for us. Talking to others begins with talking to yourself and with being yourself in talking. (Hoggart 1972: 29)

For Hoggart individuals are worth more than the 'mass'. This is the basis of all his ideas about language and communication. There is a passionate urgency about the difficult task of finding a style and tone of one's own in order to genuinely reach others. What he means by this is clarified later in Lecture 2:

There are a great many tones. All of them, unless they are remade for our own person and voice, are barriers. Barriers between us and our material; barriers between us and the people who read us; barriers between us and those parts of our personality we need to reach down to. They are smooth, they are easily picked up, they can give a range of pleasantly-acceptable images of ourselves. And they are all useless if not fought for. They all assert staggeringly assured but unproved relationships. (Hoggart 1972: 37)

These ideas of 'reaching down' within the self and that a personal tone has to be 'fought for' are not just the underlying basis of Hoggart's ideas about literature and broadcasting in the Reith lectures. They also underpin *all* human communication in his view. Even in the early seventies such ideas are 'out of sync' with postmodern theory's questioning of the idea of a 'self'; but what Hoggart says resonates for the working class and for women who have been denied an identity. Oppressed groups may be ill-served by a rupture with ideas of selfhood when they have found it so hard to achieve self-expression in the first place.

Hoggart discusses two main assumptions which underpin his work in the sixth and final Reith Lecture, 'A Common Ground'. The first assumption relates to 'the primacy of the individual conscience, the belief that any wider commitment has to start from and satisfy that conviction' (Hoggart 1972: 104). Full, rich cultures start from fulfilled individuals: 'Individual opinions are not aberrations or self-indulgences; they are the only foundation for collective positions which do not deny the fullness of human nature ... An ideology is always less than a culture, and a state is always less than a community' (Hoggart 1972: 105). For Hoggart, this is the grounding of true 'disinterestedness'; something that is always worth pursuing. Again, this may be unfashionable. Others, Bourdieu for example, have questioned the very notion of disinterestedness. But for Hoggart it is a valid notion, not for reasons of abstract essentialism, but because ordinary people need arming against false opinions and partial truths:

> It follows that there is what feels like an absolute difference in kind, a difference most people are given little opportunity to recognize, between a disinterested statement or analysis or exploration, made by a man free to go to the limits of his own strengths, weaknesses and courage, and all those other kinds of trimming which so greatly outnumber disinterested work ... for most people all over the world virtually everything that is publicly offered, in print or over the air, is *interested*, meant to tickle their fancies or arouse their emotions or hammer them for the sake of some other purpose — to get their money or their votes, to sell to them and go on selling, to keep them in line; not because the truth is great, and should prevail. If you have been much used to disinterested writing it is almost physically claustrophobic to read this stuff for any length of time. (Hoggart 1972: 105-106)

Literature, then, is the epitome of disinterestedness for Hoggart and therefore helps people recognise when they are being conned. Obviously this is not new: the idea that good literature can arm us against corruption underpins Part II of *The Uses of Literacy*. But it is important to note that this differs strikingly from the elitist valorisation of good literature by T.S. Eliot, the Leavises and others precisely because Hoggart sees disinterestedness as the grounds of all human self-expression.

Literary 'Quality'

I want to digress for a moment here to examine a little more deeply Hoggart's ideas about literary quality, as these have been misunderstood. Hoggart makes it clear in *The Uses of Literacy* that people can be 'wise in their own way' and that working-class people are more capable of appreciating 'good' writing, that is to say, the kind of literature valued in university English departments, than they are given credit for. For example, In 'Teaching Literature to Adults' Hoggart asserts that working-class adult students can appreciate good literature:

> But our students' response to experience is usually richer and more courageous than we suspect. We should base our work on this, should aim more at encouraging and developing what is already there, instead of behaving like an anti-tetanus team in a primitive community. (Hoggart 1973c: 209)

This is important and helps us avoid parodying Hoggart's position or mislabelling him purely Leavisite. A supporter of Leavis's views might think that good literature could immunise the working class against trite or manipulative discourses but Hoggart thinks it can nurture their *own* inbuilt resilience and resistance to it:

> But the answers must as far as possible be drawn from the students ... we are not there to give them something so much as to bring their own latent powers into play. (Hoggart 1973c: 219)

> And we for our part often don't see how good their answers are (or may be, if they are encouraged to develop them) because we don't always try, not to find a gold nugget in every proffered item, but to see what they are in fact saying. (Hoggart 1973c: 227)

In 'The B.B.C. and Society', first published in 1965, he argues that the working class can appreciate intelligent satire and that we should assume ordinary people have intelligence and imagination, and that we should not have limiting preconceptions (Hoggart 1973a: 173). Central to all his writing about culture, then, is the idea that working-class people can appreciate more and are worth more than they are given credit for. This notion has tended to get lost in interrogating the very notion of cultural quality in recent decades.

Linked with the notion of working-class cultural versatility and potential in Hoggart's thought is the belief that good writing does not necessarily mean 'highbrow' (his term). These linked points underpin many of Hoggart's writings on education, culture and broadcasting. In 'Culture: Dead and Alive' (published in *The Observer* in 1961), he explains his 'Good of its kind' argument which runs through all his writings about culture:

The crucial distinctions today are not those between the *News of the World* and the *Observer*, between the Third Programme and the Light Programme, between sex-and-violence paperbacks and 'egg-head' paperbacks, between Bootsie and Snudge and the Alan Taylor lectures, between the Billy Cotton Band Show and the Brains Trust, between the Top Ten and a celebrity concert, or between 'skiffle' and chamber music. The distinctions we should be making are those between the *News of the World* and the *Sunday Pictorial*, between 'skiffle' and the Top Ten; and, for 'highbrows', between the *Observer* and the *Sunday Times*, or, in 'egghead' paperbacks, between Peter Townsend and Vance Packard. (Hoggart 1973b: 129-30)

Jim McGuigan believes Hoggart later recanted, noting that in *Mass Media in a Mass Society* (2004) 'Hoggart repudiated the position that he himself had argued for so strenuously over forty years previously' (McGuigan 2008: 81). McGuigan certainly has a point when he cites this passage from *Mass Media in a Mass Society* as evidence:

That favourite exculpatory phrase on the lines of 'Agreed, it's not very high-brow but at least it's good of its kind' is especially tempting. It seems to avoid the awful business of having to say that some things might be better than others, that some things show the feebleness of their authors' talents and others are no more than market-invented hogwash. In such a world all products should be without distinguishing value-judgements, never set against any other things. All views are horizontal, never vertical. The excusing phrase above is used as a blanket acquittal to avoid any criteria of value being applied, especially to all of what could be called 'the popular arts'. This is a pity because it can have a valid as well as an invalid use. (Hoggart 2005: 59)

I think McGuigan has done us a real service by raising this important point. However, I would like to argue that, rather than representing an outright repudiation of Hoggart's former position, this passage elaborates it in a different context, forty-three years later. In the noughties Hoggart is among those who think it is important to reassert some emphasis on literary or artistic quality a context in which cultural relativism seems to have triumphed. In the context of the 1960s, a different emphasis was needed to get people to look seriously for the first time at the popular arts. In other words, Hoggart still retains a sense of the separateness of quality from 'height of brow'. In 'Broadcasting, Democracy and the Enabling Principle', originally published in 1990, and republished in modified form in 2001, he laments the increasing tendency to cater only for existing tastes and looks back to a time when freedom to try out new ideas led to good programmes. His list is quite eclectic and down-to-earth:

> Without that non-stereotyped approach we would not have had so wide a range of those good comedy series, from *Dad's Army* through *Steptoe and Son* to *Till Death Do Us Part* to *One Foot In The Grave* and after; or news and current-affairs programmes on the arts; or, perhaps most surprisingly of all, earthy, unsentimental, documentary programmes about where we fall down as a society – on drugs, violence, home-grown poverty – programmes which would predictably be 'a turn-off' for mass audiences but which ought to be made, had to be made, for those who would look and listen. We know by now that that last group can be larger than market indicators might suggest. (Hoggart 2001: 40)

He praises some soaps because they 'tackle subjects the earlier stories dared not tackle'. Thus, 'from time to time *EastEnders*, for example, might without much flannel or periphrasis, but sometimes over-theatrically, treat homosexuality, lesbianism, racism, violence in the home, drunkenness, one-parent families, prison' (Hoggart 2001: 42). His idea of 'quality' is non-elitist: quality does not automatically inhere in 'highbrow' programmes and rubbish in the rest. A popular programme may be of high quality; a 'highbrow' programme may be conventional, snooty rubbish (Hoggart 2001: 42). In other words, Hoggart's ideas about cultural 'quality' are consistent. On the one hand, he was never a relativist, never thought The Beatles as good as Beethoven. In his fifth Reith Lecture, 'Private Faces in Public Places', he discusses 'The Beatles are as good as Beethoven' argument and says, 'To imply ... that the two are, in all important senses, as good as each other is to give up thinking' (Hoggart 1972: 84). But he does want people to make 'crucial distinctions', to use careful discrimination to discern the difference between what he terms a living and a processed culture. A living culture is one in which people have the freedom to experiment and to put forward their own ideas.

The Bases of Human Communication

This brings me neatly back to the main thrust of my argument. I want now to return to the primacy of individual conscience in communication which was my theme before my digression. I think it would be problematic if Hoggart's basic idea about literature and about human communication was that individuals need to be true to themselves. However, there is a second assumption which he says in the final Reith lecture underpins all his thought. This has to do with the possibility of fellow-feeling. It is worth quoting a passage from this lecture at length:

I reach down now to an even more basic sense, one which underpins the wish itself to speak straight to one another. It is the idea, which I never used to think about, but now I find it extraordinary, strange and compelling, of fellow-feeling; fellow-feeling based not on the fact that we all belong to a particular national culture, are Frenchmen or Russians or Americans or British, nor on an abstract internationalist commitment, but based on recognizing our common experience, and on realizing that it is the facing of common sorrows which above all links us. Then I always remember Keats' quietly astonishing remark: 'Men, I think, should bear with one another'; or Yeats' old men looking out at the world: 'Gaiety transfiguring all that dread'; or a less well-known statement but of the same general kind, George Orwell's about the postcards of Donald McGill – the cards you can buy at the seaside, full of middle-aged wives with enormous bums, and little beery husbands leering at what used to be called 'flappers', and nagging mothers-in-law. After he had looked at the cards for a long time, Orwell said: 'When it comes to the pinch, human beings are heroic'. One will go a long way with a man who can look at what seems shabby and unheroic material and come up with a conclusion like that … The sense of fellow-feeling denies all abstractings, all hierarchies and all rationalizations; it provides the basis – the only basis – for moving out beyond national cultures to make contact wherever someone else is willing and free to listen. (Hoggart 1972: 108)

We may notice again the language of reaching down inside himself: Hoggart's method in the Reith lectures, at a time in the early 1970s when others in Cultural Studies were turning to high theory, was to reach down inside himself, not just once but again and again. This is deeply humanistic but it is not a crass universalism which elides differences, as the idea of common humanity is premised on the integrity of the individual. His method has something in common with psychotherapeutic discourse, perhaps also with some strands of feminism, as I have discussed in my 'Hoggart and Women' (Owen 2008e). It is interesting that, once again, Hoggart immediately reaches for literary examples both to illustrate and to express his point about the possibility for fellow-feeling. Literature, for Hoggart, not only gives us a *language* to express 'our common experience' but is itself a *proof* of the *possibility* of sharing such experience, a proof that, as he puts it in the final Lecture, 'we can in fact reach each other' (Hoggart 1972: 109). He believes 'that our attempts to come together are not simply defensive groupings by existential galley-slaves, or huddlings together by frightened kittens, but something more: a sign that we have a regard for truth and a wish truthfully to discuss the nature of our common lives'

(Hoggart 1972: 110) He thinks, though there is no proof, that true listening to each other does go on, though not all the time.

Hoggart's statements about communication could seem banal if taken out of context but in fact he gently undercut many false assumptions. His vision in the Reith lectures is in a sense both political and moral. These are fraught terms, and a focus on the 'moral' seems rather unfashionable in 1971, whilst Hoggart is political in a way which is different from the Marxisant perspective of others in cultural studies at that time, as he notes in his *Life and Times* (Hoggart 1993: 98). Hoggart's writing is political in the sense that it embraces the way in which a society should conduct itself and the basis on which it might form social and cultural policy. Hoggart was already thinking about literature as political and moral engagement in his writings on adult education in the 1950s. In 'Teaching Literature to Adults' he talks of the motivation of adult, working-class students:

[...] many come because *they feel morally and politically confused* [...] probably the most important reason, common to almost all who stay after the first month (however hidden this may be from the student himself), is that each of them is in some way dissatisfied with the terms of his life, and seeks a basis for criticism and perhaps for action. He feels that literature will speak to his condition. (Hoggart 1973c: 205-6, my emphasis)

The same yoking of the moral and the political occurs in Hoggart's thinking on the literary within cultural studies. I have argued elsewhere that Hoggart effectively made a political stand when he argued in his Inaugural Lecture at Birmingham in 1963 that the literary critic is uniquely fitted to expose debased uses of language by the persuaders and manipulators (Owen 2008d: 7). In this lecture Hoggart asserts the importance of literary criticism within Cultural Studies in the context of the founding of the Centre for Contemporary Cultural Studies. The lecture also offers a moral vision, both for cultural studies and for literary method within cultural studies, as Hoggart says good literature is important because:

It works not by precept and abstraction but by dramatization, by 'showing forth', in a fullness of sense and feeling and thought, of time and place and persons. In ordering its dramas it is driven by a desire to find the revelatory instance, the tiny gesture that opens a whole field of meaning and consequence. *It does not do this pointlessly*, nor explicitly to reform; it aims first at the momentary peace of knowing that a little more of the shifting amorphousness of experience has been named and held, that we are now that bit less shaken by the anarchy of feeling and the assault of experience. To push for this kind of truth, no matter how much it may hurt, is *a kind of moral activity*. (Hoggart 1973d: 233, my emphasis)

The ending of the Reith lecture series seems to go beyond the moral and to border on the spiritual, as he says his assumptions are 'acts of faith' (Hoggart 1972: 110). He offers a vivid image: 'We are like the insects called pond-skaters: we assume that there is a skin over the water of our shared experience and then set out across it and hope to meet, because if we assumed otherwise we would sink without trace' (Hoggart 1972: 110). Reaching down (as he would say) below both his main assumptions is another: 'that experience is exchangeable' and 'that our personal experiences can have more than a personal meaning, can be shared, can be typical, symbolic, significant' (Hoggart 1972: 110). Hoggart is not a Christian, but his chapel upbringing counted and he has a quasi-Christian outlook at times, for example in the belief that 'other people count as we feel we count ourselves'. There is also an important general point running throughout the lecture series about the need to look beneath. The conclusion of the Reith Lecture series may seem at first very modest in comparison with the rhetoric of parts of the Inaugural Lecture, as Hoggart reasserts his core beliefs and concludes 'that our wish to tell and listen is more than disguised self-seeking or self-involvement, and that that shared wish is sometimes gratified' (Hoggart 1972: 111). However, this modesty of tone fits with the point he is making. What he seems effectively to be saying is that human communication, and literature as the best expression of that communication, is not just a social or cultural — or even a political or moral — activity, but a kind of spiritual experience. It would be easy to dismiss this, but it is hard not to feel challenged by it.

Bibliography

Collini, S. (2008) 'Richard Hoggart: Literary Criticism and Cultural Decline in Twentieth-Century Britain'. In Sue Owen (ed.), *Richard Hoggart and Cultural Studies* (London: Palgrave), pp. 33-56.

Gregg, M. (2006) *Cultural Studies' Affective Voices* (Basingstoke: Palgrave Macmillan).

————— (2007) 'The Importance of Being Ordinary', *International Journal of Cultural Studies*, 10 (1), pp. 95-104.

Hall, S. (2008) 'Richard Hoggart, *The Uses of Literacy* and The Cultural Turn'. In Sue Owen (ed.), *Richard Hoggart and Cultural Studies* (London: Palgrave), pp. 20-32.

Hartley, J. (1999) *The Uses of Television* (London. Routledge).

Hoggart, R. (1957/1998) *The Uses of Literacy* (New Brunswick, NJ:

Transaction).

————— (1972) *Only Connect: On Culture and Communication* (London: Chatto and Windus).

————— (1973a) 'The B.B.C. and Society'. *Listener*, 5 August 1965. In *Speaking To Each Other Vol. I: About Society* (Harmondsworth: Penguin), pp. 173-181.

————— (1973b) 'Culture: Dead and Alive'. *Observer*, 14.5.61. In *Speaking to Each Other, Vol. I: About Society* (Harmondsworth: Penguin), pp. 129-132.

————— (1973c) 'Teaching Literature to Adults', articles 1951-1959, first printed together in *Teaching Literature* (National Institute of Adult Educational and Department of Adult Education, University of Hull, 1963). In *Speaking to Each Other, Vol. II: About Literature.* (Harmondsworth: Penguin), pp. 205-230.

————— (1973d) 'Schools of English in Contemporary Society': Inaugural Lecture, University of Birmingham (1963). In *Speaking to Each Other, Vol. II: About Literature* (Harmondsworth: Penguin), pp. 231-243.

————— (1993) *An Imagined Life: Life and Times 1959-1991* (Oxford: Oxford University Press).

————— (2001) 'Broadcasting, Democracy and the Enabling Principle'. First pub. in R. Carver (ed.), *Aeriel at Bay: Reflections on Broadcasting and the Arts*, Essays in Honour of Philip French (Manchester: Carcanet, 1990). Republished in modified form incorporating elements from pieces in the *Political Quarterly* and the *Daily Express* in *Between Two Worlds* (London: Aurum Press), pp. 34-45.

————— (2005) *Mass Media in a Mass Society: Myth and Reality* (London and New York: Continuum).

Matthews, S. (2008) 'The Uses of D. H. Lawrence'. In Sue Owen (ed.), *Re-reading Richard Hoggart, Life, Literature, Language, Education* (Newcastle: Cambridge Scholars), pp. 85-101.

McGuigan, J. (2008) 'Richard Hoggart and The Way We Live Now' in Sue Owen (ed.), *Richard Hoggart and Cultural Studies* (London: Palgrave), pp.75-87.

Owen, S. (2005) '*The Abuse of Literacy* and the Feeling Heart: the Trials of Richard Hoggart', *Cambridge Quarterly* 34(2), 147-76.

————— (2007) 'Richard Hoggart as Literary Critic'. *International Journal of Cultural Studies*, 10 (1), pp.85-94.

————— (ed.) (2008a) *Re-reading Richard Hoggart, Life, Literature, Language, Education* (Newcastle: Cambridge Scholars).

————— (2008b) Introduction. In *Re-reading Richard Hoggart, Life, Literature, Language, Education* (Newcastle: Cambridge Scholars), pp. xvi-xlv.

————— (2008c) 'Hoggart and Literature'. In *Re-reading Richard Hoggart, Life, Literature, Language, Education* (Newcastle: Cambridge Scholars), pp. 58-84.

————— (2008d) *Richard Hoggart and Cultural Studies* (London: Palgrave Macmillan).

————— (2008e) 'Hoggart and Women'. In *Richard Hoggart and Cultural Studies* (London: Palgrave Macmillan), pp. 227-242.

ETHICS, WRITING AND SCHOLARSHIP: DOES HOGGART MEET HIS OWN STANDARDS?
Macdonald Daly

Having recently been engaged on a project to do with British public radio, I decided to read Richard Hoggart's *Mass Media in a Mass Society: Myth and Reality* (Hoggart 2005), not simply because, as a colleague told me, it has a few pages on radio, but because I thought that Hoggart's considered opinion on a whole range of issues informing contemporary society and its mediation would be useful for me to know. In this decision, the element of recognition — in short, of Hoggart's reputation — undoubtedly played a part, given that, for the purposes of my project, I have ignored (because they say nothing or very little about radio) a whole raft of books of the 'mass media/mass society' type. Note that, for me at any rate, that recognition is not bound up with any sense of Hoggart as a media or sociological specialist, while the books I ignore are often written by academics who could creditably claim one or both of those labels. Indeed, I did not consciously even expect Hoggart to answer the kinds of questions those other authors might debate; what is more likely is that I expected Hoggart to ask different questions and perhaps venture interesting answers.

I certainly expected a view that I considered 'of the Left'. In fact, the book is either an ideological hodge-podge of Left, Centre and Right, or at best is cut adrift from any coherent position designated by such terms, as Charlie Ellis in part argues (Owen 2008: 198-212). What I did not expect was to read a book that should never have been published. I did not expect a book whose public existence can owe little to its impoverished intellectual content, but is validated by the flimsiest of supports, its author's reputation alone (a reputation not regenerated by the book itself, of course). 'Reputation' in this context is what creates the market for something no matter how unnecessary it is, a feature of contemporary capitalism which Hoggart repeatedly criticises in the book itself. But it is probably the only reason why my edition of the book, first published in 2004, is the 2005 reprint: without the name of Hoggart acting as a kind of brand, I doubt that it would have sold so respectably, and so quickly, that it required reprinting within a year. I am obliged to try to justify my adverse evaluation of the book in what follows, but if I do so persuasively then the first of several ironies would have to be registered. For example, here we would have Hoggart churning out a book that is otiose, out of touch, miles wide of its mark because it seems to have paid little attention to the scholarship of the past twenty years, in either media studies or sociology;

and yet is probably read and bought many times more than academic volumes to which it is, methodologically and conceptually, inferior. Hereby we would find Hoggart involved, in a small way, in precisely the market-determined routines his own book repeatedly rails against.

And that was, I have to say, my continuous response all the way through my first reading of the book. I found it, indeed, nothing short of shocking and on occasions vulgar. Charlie Ellis (Owen 2008: 198) cites a number of early reviews which point out that, at worst, it is a rant by a grumbling old man; at best it is an intellectually rickety construction in which rather subjective views of contemporary British society (or the views of a particular social group, perhaps, namely those who remember the War) are offered in a discourse which attempts to deploy many of the devices of impersonality and objectivity, but which is really being pressed into self-serving ends (either of the author or of the putative social group). Most charitably, one might simply consider the author to belong to a much smaller sub-culture than he thinks he does and to have made the mistake of overrating the general social import of the views he holds. But Hoggart would not see that as a criticism, as he is militant in his absolutely correct conviction that the widespread popularity of something is no argument in favour of its quality.

However, when I re-read the book I tried to gain a perspective from which I could view it with less hostility, and I shall try to suggest how that might be possible: it devolves on the question of what kind of writing, now, in the early twenty-first century, might answer the lack which, despite his very dubious arguments about this and that, Hoggart does, I think, correctly identify. That lack is caused by the ejection of moral and aesthetic evaluation from discourses around culture which has been effected by postmodernism (a word Hoggart uses only once in the book, incidentally), in society at large but also (in his view, and my own) in academic work, a serious business where one might expect it to have remained alive. In this latter respect — the general failure of the academic disciplines we variously sub-divide the field into, namely Literary Studies, Media Studies, Cultural Studies, to maintain in their discourses any strong sense of objective ethical and artistic worth, but to have witnessed and in many ways facilitated the relativisation of both — we can see why Hoggart might not have wished to bother to meet the contemporary scholarly standards of even the best academic practitioners in these disciplines. (My point here is not that there are no individual exceptions to the relativising tide within every discipline, but that the individual exceptions within the named disciplines have the appearance of being King Canutes.) In Hoggart's book there is a heavy reckoning to be paid for that divorce between ethics and evaluation on the one hand and intellectual discourses about culture on the other, although he does not describe the likely reckoning very well, nor does he suggest more than a handful of remedies to assuage the social wounds it will cause or maybe prevent its axe from falling so heavily.

Nonetheless, I do agree with Hoggart about this damaging dissolution of evaluative responsibility, and it may therefore be that his abiding worth is that he maintains, at this unfashionably late stage, this Arnoldian/ Leavisite torch alight at all in the very high winds surrounding it without subscribing to the pompous elitism of someone like Harold Bloom (1995), whose *The Western Canon* builds a pyramid of worthy books around the notionally solitary reader as a protection against the chaos and vulgarity of the social life deemed to be outside it. I tend to think I knew in advance, no doubt from Hoggart's other writings, that this was the row he would continue unfashionably to plough in this book, and, though I found the volume an extremely disagreeable folly, it does prompt the question: what would writing that could properly rejuvenate the integration of moral and aesthetic evaluation with the study of culture have to be like, now, in the world in which we find ourselves? I shall fail to answer this question (which is more of an invitation to discussion than an enquiry to which I have a ready-made answer) except in the negative: such a discourse cannot now be like Richard Hoggart's. But I do believe that Hoggart's writing, although in my mind it is now an intellectually superannuated venture, is one of the few sources which still forces us to confront the question. In that alone, we might say, inheres *its* persistent value — and just as a return to the discourse of Arnold or Leavis or even (the comparison may be better in respect of Hoggart) Raymond Williams would these days be a kamikaze act for its author, nonetheless I know I am not alone in thinking that, post-postmodernism, someone with considerable intellectual authority is likely to arise who will, after some new design, successfully sail that battered boat on the waters once more.

I mention Williams also because Hoggart's book on the mass media seems to me an attempt to replicate the kind of discourse in which Williams engaged in his essay 'Britain in the 1960s' in *The Long Revolution* (Williams 1961: 319-83): both are expansive attempts to write a kind of sweeping sociological survey about the contemporary, and both mix what one might call their 'high' and impersonal ambitions with some very 'low' and idiosyncratic perceptions. But whereas what Williams was doing, in those pre-Cultural Studies days, when academic sociology and political science were also in what we might now consider their childhood if not their infancy, had the impact of a genuinely new approach to questions of the contemporary, Hoggart's prose, more than forty years later, reads as if it were a kind of last resort, the sort of limited thing one is able to produce out of a self-imposed refusal to engage with the developments that have occurred in the interim. The difference may simply be that the two authors wrote these books at quite different points in their careers. But it is no longer intellectually tenable to produce such wide-ranging surveys if they are invertebrate; that is, if they lack the spine of evidential data, tending towards pronouncement and judgment on their many subjects without seriously engaging with the empirical realities towards which they gesture. Moreover, Williams's essay was only one (the last) in a long and highly original book, which had a clear central thesis; Hoggart's book has no opportunity for the kind of contrapuntal effects that Williams is able to produce. Perhaps most significantly, Williams's essay could easily be recognised as an enterprise firmly rooted in left-wing politics. Hoggart's, by contrast, is ideologically kaleidoscopic: if anything, although I am not qualified to carry out the discourse analysis which would prove it, it resembles the kind of discourse which elected members of Parliament probably consider intellectual. It reaches, in other words, the level of something like a Fabian Society pamphlet.

I should say that I recognise that there are all kinds of writing outside of academic and/or scholarly writing which are intellectually valuable and socially necessary: Hoggart's (and for that matter Williams's) own project is such that one could never give any of their works the dispiriting and limiting label of 'monograph'. From the very first, in the opening words of *The Uses of Literacy*, Hoggart has genuinely, and I think valuably 'thought of myself as addressing first of all the serious "common reader" or "intelligent layman" from any class'. But while he acknowledged there that that same book 'does not purport to have the scientifically-tested character of a sociological survey', he explains: 'There is an obvious danger of generalization from limited experience. I have therefore included, chiefly in the notes, some of the findings of sociologists where they seemed necessary, either as support or as qualification of the text' (Hoggart 2004: xli). In my edition of *The Uses of Literacy* there are twenty-five pages of notes and a five-page select bibliography: almost exactly a tenth of the book when taken together. *Mass Media in a Mass Society* has not a single footnote and no bibliography, and shows every sign of being written without any heed whatsoever to the 'obvious danger of generalization from limited experience' — a danger that, elsewhere, we usually call prejudice and/or ignorance.

And so much of the book is simply ignorant of what it speaks. The list of idiosyncratic opinions Hoggart holds, but which he presents in the book as if they have a basis in fact (while not citing or otherwise producing any evidence informing them) is very large: the book mainly consists of these opinions being delivered up out of the most slender, and often demonstrably false, certainly unverifiable, assumptions and suppositions.

For example, the following, from quite early in the book, is paradigmatic (a word his chapter on language castigates, incidentally). He condemns an entire educational (or, if you prefer, training) endeavour thus: 'Do these schools of journalism in British universities and further education colleges ask their students to face the ethical questions raised by their desired profession? From the answers recently given on the radio by a professor from one such school, it seems not' (Hoggart 2005: 21). He then spends a couple of sentences summarising the ethical deficiencies of what the unnamed professor from the unnamed school of journalism on the unnamed radio programme on an unnamed station on an unspecified date is purported to have said ('purported' because Hoggart provides no data which would allow us to check) and rounds off his condemnation with an irony of some enormity: 'Not to raise such questions seems a dereliction of duty in an academic at any level' (Hoggart 2005: 22). But Hoggart himself can hardly lecture an academic on a duty he himself has abandoned, namely the duty to allow readers to verify one's conclusions with reference to the sources which prompted them. That is what is ethical about scholarly discourse. One could give *dozens* of examples from the book to show that this is Hoggart's habitual tendency throughout. Indeed, I do not recall a single instance in the book in which Hoggart adequately sources claims about what x or y said or wrote.

If one trusts Hoggart's judgment unquestioningly, this will not be a problem. He truly thinks that major shareholders of and members of the boards of most companies 'probably' have degrees from Oxbridge (Hoggart 2005: 25). The 'probably' means that one cannot say that this is factually wrong because the degree of probability he neglects to specify: but in a context such as this one there is no ethical justification for the word at all. The scholarly thing to do would be to find out, not to rely on the 'probably' of one's prejudices. I suspect (but admit I do not know) that far fewer people in this category went to Oxbridge than he thinks. In print, however, I would commit myself to a claim only after I had undertaken the necessary enquires. At times the bathos of these utterly bogus claims is embarrassingly laughable: for instance, Hoggart cannot believe that 'Smillie' (pronounced as 'smiley') is really TV celebrity Carol Smillie's name: 'surely a pseudonym, or coincidence has become almost unbelievable' he says parenthetically (Hoggart 2005: 87). Of course, this may just be a cheap joke at the perennially cheerful Ms Smillie's expense, although cheap jokes are something Hoggart usually disapproves of. But Smillie is nonetheless her real name, there is no reason to think it is not, and the fact can very easily be verified. It is not an unusual name in Scotland, and Hoggart himself probably knows that Robert Smillie, born in Belfast, was a founder member of the Scottish Labour Party in 1888 and of the Independent Labour Party in 1893, Keir Hardie's right hand man in many ways. President of the Miners' Federation of Great Britain from 1912 until 1922, MP for Morpeth in the 1920s, he did not die until 1940, when Hoggart turned twenty-two. The name is not unusual for anyone with a passing historical interest in the British labour movement.

I do not wish to suggest that Hoggart's text is laced with personal jibes like these (Smillie is one of the few people he sees fit to name), but it is bedevilled by regrettable and unsupported prejudices of this kind. The apotheosis of this low-level hubris is the dismal chapter 'Language and Meanings' (Hoggart 2005: 140-57), which reads like the outpouring of a pedantic *Daily Telegraph* reader glorying in his own out-of-tuneness with the mass of ignorant unlettered people he criticises. So (extreme laments at the passing of 'sir' and at the rise of a redefined 'gay' aside) we get the most astounding linguistic prescriptivism for eighteen entire pages, the spirit of which might have moved the pen of Ernest Gowers, except that Hoggart's suggested amendments are not of the kind that would have made it into Gowers' *The Complete Plain Words*. Thus Hoggart complains about titles such as 'Chief Environmental Planning Officer' and suggests, absurdly, that a more appropriate term might be 'Chief Environmental-Rape Officer'. It would, of course, be some salvation if Hoggart's English were impeccable. But throughout his writing career he has misused the word 'since' to indicate causation when in fact, for a prescriptivist, it can indicate only duration. He similarly misuses 'due to' to mark causation when in fact it 'properly' marks only temporal imminence. And every five or six pages in *Mass Media in a Mass Society* there pops up a sentence without a primary verb. Again, one need not labour the point too much: if you are going to use an ethical slingshot, you'd better look to the beam in your own eye, or your aim may be misdirected.

But Hoggart is consciously writing as a David facing a Goliath, and the book is a kind of desperate last wail from someone whose resources are running out and whose material is thin and whose strength is no longer great in this fight. We must remember that he published the book when he was eighty-two years old. Thus I may seem simply uncharitable and perhaps a little cruel in the criticisms and comparisons I have made. There is quite a different way of looking at the book which ignores and perhaps explains its very shortcomings: namely the impulse, in an old man, not to go down quietly, without a fight, even if the result is that he is ranting half the time. And the fight here is precisely borne out of a worthy insistence that ethics — and the corresponding duty to make aesthetic evaluation — remain at the heart of the study of art and culture. I believe Hoggart is the last surviving remnant of this tradition — he would probably be relatively happy with the word — which, despite all their differences, binds Arnold to Leavis to Williams to Hoggart. I have never thought that Hoggart had the intellectual stature or gravitas of the other three I have named. But, in his own way — grossly distorted in the book I have discussed — he refuses to cease whispering (as he puts it in the book) in that wind. And it is because of this insistence — not the bizarrely confused and worryingly out-of-touch discourse it has produced in this case — that I think Hoggart's life-work remains salutary, and something to carry forward.

I think he is right (both factually and morally) that the decoupling of ethical considerations (and the concomitant evaluation of cultural products and procedures) has — and I suspect we are at the apex of this development — been a disaster which the academy, and especially Cultural Studies, has all too helpfully aided. I now work in a discipline which, at its inception (for the sake of argument, let's assume that to be the Birmingham Centre, which Hoggart founded) was reworking that ethical stress in terms of politics and ideology. Twenty-five years ago, when I was an undergraduate studying English Literature, I saw this belatedly working its way through Literary Studies, as 'Theory', apparently bent on destroying the seeming ideological naïvety of liberal humanism, was still doing so within the relatively clear ethical framework of socialist politics. But not any more: Literary Studies, but especially Cultural Studies, are both now awash, if not drowned, in a tide of relativism caused by the crisis of pluralist and identity-based politics to which, ironically, 'Theory' opened the gates. One still has straightforward discussions about what is 'good' and 'bad' but one hesitates to commit these to the illusory objectivity which writing seems to bestow. The institutions in which we carry out our teaching and research have similarly, in my experience, migrated from the collegiate public service model which I got a last glimpse of when I joined a University's staff in 1991, to the competitive business models we are now all too familiar with from experience, and, in the process, their watchword has become not what is good and right, but what, practically, in the world of education, sells and can be marketed, or can be exploited to raise research funds.

My aim in what I have said, therefore, and despite what it may have sounded like, was not simply to launch a partial attack on Hoggart by choosing one of his obvious Achilles' heels. Actually, I think what I am trying to do with Hoggart is to praise him with faint damning. When his voice is lost, the Humanities loses the last of the uncompromising ethicists and, although his practice went sorely awry in this book, he articulates the principle bravely, unwaveringly and unfashionably, at an incredibly late and unpropitious stage. He does not practise what he preaches because the slapdashness of his scholarship and argumentative procedures is no longer acceptable, just as one would be mistaken to try to reproduce in today's conditions Williams's clotted complexity, Leavis's icy and Olympian moral superiority, or Arnold's wistful, analysis-shy classicism. There is, to my mind, no one left alive in the field of the required intellectual stature who can take the baton he wishes to pass. That is what makes it difficult to see, now, what an ethically rooted study of literature, the arts, culture more generally and the social conditions which modulate it, would look like — above all, what intellectual writing, in these new conditions but with a wish to keep that strain alive, would look like. Despite all his shortcomings, then, I believe that that is Hoggart's challenge to the future of those disciplines, and I invite us to discuss whether or not it is a challenge we wish to take up or turn our backs on.

Bibliography

Bloom, H. (1995) *The Western Canon: the Books and School of the Ages* (London: Macmillan).

Hoggart, R. (2004) *The Uses of Literacy: Aspects of Working-Class Life* (New Brunswick: Transaction Publishers).

———— (2005) *Mass Media in a Mass Society: Myth and Reality* (London: Continuum).

Owen, S. (ed.) (2008) *Richard Hoggart and Cultural Studies* (Basingstoke: Palgrave Macmillan).

Williams, R. (1961) *The Long Revolution* (London: Chatto and Windus).

EXCURSIONS INTO THE 'BAROQUE':
HOGGART, *ANGEL* AND THE USES OF ROMANCE
Alice Ferrebe

Elizabeth Taylor's novel *Angel* was published in 1957, the same year as Richard Hoggart's *The Uses of Literacy*. It is the story of a grocer's daughter from the fictional town of 'Norley' who begins at fifteen a commercially triumphant and critically derided career in racy and heavily ornate romantic fiction. As such, she appears at first to be a feminine member of the abusers of literacy that Hoggart's work so condemns, as he decries the increasing dominance of mass-produced, corrupting, fake-cultural forms; as he puts it, persistent and seductive 'invitations to a candy-floss world' (Hoggart 1958: 169). Yet both Taylor's and Hoggart's texts enact a far more complex apprehension of the relationship between gender and literary consumption, as well as sharing a preoccupation with the politics of representation we might consider as indicative of 1950's British intellectual culture.

Writing and reading romance

Angelica Deverell, the protagonist of *Angel*, is on one level a parody of Marie Corelli, the best-selling Victorian romance writer, whose life had been examined in Eileen Bigland's 1953 biography. Angel (as Angelica is most often known) is quick to condemn her 'rival's' work — when a young journalist from the *Norley Advertiser* suggests Corelli as an influence, she responds acidly: 'I am afraid that in my opinion Miss Corelli writes like a Sunday-school teacher' (Taylor 2001: 108). Yet Taylor evokes Corelli on a number of occasions to suggest Angel's condemnation stems from discomfort at the closeness of their careers. On discovering that Gilbright and Brace are to publish her first novel, Angel experiences 'a delightful sensation of being lifted up' (Taylor 2001: 50), and *Lifted Up* was the original title for Corelli's first novel (Bigland 1953: 66). Subsequently, Mrs Gilbright notices a photograph on Angel's piano in which the now-famous novelist is 'garbed as one of the muses, sitting on a marble seat in a trance' (Taylor 2001: 78): the pose is deliberately reminiscent of one of Corelli's kitsch, po-faced frontispieces. Harold Rosenberg's 1959 study *The Tradition of the New* described kitsch (certainly a concept applicable to the glimpses we get of Angel's writing) as art that 'follows established rules' with 'a predictable audience, predictable effects, predictable rewards'. His objection centres upon not the commercialism of this brand of art but on what he calls a 'muscular slackness associated with finding an audience responsive to certain norms' (Rosenberg 1965: 266-8). In this way,

Rosenberg shares a key concern with *The Uses of Literacy* — that of the social and moral effects of mass-produced, popular art — but also, with that phrase 'muscular slackness', a particular Hoggartian discourse which positions that art as antithetical to values of healthiness, vitality, and wholesomeness. During the twentieth century, British women were the buyers and borrowers of almost three-quarters of all the fiction in circulation (Bloom 2002: 51). Also apparent and inherent in that phrase 'muscular slackness' is a gendered inflection upon cultural consumption, as the suggestion of physical and psychic softness feminises the phenomenon as it is condemned.

In her exploration of the reading and writing processes of romance in *Angel*, Taylor seems similarly intent upon suggesting the debilitating effects of the genre. Angelica Deverell writes her first novel *The Lady Irania* when she is only fifteen, feigning illness and recumbent in bed:

> The words flowed without effort all the evening and she seemed to be in a trance. [...] By bedtime, she was both excited and exhausted. Her right arm and shoulder were aching and her fingers were cramped. She had scarcely paused, either to consider what she should write or judge what she had written. (Taylor 2001: 29)

Hoggart claims of what he calls 'cheap romances' that:

> They are [...] produced by people who possess some qualities in greater measure than their readers, but are of the same ethos. 'Every culture lives inside its own dream'; they share the common dream of their culture. They can publish in great quantity and over year after year, without the phases which in a serious writer mark developments in his experience and consequent changes in his manner of expression because they write semi-automatically. (Hoggart 1958: 171)

Angel exemplifies this flawed creative process: her fiction is produced from an adolescent and trance-like writing state which is portrayed as unhealthily onanistic. The man who is to become her husband, Esmé Howe-Nevinson, observes: 'I think that the secret of your power over people is that you communicate with yourself, not with your readers' (Taylor 2001: 133). A familiar generic affiliation is in place here, between Angel's febrile and feminised writing practices, and reading practices characterised in the same way. Alan Boon, of Mills and Boon, whose reputed charm and solicitousness toward his authoresses is shared by Angel's gallant publisher Theo Gilbright, was quoted in the *Daily Citizen* (3 January 1913) as saying: 'I am certain that to-day the bulk of novels

95

published are devoured by women before they reach the men.' Theo asks his colleague if his wife has also read the manuscript of *The Lady Irania.* Apeing Angel's writing style, Willie Brace replies:

'Read it? She devoured and gobbled every iridescent word.'
'So will other women.'
'I should hope more reverently.' (Taylor 2001: 51)

In her still definitively interdisciplinary study of the reading cultures of the genre, *Reading the Romance,* Janice A. Radway identified a particular commercial relationship between romance and its readers: the publishing of romance fiction, she claims, accentuates 'the book as an endlessly replicable commodity' (Radway 1994: 23), and notes that '[r]omance readers are generally heavy consumers' (Radway 1994: 60). The 'devouring' of Angel's work by a female readership evokes a similar disquiet at the mindless consumption of a mass-product.

The diegesis of *Angel* runs between 1885 and 1947, but the novel's cultural perspective is fraught with concerns contemporary to its publication. Taylor represents the romance genre as a nexus of the moral and social anxieties surrounding consumerism and art. Like Radway, she uses romance in an anthropological way: as a phenomenon to yield insights into 'the spatial and temporal specificity of culture' (Radway 1994: 10). It is both this investigatory technique and these anxieties, of course, that so animate *The Uses of Literacy,* in which, Hoggart claims, piles of magazines and novelettes at railway-bookstalls 'make a picture of some of the stresses inside our culture' (Hoggart 1958: 211). Joseph McAleer's history of Mills and Boon records how, in the case of both World Wars, 'wartime stimulated reading and the desire to "escape" with a good book, and demand was up, mainly from the libraries' (McAleer 1999: 36). Hoggart reads escapism as a definitive factor in the working-class response to art:

Art is marginal, 'fun': 'It teks y'mind *off* things'; 'It teks yer *out* of y'self'; 'It meks a *break*, and a bit of a change' (the italics are mine). Whilst they are enjoying it, people may submit themselves, may identify themselves; but at the back of their minds they know it is not 'real'; 'real' life goes on elsewhere. (Hoggart 1958: 196)

The quotation in the title of this chapter is taken from one of Hoggart's sub-headings, to a section in which he describes a working-class attitude which emulates artistic extravagance and ornament: 'It loves what might be called (without necessarily implying a historical link) the "baroque"

[…]. It loves the cornucopia, all that is generous and sprawling, that suggests splendour and wealth by sheer abundance and lavishness of colour. It loves the East, because the East is exotic and elaborate' (1958: 114). Taylor's meticulous description of the cramped sitting room about the grocery shop in Norley, in which Angel has been raised, situates it precisely within these elaborate tastes:

> A crochet-work cloth was spread over the green chenille one and the light shone down on the cups and saucers on the table. The room was overcrowded and it was difficult to push between the table and the other furniture, the horsehair sofa, the chiffonier, the treadle sewing-machine and the harmonium. Photographs covered every surface. The chimney-piece was draped with ball-fringed velvet and a bead fringe hid the incandescent gas-mantle. (Taylor 2001: 11)

On her first visit to London, Angel is disappointed in Theo and Hermione Gilbright's house — she despises 'the modern furnishings, the lack of sumptuousness. Instead of gilt and marble there were plain oak and pottery tiles' (Taylor 2001: 61). This represents, of course, a carefully calibrated sense of transition between Victorian and Edwardian taste, but there is also an explicit class inflection at work. The word 'baroque' comes from the Spanish (it is a jeweler's term for an 'imperfect pearl') and for both Hoggart and Taylor the idea invokes a sense of flawed imitation. 'She writes like a servant-girl!' an exasperated Hermione tells her husband (Taylor 2001: 65), and Taylor's readers are repeatedly prompted to make the link between Angel's working-class origins, the distastefully baroque, Orientalised style and settings of her fiction and the escapist desires of both herself and her devoted readers.

Cultural and class concerns

Elizabeth Taylor's work has routinely been critically classified in the literary sub-section of 'women's novels', and has thus, until recently, been largely overlooked. Such writing has traditionally been understood to attend to female experience as 'special', rather than culturally integrated with or indicative of its period, and to cater exclusively to a female readership of feminised tastes. Of late, however, numerous literary critics have sought to reassess and rehabilitate the 'feminine middlebrow' (the term is Nicola Humble's) as a dynamic genre animated by 'a powerful force in establishing and consolidating, but also in resisting, new class and gender identities' (Humble 2001: 3). Hilary Hinds characterises the genre as 'a body of work in which domesticity is repeatedly an arena for feminine disappointment' (Hinds 2009: 300), and in which such disappointment is frequently 'associated with a deluded romanticism' (Hinds 2009: 307). Deluded romance is certainly Angelica Deverell's *modus operandi* in her writing. However, of all Taylor's novels, *Angel* stands alone in its disruption of the standard feminine middlebrow formula of domesticity focalised through middle-class female experience. For all Angel's baroque sensibilities, the novel is a stark *bildungsroman* about a working-class woman's pain at her unaccustomed affluence, dislocation from the community of her birth, and class mobility. Her disorientation is aggravated by hypergamy, a staple plot device not only of romance fiction, but also that of the canonised definitive of 1950's literature, the Angry Young Man novel. Angel's husband, Esmé Howe-Nevinson, as his name indicates, is upper class, albeit an impoverished aristocrat whose social standing and confidence is indicated, paradoxically, by the squalor of his studio: 'No one in Volunteer Street would have left a greasy newspaper lying on the table. There were even a few dried-up chips left in it. That the nephew of a Lord — as she thought of Esmé — should do so, troubled her' (Taylor 2001: 124).

In this way, Taylor's novel reworks another crucial trope of the literature of its period. 'The Uprooted and the Anxious': this is what Hoggart famously called those definitive figures of the British 1950s, and the tenth chapter of *The Uses of Literacy*, 'Unbent Springs', focuses upon the social and cultural dislocation experienced by the 'scholarship boys' among whose ranks he is numbered. In fiction, it is the (allegedly) Angry Young Men – Kingsley Amis, John Braine and John Wain in particular– whose work is traditionally assumed to provide a diagnostic for the social and psychic stresses of class difference during the decade. Alison Light has argued that 'being "middle-class" in fact depends on an extremely anxious production of endless discriminations between people who are constantly assessing each other's standing' (Light 1991: 13). Under Light's definition, though they are rarely read in this way, these AYM narratives might be considered to be profoundly (if newly) middle-class in their concerns, negotiating as they do so explicitly the anxieties of class discrimination in a new (Welfare) state of affluent meritocracy. Nicola Beauman's recent biography portrays Elizabeth Taylor's middle-class existence as a constant, uneasy negotiation of class difference in both public and private: in the mid-1930s Taylor was selling the *Daily Worker* in High Wycombe High Street (Beauman 2009: 77), and by the 1950s, still a socialist (as she remained all her life), she is attempting to orientate herself ethically in relation to her acquisition of a modest domestic staff to assist her in running her household. Increasingly then, rather than a narrative of marginalised existence, *Angel* is revealed as inextricably engaged with the definitive 1950's cultural project in Britain: a renegotiation of the representational politics of fast-evolving class experiences in writing. This project spans both literature and the newly-emerging field of cultural studies.

Taylor's novel is riven with the kind of ethical anxieties about portraying working-class experience that so drive *The Uses of Literacy*. 'How many major English writers are there,' Hoggart asks, 'who do not, however slightly, over-emphasize the salty features of working-class life?' (Hoggart 1958: 4-5). Romances are rarely salty, but what Hoggart refers to here is that long literary tradition of romanticising salt-of-the-earth characters. Inherent in his unease is the concern that the aestheticisation of working-class realities will render them inauthentic, making the reader complicit with the kind of 'unhealthy' and escapist reading practices routinely attributed, as we have seen, to the romance genre. One of Hoggart's techniques to counter such inauthenticity is the 'thick description' of anthropological writing that holistically situates the events it describes within their physical and social context. Raymond Williams's work of the same period aims to establish a 'structure of feeling' in order to communicate the 'felt sense of the quality of life at a particular place and time: a sense of the ways in which the particular activities combined into a way of thinking and living' (Williams 1961: 47). Clustered here is a range of conceptual links that have already been well made — the coincidence of this anthropological project of authentic representation with that of literary realism, as well as the subsequent orthodoxy of literary text as a metaphor for culture — in other words, both culture and writing about culture as inescapably literary.

In a chapter called 'The "Real" World of People', Hoggart suggests that '[i]f we want to capture something of the essence of working-class life in such a phrase, we must say that it is the "dense and concrete life", a life whose main stress is on the intimate, the sensory, the detailed, and the personal' (Hoggart 1958: 81). The inverted commas around 'Real' are particularly eloquent, suggesting his sense of realism as necessarily aesthetic. In his autobiography, Hoggart was to state that 'my own experience had been overwhelmingly domestic, internal, home and woman-centred' (Hoggart 1991: 142). Sue Owen has argued that Hoggart's commitment to citing women at the heart of working-class experience, as well as his determinedly personal writing style, makes his work properly proto-feminist (Owen 2008: 240). She is right, but it is also worth noting how the radical aspects of his perspective — domestic, internal, intimate, sensory, detailed, personal — are simultaneously traditionally feminine. As such, it is these characteristics which have invited the familiar and errant accusations of *The Uses of Literacy* as 'sentimental'. Yet it is Hoggart's uses of women in his first book that serve most convincingly to refute these accusations:

The lines on the face of an old working-class woman are often magnificently expressive — but they are hard earned. We should not try to add a glamour to such a face; it has its fineness without any artificial light. It is often a face with a scaly texture and the lines, looked at closely, have grime in them; the hands are bony claws covered with densely lined skin, and again the dirt is well-ingrained there: years of snatched washes, usually in cold water, have caused that. The face has two marked lines of force — from the sides of the nose down to the compressed lips; they tell of years of 'calculating'. (Hoggart 1958: 33)

Profoundly detailed, unromantic without being 'salty', and affectingly visceral (by contrast, little attention is paid to the male body in the text), Hoggart's women function as much as reality effects as they do emotional foci.

Crossing classes

Taylor's text, like *The Uses of Literacy*, tries to produce a structure of feeling rooted in accurate description that will allow its readers a properly productive combination of emotional and intellectual identification with lives outside their own experience. In order for *Angel* to achieve its educational and emotional goals as a *bildungsroman*, this identification must most often occur across a class divide, between middle-class readers of middlebrow novels, and a working-class protagonist. A literature of 'the intimate, the sensory, the detailed, and the personal': these are the directives of the thick description of Hoggart's cultural study, but we might also note their coincidence with an important tenet of romance writing. Radway's analysis notes in the romance text a marked attention to the material details, or reality effects, of the fantasy world, expostulating that 'this peculiar blend of a deliberately referential language with the signs of "the literary" serves the dual purpose of signaling "escape" while suggesting to the reader that the imaginary world is congruent with her own and, therefore, dominated by events that might well occur in a life such as hers' (Radway 1994: 192). Rather than the model of consumption without discrimination (by which both Hoggart and Taylor understand romance), Radway upholds a more intricate reading process for the genre that involves both cognitive and affective identifications. In contrast to the authors Radway considers, Angel Deverell is notoriously inaccurate in the contextual minutiae of her romance writing, preferring to fantasise details rather than research them. After the death of her mother she is able to deploy this labile process with the details of her own early life too, publicising the story of an errant, aristocratic father rather than that of the grocer who 'coughed his way though only a year and a half of married bliss' (Taylor 2001: 14). Taylor emphasises the unhealthy nature of Angel's unbridled and unrealistic imagination to once again condemn the undesirable practices of popular romance.

Clare Hanson has noted of Elizabeth Taylor that she 'foregrounds the hybridity of her own art and opens up the whole question of what "art" should be' (Hanson 2000: 22). Taylor's writing is notable for its synaesthetic qualities, as it explores the politics of representation through a range of artistic forms. Ultimately, the author suggests that Angel's artistic flaws are peculiar neither to herself, her gender, nor her chosen genre. Aristocratic Esmé is a realist painter, his style and subjects seemingly utterly at odds with those of his wife's work. The couple are introduced by his uncle:

> 'Esmé is a painter himself, you know,' said Lord Norley, glad that the awkwardness was passing off so well.
> 'I *see*,' Angel said softly.
> 'Such horrible pictures! Barmaids and jockeys, barges in the fog, back-streets in the pouring rain, slag heaps ... the seamy side of life ...'
> 'And allotments,' Nora said spitefully. 'Don't forget the allotments, Uncle, with all the horrid little tool-sheds and rubbish-heaps.'
> 'And cemeteries,' Esmé said cheerfully. 'I am particularly fond of my cemeteries.' (Taylor 2001: 89)

This is part of a game of allusion Taylor plays throughout the novel to Virginia Woolf's essay on Walter Sickert (Woolf 1992), but for her contemporary and subsequent readers these descriptions surely summon the work of another painter, that of Lawrence Stephen Lowry (1887-1976), whose work saw a surge in public popularity in the post-Second World War years, along with a prominent critical reinterpretation. During the 1930s, journalist Howard Spring had upheld Lowry's work to have a realism of enormous political potential in a way that chimes with Chris Waters's much more recent description of Lowry's paintings as 'Geertzian exercises in thick description of a vanished past' (Waters 1999: 142). Waters's article catalogues a range of differing interpretations of Lowry's work, including this 'political Lowry' and also an 'existential Lowry'. However, by 1957, Spring is claiming that Lowry's paintings capture 'the romance that is there when you open up the door any morning in an industrial town' (Spring 1957: 228). Waters notes that it was this urban pastoral reading of Lowry's work — an 'aestheticized, fairyland version of the North' — that was prevalent during the 1950s: 'It was this particular construct of Lowry's importance, disseminated through many radio chats and television documentaries, that framed popular readings of the millions of prints of his industrial scenes that rolled off the presses after the war' (Waters 1999: 133). Texts which give accounts of the industrial North — the landscape that, in the popular consciousness, has become, in Philip Dodd's phrase, a 'Lowryscape' (Dodd 1990) — are regularly branded by the addition of Lowry's work. Hoggart's writing is no exception, and the cover of the 1969 Pelican edition of *The Uses of Literacy* exhibits an unnamed piece of Lowry's work from Penguin's own collection. This sense of 'romantic Lowry' is obviously at aesthetic odds with Hoggart's project to produce a 'felt sense' of working-class experience. Yet, like Hoggart the scholarship boy (and Taylor, writing *Angel*), Lowry the white-collar rent-collector found himself an outsider of the experience he sought to represent: the elevated and objectifying perspectives of his landscape paintings are a visual demonstration of this social and psychological distance, at the same time that their detail communicates his empathy with his subjects' lives.

Esmé's self-esteem as an artist is founded upon his sense of the authenticity of his depictions of working-class urban landscapes and interiors which sets him apart, he feels, from the fantasy-elements of his wife's work: 'those subfusc bars, with their ferns and patterned glass, marble-topped tables, immense hat-stands. When he showed Angel what he had done, she praised him as soon as she recoiled' (Taylor 2001: 136). Eventually, utterly emasculated by debt, the loss of his leg in the First World War, and his wife's fantastical financial success, he kills himself. Years later, Angel is delighted when a young academic, Clive Fennelly, visits to research an article on Esmé's painting: 'She took his essay to the window, straining her eyes to read it. "A literary painter," she said. "I like that very much. That would have pleased Esmé". It seemed to her to be praise indeed; but Clive looked away, blushing' (Hinds 2009: 240). Clive is embarrassed, of course, because that 'literary' is derogatory. The *O.E.D.* gives this example of usage from 1962: 'R. G. HAGGAR *Dict. Art Terms* 196 *Literary art* ... The term is frequently used in a pejorative sense, but most romantic painting is dependent upon a text.' This moment in the novel forces the instructive reassessment of Esmé's work in relation to Angel's, as it implies that his allegedly 'realist' paintings are as much an exercise in romanticising reality as his wife's art of romance. Hoggart's work, of course, has not escaped similar accusations of sentimentality.

Double readings, double relationships

In *Angel* Taylor poses that double bind common to art, ethnography and literature: realism is a literary construct, yet self-consciously 'literary' work draws attention to its constructed, 'unreal' nature. In aligning realism with romance as literary devices, she has her own agenda. Angel's reputation

102

with literary critics is derisible. Taylor's critical reception, characteristic of that of 'the woman's novel' more generally, tended instead towards a genteel damnation with faint praise: 'Save me', wrote Norman Shrapnel in *The Guardian*, in response to her 1961 novel *In a Summer Season*, 'from the wise, witty, sensitive, accomplished, charming female novelist'. However, one of the many doubling effects produced by the novel is between the two writers, Angel and Taylor herself, united in their production of fiction judged by the intellectual establishment as sappingly inconsequential — writing which infantilises, or at least (and still worse) effeminises, its reader. One of the notable aspects of Angel's work, in its heyday at least, is its ability to gain popularity (for entirely different reasons) in completely different sections of the market. Her publisher says of *The Lady Irania* that "'It will be nice strong meat for the unsophisticated, and delicious stuff and nonsense for some connoisseurs". After a moment Theo said: "When I think of her, I dislike myself for saying that"' (Taylor 2001: 58). This moment is metonymic of the novel's narrative voice and its emotional effect: an assertion of intellectual superiority over the unsophisticated reading practices that Angel shares with her own readers, followed immediately by an enforced unease at the condescending nature of this assertion. Laughing at her preposterous stand against her new-found publisher, refusing to change a word of *The Lady Irania* (even the incident when the champagne is opened with a corkscrew [Hinds 2009: 52]), the reader is brought up short in their mockery by Angel's abrupt and epiphanic realisation of reality, as she beholds her profoundly unromantic appearance: 'In the Ladies' Waiting Room, she glimpsed herself in a looking-glass. She was an absurd figure: her straw hat was crooked above her pale and glistening face, her hair untidy, and her dress creased. She was not at all her own idea of Angel Deverell' (Hinds 2009: 57). Angel's moment of self-recognition is mirrored by that which is created in the reader, of an unjust and ugly assumption of superiority.

Taylor's novel works to make a case for the double reading of her own fiction — as work that is both traditionally feminine (in its focus on the female experience, its domestic settings, and its middle-classness), yet socially profound: not despite, but because of this. Angel seeing herself in the mirror is an intensely literary moment, open to a range of intellectual interpretation from the existential to the Lacanian. In her study of middlebrow fiction, Clare Hanson's interpretation of the genre identifies a double reading process that recalls Radway's understanding of the complex romance-reading strategies of the Smithton women:

On the one hand, the woman's novel offers a discourse of mastery and a regime of pleasure modeled on obsessional rather than hysterical structures. The intelligence, the psychological and sociological acuity of the novel, its 'high' cultural references, all reflect/create a discourse of mastery. However, this kind of novel also works in the identificatory mode, allowing the reader to give herself over to the novel as a process, reading (hysterically) for the pleasure of the text. (Hanson 2000: 5-6)

In its configuration of reading as the interplay of states of intellectual detachment and emotional engagement it also recalls the 'double relationship' which, in the 'Questions of Approach' section with which Hoggart begins *The Uses of Literacy*, he establishes at the core of his own developing methodology:

A writer who is himself from the working-classes has his own temptations to error, somewhat different from but no less than those of a writer from another class. I am from the working-classes and feel even now both close to them and apart from them. In a few more years this double relationship may not, I suppose, be so apparent to me; but it is bound to affect what I say. It may help me to come nearer to giving a felt sense of working-class life, to avoid some of an outsider's more obvious risks of misinterpretation. On the other hand, this very emotional involvement presents considerable dangers. (Hoggart 1958: 6)

As Helen Wood has pointed out, this ethical debate of a 'double relationship' remains live among feminist critics today in, for example, issues surrounding the 'pleasure' of the consumption of mass art, the extent to which its value might counteract perceived personal and cultural debilitation, and related concerns regarding the relationship between feminist discourse and 'real' women (Wood 2004: 148). We might compare Hoggart's guarded suggestion that the working-classes have a more febrile response to those fallacious 'invitations to a candy-floss world' (Hoggart 1958: 169) from the mass-publicists. Such critical issues have bedevilled Radway's *Reading the Romance* (see, for example, Modleski 1986), and they remain alive today in the wider cultural studies project.

Conclusion

Ultimately, Angel is unable to maintain her fantasy: her relationship with Esmé is so fraught with harsh emotional, political, economic and sexual realities that romance fails her as a escapist genre. Her career swiftly collapses as she begins to freight her work with realist settings and pacifist ideologies while Esmé is away at war, alienating her mass audience, 'the bread-and-milk brigade' (Taylor 2001: 56), as publisher Willie Brace calls them. 'Aim Low, Angel' urges the title of one of Hoggart's spoof 'sex-novelettes' (Hoggart 1958: 213), and Angel gets ideas above her station in the aims of her work. Unpracticed (and uneducated) as she is, she cannot forge the 'double relationship' in her own writing that mediates between emotion and detachment in a process both affective and cognitive. Taylor, however, has used her protagonist precisely to achieve that combination, engendering a literary realism that stands outside the dominant (and masculine) models of the literature of the 1950s, and that her own, middlebrow novels will go on to exemplify. In 1984 a committee including Richard Hoggart (and also Elizabeth Jane Howard and the industrialist Peter Park) chose a list of what they called the 'Best Novels of Our Time' for a Book Marketing Council promotion. Controversially, *Angel* was among them. This chapter has sought to show why, alongside Hoggart's work, and along with his vote, we should consider Taylor's work afresh as engaged with the politics of representation so definitive of its decade, and so vital in literary and cultural studies since.

Bibliography

Beauman, N. (2009) *The Other Elizabeth Taylor* (London: Persephone Books).

Bigland, E. (1953) *Marie Corelli: Her Life and Legend* (London: Jarrolds).

Bloom, C. (2002) *Bestsellers: Popular Fiction since 1900* (Basingstoke: Palgrave Macmillan).

Dodd, P. (1990) 'Lowryscapes: Recent Writings about "the North"', *Critical Quarterly*, 32 (2), pp.17-28.

Hall, S. (1980) 'Cultural Studies and the Centre: Some Problematics and Problems' in *Culture, Media, Language: Working Papers in Cultural Studies 1972-79* (London: Hutchinson), pp. 3-33.

Hanson, C. (2000) *Hysterical Fictions: The 'Woman's Novel' in the Twentieth Century* (Basingstoke: Palgrave Macmillan).

Hinds, H. (2009) 'Ordinary Disappointments: Femininity, Domesticity, and Nation in British Middlebrow Fiction, 1920-1944', *Modern Fiction Studies*, 55 (2), pp. 293-320.

Hoggart, R. (1991) *A Sort of Clowning: Life and Times, Vol. II: 1940-1959* (Oxford: Oxford University Press).

———— (1958) *The Uses of Literacy: Aspects of Working-Class Life* (Harmondsworth: Penguin).

Humble, N. (2001) *The Feminine Middlebrow Novel 1920s to 1950s* (Oxford: Oxford University Press).

Light, A. (1991) *Forever England: Femininity, Literature and Conservatism between the Wars* (London: Routledge).

McAleer, J. (1999) *Passion's Fortune: The Story of Mills and Boon* (Oxford: Oxford University Press).

Modleski, T. (1986) *Studies in Entertainment* (Bloomington: Indiana University Press).

Owen, S. (2008) 'Hoggart and Women'. In S. Owen, (ed.) *Richard Hoggart and Cultural Studies* (Houndmills: Palgrave Macmillan), pp. 227-242.

Radway, J. A. (1994) *Reading the Romance* (London: Verso).

Rosenberg, H. (1965) *The Tradition of the New* (New York: McGraw-Hill).

Shrapnel, N. (1961) 'Lady's-eye-view', *Guardian* (28 April), p. 9.

Spring, H. (1957) 'The World of L.S. Lowry', *The Saturday Book* 17. 228, quoted Waters 1999: 129.

Waters, C. (1999) 'Representations of Everyday Life: L.S. Lowry and the Landscape of Memory in Postwar Britain', *Representations* 65 (Winter), pp. 121-50.

Williams, R. (1961) *The Long Revolution* (London: Chatto and Windus).

Wood, H. (2004) 'What *Reading the Romance* Did For Us', *European Journal of Cultural Studies*, 7 (2), pp. 147-54.

Woolf, V. (1992) *Walter Sickert: A Conversation* (London: The Bloomsbury Workshop).

THE USES OF LITERACY, THE 'ANGRY YOUNG MEN' AND BRITISH NEW WAVE

Tracy Hargreaves

The publication of *The Uses of Literacy* in 1957 coincided with popular interest in the 'Angry Young Man'. Briefly fashionable and vigorously rejected by those whose work was attached to it, the nomenclature has nonetheless endured alongside other literary, theatrical and cinematic labels that emerged in the decade: the Movement, Kitchen Sink Drama and British New Wave Cinema. The 'Angry Young Man' was always an inexact term, a 'catchphrase' and a 'slogan' as Harry Ritchie (1988: 26, 39) has redefined it and it was used to describe individual writers, fictional and dramatic characters, and a number of texts published in the 1950s that made up an illusory 'group' 'I suppose you're really - an angry young man' George Fearon, Press Officer for the Royal Court Theatre told John Osborne (Osborne 1999: 298) as he set about publicising *Look Back in Anger* in 1956. The phrase caught on so that when *The Uses of Literacy* was published a year later, Richard Hoggart was invoked as an Angry Young Man: 'bawling above the din of mass-made entertainment, [he] flings an angry question at us: Are we becoming a nation of robots?' (Carpenter 2002: 167).

Harry Ritchie has suggested that the media coverage of the Angry Young Man, at its peak in 1957, had become so indiscriminate that 'almost any youngish contemporary author could be enlisted as a (temporary) member of the "group"' (Ritchie 1988: 39). Whilst the *Daily Herald*'s inclusion of Hoggart as an Angry Young Man was arguably more opportunistic than analytical (Angry Young Men boosted sales circulations), I want to return to their description of Hoggart as an 'Angry Young Man' in this essay. This is not to uphold the connection or indeed the term which was mostly a misnomer. Hoggart himself dismissed the 'Angry Young Man' in his Birmingham inaugural lecture as one of those 'new little cultural patterns', the promotion of which was 'almost wholly lacking in precision or historical perspective' (Hoggart 1970: 255). But it is the 'new little cultural pattern' that I want to revisit in this essay by tracing its delineations and intersections across *The Uses of Literacy* and across the literature and film of the period; in particular my focus is John Braine's novel, *Room at the Top*, published at the same time as *The Uses of Literacy* in 1957. Braine's novel was then adapted to film in 1959, a film that Dilys Powell claimed 'gives one faith all over again in a renaissance of the British cinema' (Sinyard 2000: 37). Her faith was not misplaced and it is that renaissance, what became known as British New Wave Cinema (1959-1963) that I wish to turn to in the final part of this essay. I do so in the spirit of Sue Owen's call for 'an informed re-evaluation of "totalizing" theories of working-class culture' (Owen 2008a: 227) in order to trace the intimate connections and cultural changes that evolve so tentatively across *The Uses of Literacy, Room at the Top* and British New Wave Cinema.

The literariness of *The Uses of Literacy,* together with Hoggart's origin as a literary scholar has been much commented on, from F. R. Leavis's ambiguous response: 'he should have written a novel' (Hoggart 1991: 206) to more explicit comparisons which link *The Uses of Literacy* with *Sons and Lovers* (Collini 2008: 53). In a BBC2 programme, *Mirror on Class,* Melvyn Bragg hailed *The Uses of Literacy* as a 'literary breakthrough' alongside the works of John Osborne, Kingsley Amis, and Arnold Wesker (Wales 103: 2008). David Lodge is one of a number of critics to have noted 'the almost novelistic quality of the writing' (Lodge 2007: 30; see also Long 2008: 124-5; Hall 2007: 27; Owen 2008a: 64; Collini 2008: 52-3; Clarke, 2008: 49-50). Like Bragg before him, Lodge aligned *The Uses of Literacy* with other contemporary literary texts that 'belonged to the same seismic shift in the English literary landscape in the 1950s' (Lodge 2007: 31). John Braine summarised this shift in an unpublished and undated notebook where he described it as one that moved 'from the Home Counties to the Provinces, from the middle-class to the working-class, from the wet hero to the dry and tough hero'. Braine was drafting a talk called 'The New English Novelists' in which he, too, dismissed the Angry Young Man. It was misconceived, he suggested, there never was such a group: 'What the talk, what all the articles amounted to was this: something had happened to the English novel. Something had happened to the English theatre drama too: but that in itself is material for another talk.' The 'something' that had happened, summarised by Braine in those clipped binaries, was a dedicated representation of the Midlands and the North, of working-class cultures, and of working-class masculinity. But it was also a far more exploratory shift than either the seismic shift or the dynamic trajectory alluded to by Lodge and Braine. Hoggart dismissed the 'cultural pattern' of the Angry Young Man as not much more than an idiom from 'the organs of opinion' (Hoggart 1970: 255). He does not name them in his inaugural lecture, but he is presumably referring to magazines like the *Spectator,* the *New Statesman, Encounter* and *The London Magazine* who created and despised the new cultural taxonomies of the decade. Both 'the Movement' and the 'Angry Young Men' evolved, on one level at least, through a desire to create a cultural post-war identity from what John Lehmann described as the dearth of 'new impulses' (Ritchie 1988: 24). As that identity emerged, it got mired in snobbery and caricatures of undistinguished 'grim young people' as Evelyn Waugh described 1950s writers, 'coming off the assembly lines in their hundreds every year and finding employment as critics, even as poets and novelists' (Ritchie 1988: 71). Somerset Maugham dreaded their influence as teachers, journalists and politicians who might be capable of forming public opinion and ruling the country and he denounced the new type (gleaned through Kingsley Amis's *Lucky Jim*) as 'scum' (Ritchie 1988: 72). Reading these 'grim young people' and this 'seismic shift' through Hoggart's cultural study, contemporary literature and film both constitutes and reveals a far more nuanced and always evolving engagement with social class and culture than the descriptive labels attached to this period could ever suggest. These engagements are at once radical *and* tentative; read alongside each other, they offer a far subtler understanding of what is at stake in the relationships between literature and society, and between cultural and sexual politics.

Stefan Collini has recently suggested that *The Uses of Literacy* has more in common than is usually acknowledged with a 'highly-visible strain' of post-war literary criticism (Collini 2008: 35). In assuming 'some kind of pre-existing community of values', Collini argues, the persuasive force of literary criticism could be made on the basis of assuming shared values. It is an assumption that Hoggart himself has both acknowledged and questioned as one that underlines his own critical style (Hoggart, 1991: 90). Such assumption informed understanding about post-war culture in a particular way: 'The combination of its ethically strenuous idiom with the confident presumption of agreement made it fatally easy to project the contrast between, on the one hand, what is "genuine", "grounded", and "humanly representative" and, on the other, what is "shallow", "inauthentic", and "commercially driven" onto a temporal contrast between a past simplicity and a present corruption' (Collini 2008: 37-8). Collini's characterisation of a certain tendency in post-war literary criticism has an evident (though by no means complete) resonance in *The Uses of Literacy* both in the book's overall structure and within individual chapters that evaluate the past against the present and that imbricate ethical decline with cultural decline (Collini 2008: 52). The causal effect of that relationship produces a decaying and depthless ontology in *Room at the Top* that evolves through the specific linkage of mass-market publications with the failure of affect and intimacy. In Chapter 10 of *The Uses of Literacy*, 'The Uprooted and the Anxious', Hoggart depicts the scholarship boy as securely grounded in a social and domestic environment: 'The boy spends a large part of his time at the physical centre of home, where the woman's spirit rules, quietly getting on with his work whilst his mother gets on with her jobs - the father not yet back from work or out for a drink with his mates' (Hoggart 1992: 295). The fruits of his learning, though, are not dissimilar to those of the autodidact for whom the acquisition of 'culture' is a social embellishment: what these two types share in common is less the acquisition of knowledge as 'genuine', 'grounded', 'humanly representative', and more the accumulation of information as 'shallow', 'inauthentic', 'commercially driven'. Knowledge thus becomes a matter of information over ideas, as Hoggart describes this in *A Sort of Clowning* (Hoggart 1991: 160). It is precisely this usurpation of surface over depth that Braine describes in *Room at the Top*, a kind of cultural fatality mapped across a similar historical time frame used by Hoggart in *The Uses of Literacy*: the 1920s and 1930s up to the late 1950s. And what I am interested in looking at is a concern that both Hoggart and Braine share: the troubling eruptions of mass-market publications in the fabric of everyday life and in the quality of felt experience.

Room at the Top was John Braine's first and most successful novel. Published in 1957, it sold well: 35,000 copies in its first year and sales rose dramatically to around 300,000 following Jack Clayton's film of the novel in 1959. Lauded as one of the most important films of that year, it won recognition for its sophisticated approach to sexuality and is regarded as inaugurating the 'New Wave' in British film (Sinyard 2000: 37). Braine's diaries from the early 1950s record a series of frustrated stops and starts as he tries to get going with his first novel. Convinced that he was 'born to make a memorial for western civilization' he dallied with his subject: 'I can memorialize Bingley, but something more is needed. Or is it? Haven't I, in Bingley, all that I need?' Like Hoggart, he celebrated concreteness and his region. Reading Robert Liddell's *Some Principles of Fiction* (1953) he agreed with 'The first bit about rootlessness and lack of community sense in modern urban society [...] This is why I like Bingley — it is a *place*'. *Room at the Top* has two 'places': working-class Dufton and well-to-do Warley. The novel negotiates Joe Lampton's 'embourgeoisement' (or 'deproletarianisation') as he moves from his birthplace to a place of cultural reinvention. His geographical move is also indicative of a more broadly temporal and economic one as the narrative shifts around the 1930s, 1940s, and 1950s (the events in the narrative take place in 1946 but are narrated by Joe from his present-day perspective a decade on in 1956). Those three decades evoke the dominant socio-economic shifts of the period: poverty, austerity and affluence. Following Collini's suggestion that 'ethically diagnostic' criticism should to be able to support a narrative of progress (Collini 2008: 38), those socio-economic shifts *ought* to enable the telling of a passage from hardship to ease in *Room at the Top* but on the whole such a move is resisted. Joe's birthplace, Dufton, is devoid of 'culture' (as he narrowly perceives it); its people's energies seem sapped by deadly industrialism. But his recollection of his kindly Aunt Emily 'sitting by the fire with her hands folded' (Braine 1989: 89) makes him tearful because she also reminds him of his mother who, recollected along with his Labour-voting father, is moral, virtuous, loving, reliable, dependable, fair, hard-working. Recalled by Joe as sitting at either side of the coal fire they resemble two bookends (as Tony Harrison would later remember his mother describing himself and his father) but ones that frame a world of perfect order and social commitment. They recall, too, Hoggart's arrested and arresting figures in a landscape. But Joe Lampton's parents were killed, and the order that they represented was obliterated in a bombing raid that obliges him to re-conceive the setting in fragments across the course of his narrative.

Room at the Top is told though Joe's first-person narration as he gives an account of his social ambition and his moral ruin. This is measured, significantly, by his relationships with two women, Susan Brown and Alice Aisgill, women who are at once incidental, since the narrative is ostensibly about Joe's social mobility, but also crucial since they are indexed to his shabby morality which in turn is a measure of susceptibility to mass-market cultural production. One of the most striking aspects of the novel, normalised by sheer repetition, is that every experience that happens to Joe Lampton during the 1940s and 1950s is compromised or negotiated through mass-market publications. In Joe's narrative, everyone thinks and feels through such publications because this is how Joe has learnt to apprehend his experiences. His narrative voice is a collage made up of advertising jargon, mass-market fiction, popular women's magazines, and popular films. Even a working-class man spotted by Joe has a 'mass-produced face' (Braine 1959:153). There is rarely an unmediated frame of reference for anyone in this narrative apart from one occasion when Joe's colleagues in the Town Hall remember their direct experiences in the Second World War, a remembrance that swiftly prompts the need to forget.

The time lapse in Joe's narrative, from 1946 to 1956, generates a number of anachronisms in the text. The Fiat 500 that Joe remembers Alice driving in 1946, for example, was not made until 1957. The American Hamilton watch that Susan might be the recipient of was possibly one of the new (and first) electric watches, also produced in 1957. The ballet that Joe takes Susan to, Geoffrey Toye's *The Haunted Ballroom*, had just been aired for the last time in the Sadler's Wells repertoire on the BBC in February 1957. If these are all coincidences (Braine records in his diary that his novel, then called *Joe for King*, had just been accepted for publication in 1956) the references are nonetheless easy to register for a culture that supposedly celebrates novelty and youth as the very index of contemporaneity, as Hoggart suggests in *The Uses of Literacy* (Hoggart 1992: 193). Nobody has to try too hard to understand how modish this car is, how sexy or expensive this watch is, how popular this ballet is: gratifyingly, it is all there

111

for immediate consumption. *Room at the Top* is, then, a text that, like *The Uses of Literacy*, realises and recognises the new texture and material fabric of the 1950s.

Without exception, the text's cultural references derive from American advertising, women's magazines, unidentified mass-market fiction and films. Susan Brown reminds Joe of a girl in an American advert selling Cannon Percale sheets. She is the kind of girl who would be given a Hamilton watch or a Nash Airflyte Eight car. Everything that Joe sees, ostensibly for the first time on his arrival in Warley, has in a sense already been seen for him. When he visits his new lodgings (the first chapters of his narrative realise Freud's 'Family Romances') he recognises everything as belonging to 'a pattern of gracious living' and he realises that the phrase is not his but 'straight from the women's magazine...' (Braine 1989: 12). Throughout the narrative Joe, and Susan as she is focalised by Joe, narrate and experience events through similes that either defer or constitute anything they might feel or think, as though everything is, as the simile promises, the same as. Such instances are spread like an infection through the narrative. Shortly after his arrival in Warley, Joe has difficulty in describing a car he sees — and wants — outside a café: 'it's a quality which is difficult to convey without using the terms of the advertising copywriter...' (Braine 1989: 26). The scene is similar to one described by Hoggart in *The Uses of Literacy* as a series of captions designed by a pools firm are clearly managed by the extremes of cynicism and gullibility: 'In block four, having won several thousands, [the young man] is flying round the corner in a snappy sports car with one of the girls from the first picture behind him' (Hoggart 1992: 139). Authentic feeling is seriously compromised. When Joe tries to tell Alice what he feels, he thinks he sounds 'like a cheap film' (Braine, 1989: 62). When he returns to Dufton, it reminds him of 'one of those detective stories in dossier form...' (Braine 1989: 97). When he tries to tell Susan that he is feeling sexually frustrated, her frame of reference is entirely limited by her reading matter: 'Golly. Were you blazing with pent-up desire like people in books?' (Braine 1989: 138). Even anger, that hyper-inflated emotion of the decade is motivated by docile suggestibility: 'At that moment he was enjoying what a thousand films and magazines had assured him to be a righteous anger: His Girl Had Been Untrue' (Braine 1989: 227). At one level, all of these examples (and there are many, many more in the text) indicate a contagious homogenisation. Looking at them, you might assume that the mass market now scripts affect as the depthless simulacra of emergent postmodern culture which is, after Jameson, the logic of late capitalism, or after Hoggart the logic of the new uses of literacy. But the rhetoric and flattened sensibility of mass culture inhabits a text that also suspects and disdains it and in its disdain attempts to distinguish itself from the generalised mass market.

Room at the Top has a complex relation with the pre-war past and the 1930s and it both participates in and refutes a sentimental retrieval of that past. The examples listed above speak to the visible temptations of 'an acquisitive society' (Hoggart 1992: 139), the frustration of 'true' love or authentic feeling, the conflation of acquisition with the performance of love, and the performance of feeling spurred to action as that is determined by mass-produced pulp fiction. These examples all relate to very different things: Joe's recollection of his home town, the woman he loves (Alice), the woman he pretends to love (Susan), and the woman he picks up in a pub (Mavis), a stranger whose fickle disregard for her boyfriend causes him to beat Joe up because, as Joe observes, that happens in popular fiction which seems to function like an eighteenth-century Conduct Book. When the fantasies of pulp fiction get re-enacted in the moral logic of the everyday, something is very wrong. At least, this is what *Room at the Top* tells us because although those examples do relate to different histories and feelings, they are related flatly as though there is no qualitative distinction between them. This kind of flat repetition is starkly visualised for us in Jack Clayton's film of *Room at the Top*. Joe first seduces Susan, daughter of a wealthy industrialist following a fairly vicious social snub at the Civic Ball where he is belittled and put firmly back in his place by the town's various luminaries. He then begins his vengeful and tactical seduction of Susan in a space that seems more mythical than real as he moves from social rebuff to regaining mastery of his preferred version of himself. But as the film illustrates, such re-mastery is the stuff of fantasy. In the scene, Susan and Joe are flanked by the impossibly cool perfection of classical statues and Joe speaks to her (and she to him) as though replicating the dialogue of a Mills and Boon novel; such fictional perfection leads in the end to his moral ruin since he is lured by the attractive placidity of the image both as that is embodied in Susan and as that is copiously illustrated in the magazines and adverts that he so clearly responds to. In that process, the virtue of the real has been sacrificed and the attention Braine draws to this clearly aligns his view of cultural loss with that of Hoggart's. It is through Joe's relationship with Alice Aisgill that a more complicated relationship emerges in the representation of nostalgia, culture and men's relationship to the maternal body.

One of the most striking things about Joe's perception of Alice is her apparent decrepitude, which seems to exercise a peculiar fascination for him; it is as though Braine shares Hoggart's imperative of not trying 'to add glamour' (Hoggart 1992: 49) to certain working-class faces. When Joe first sees Alice, she is 'pale and haggard', and though she has an 'angular fashion plate figure', she is also variously described as 'plain…downright ugly: her chin had a heavy shapelessness … the lines on her forehead and neck were as if scored with a knife'; there is 'a speck of decay' on one of her teeth whilst another seemed to be 'more filling than tooth' (Braine 1989: 78). She also has huge, sagging breasts to which he is immensely drawn, and her breasts, along with her 'low tastes' (she likes beer and salty crisps) and her bad teeth produce at first a shabby kinship that then turns into love, whereupon their first sexual encounter is strategically de-romanticised as the old charmer compares it to 'an indifferently cooked meal' (Braine 1989: 83). Joe wants many things, most of them expensive and material, but what he also wants is to recuperate the loss of his parents. Arguably he tries to do that with his playing out of Freud's 'Family Romances' through the culturally impeccable figure of his landlady/pseudo mother Mrs Thompson, whose middle-class status and disciplined body he relishes. And then he tries to redeem his loss through Alice whose bodily imperfections rebut the physical perfections of women in advertising and mass-market publications. She is the opposite, then, of Susan Brown. As such, Alice guarantees authenticity for Joe, which is predicated on natural decay; the first rupture in their relationship occurs when she discloses that she was once painted in the nude, a revelation that makes him feel betrayed, sick and dirty. Alice's defence of herself is forthright; she is not ashamed of what she has done, she makes a distinction between the real of her body and the aesthetic and formal representation of her body and she castigates Joe for his hypocrisy and his preferences for 'Leg show and lingerie' (Braine 1989: 116). This is precisely the kind of fragmented embodiment that Susan Brook has suggested Hoggart allies with an inauthentic mass culture against the solidly realised body of the quiescent maternal figure. Through a close reading of Hoggart's descriptive accounts, Brook shows how different female embodiments are made to signify authentic working-class culture in the maternal figure whereas the 'pin-up' figuratively embodies the fragmentation of mass culture. She goes on to argue that the wounded body of the scholarship boy might redeem mass culturally produced apathy since he precisely *is* granted an emotional and intellectual inner life in Hoggart's account. His contradictions, she suggests, are marked on his 'feeling body': 'The feeling bruised body of scholarship boys exemplify broader social wounds, such as the problem of rootlessness, but they also offer the possibility of healing society through their capacity for feeling' (Brook 2007: 26). Joe Lampton is not a scholarship boy but he does belong to that 'larger group' Hoggart describes in 'The Uprooted and the Anxious', the ones caught 'between two worlds, one dead, the other powerless to be born' (Hoggart 1992: 300). Joe, then, is the example of the 'minor clerk' whose aspiration for 'self-improvement' is less 'political betrayal' (which is how he reads himself when he visits his prospective father-in-law in the Conservative Club) and more 'mistaken idealism' (Hoggart 1992: 300). He is like the person who 'cannot face squarely his own working-class', who 'cannot go back' and who 'pines for some Nameless Eden where he never was' (Hoggart 1992: 300-301). Hoggart's account of the uprooted and anxious sensibility that attends class displacement is precisely realised in Joe's inevitable downfall.

When Joe reacts so angrily to Alice's revelation about posing as an artist's model, she imagines him in Dufton: 'I can just see you in Dufton now, looking at the nudes in a magazine, drooling over them. Saying you wouldn't mind having a quick bash. But blackguarding the girls, calling them shameless' (Braine 1989: 118). In return, Joe fixes her precisely and punitively as an iconic figure in a working-class landscape: 'She looked thin and bedraggled; not unlike the thin women one sees in pictures of mine disasters, disconsolate and old and ugly against the pithead wheel' (Braine 1989: 119). There seem to be many things at stake here and it is not clear that they are easily resolvable: Alice's ownership of her body and an insistence that real and image, high culture and mass culture are distinct, marks out her difference from everyone else in Joe's narrative. Location is also shown to confer meaning on culture: art is high aesthetic in a gallery; pinups are low culture in magazines and pubs. And her defiance also unsettles Joe who cannot, in this moment, accept the de-materialisation of her body as abstract aesthetic form and nor can he accept that his shedding of Dufton and the working-class might be measured by other things beside the cut of his cloth and his annual salary. When he comes to look back on this moment, Joe realises something else; that he was at that moment a person of 'higher quality' than he is in the present of 1956/7. That higher quality is in accord with Hoggart's upholding of the values of the Hunslet of his childhood: 'Of a higher quality, that is, if one accepts that a human being is meant to have certain emotions, to be affected strongly by all that happens to him, to live *among* the people around him' (Hoggart 1992: 123).

When Alice and Joe are reconciled in a final and brief interlude of happiness, Joe watches Alice washing and manages to see in the material body an aesthetic transformation which, momentarily at least, consoles his sense of loss:

...I saw its beauty impersonally, as an arrangement of colour and light, a satisfying theorem of lines which curved generously, which gave, gave, gave to the air, to the cold stinging water, to me... as long as Alice was there I wouldn't die. It was like having my father and mother alive again, it was the end of being afraid and alone'. (Braine 1989: 180)

115

It is as though in that moment the parental figures in a landscape obliterated by the war might be recuperated in a dynamic relationship that recognises the body in material and aesthetic incarnations outside the simulacra of 1950's mass culture. The irony is that the very rootedness of the social order, in this instance Alice's marriage, excludes such a possibility. Neither can survive the ruin and scandal of divorce; if the Warley community is a hotbed of infidelity (as it seems to be) it is another place of hypocritical disavowal as the mix of sensation and morality spill from the tabloids to the new middle class. Looking over the top of Warley one day, Joe sees that it is spread out like a cross (Braine 1989: 157). Susan compares his eyes to Christ's and Alice, like Mary Magdalene, washes Joe's feet with her tears and dries them with her hair (Braine 1989: 172). After his beating, and when he is at his moral nadir, he takes a tram ride and is reminded of the hymn, 'The Old Rugged Cross'; on the tram he sees one decent woman who is 'so clean and motherly...that I found tears coming to my eyes' (Braine 1989: 233). The juxtaposition is telling. The comparisons between Joe and Christ seem bizarrely aggrandising but they are also intriguing since sacrifice and redemption are aligned, rather hopelessly, with secular culture and sexuality. Alice, not Joe, is the real figure of suffering and sacrifice and Joe's train of association takes him from the popular hymn to the 'clean and motherly woman' as the proper and worthy object of his devotion. Hoggart tells us that 'Home is carved out under the shadow of the giant abstractions' (Hoggart 1992: 104); in the 'streamlined' outer world, home is a refuge, 'something that is real and recognizable' (Hoggart 1991: 104). Alice crystallises a train of associations for Joe: his parents and the ordered moral decencies of the past, the maternal body, authentic desire, realism, and these are indexed to sexual and aesthetic sensibility. The redemptive possibility that Alice embodies and upholds is squandered in the sensational manner of her death, as though the novel surrenders, in the end, to the tactics and sensibilities of mass-market fiction. Joe might have redeemed a loss of integrity that is figured in the novel as personal, emotional and cultural but it is, in the end, too much for a figure cast between two worlds to bear. Such a figure takes a suggestively sinister turn in *Room at the Top*: numbed by Alice's death and his culpability for it, Joe switches his narration from the first-person to a depersonalising third-person and characterises himself as a 'zombie'; if that suggests a re-alignment with the inhabitants of Dufton, described by him as zombies, the description points to another cultural turn as though the drift to the schlock horror 'B' movie confirms the hyperreality of identity as a permanent living death. *Room at the Top* attempts to frame that cultural shift; the narrative invokes mass culture only to stand above it but given the novel's fascination with seduction, it is perhaps inevitable that it, too, finds it difficult not to succumb to what it also critiques. When Collini describes *The Uses of Literacy* as being 'preoccupied above all with *ethical* decline, with the loss of meaning and value that are alleged to come with mobility and prosperity' (Collini 2008: 52) he could just as easily be describing Braine's novel as Hoggart's cultural study. But when *Room at the Top* was adapted to film, the move from textual narration to visual media began to unsettle the representation of women as iconic fixtures or settled tropes.

In 'The Work of Art in the Age of Mechanical Reproduction', Walter Benjamin argued that modern man had a legitimate claim to be reproduced realistically rather than through capitalist fantasies that fob him off with some unattainable vision of his life. That contention was, in its way, shared by filmmakers like Lindsay Anderson, Tony Richardson and Karel Reisz whose early films were inspired by the desire, as Reisz described it, to: 'confront the new realities which the years of the Labour government had brought about, to catch the extraordinary social changes which were in the air' (Tibbetts and Welsh 1999: 28). As filmmakers, they were committed to combining social realism with poetic realism and to reinvigorating British Cinema on the back of the cultural energy released in literature often reductively defined through the 'Angry Young Man' label. All nine films of the British New Wave were adaptations from recent fictional and dramatic texts: *Room at the Top, Look Back in Anger, Saturday Night and Sunday Morning, The Entertainer, A Taste of Honey, A Kind of Loving, The Loneliness of the Long Distance Runner, This Sporting Life* and *Billy Liar*. Including Hoggart's *The Uses of Literacy*, these texts constitute a close-knit community with shared concerns about social mobility and displacement, cultural atrophy and change, cultural vulgarity, national decline, the vulnerability of working-class culture and so on. But the nine films of British New Wave Cinema reveal women differently through the operation of the gaze and in doing so, they redirect and re-imagine their textual incarnations.

Room at the Top was hailed as the best British film since *Brief Encounter*: it has been read as a version of David Lean's 1945 film (Sinyard 2000: 44). It came to be regarded, as I have noted above, as the film that inaugurated British New Wave Cinema with its northern locations, its documentation of post-war social mobility and its depiction of sexuality not as titillating or tame but as complex, revealing vulnerability in the face of temptation. One of the fascinating consequences of the adaptation from text to screen was the dispersal of the first-person narration across potentially multiple points of view (as is the case for several of the adaptations, notably *A Kind of Loving, The Loneliness of the Long Distance Runner* and *This Sporting Life*). One of the striking features in Jack Clayton's film is that although Joe Lampton is often the holder of the spectator's gaze, he is not consistently in charge of it. If our gaze is directed through his so that we see and identify directly with what he sees and feels, as is the case with his focalisation of Susan, it is also directed *at* him because we see him, his discomfort, his objectification and his desirability through the gaze of other figures in the film, notably Alice Aisgill. One of the consequences of this is a shift in critical interest and emotional investment as the foregrounding of class and sexuality nudge the novel's detailed fascination with popular narratives aside. Alice's entrapment in an unhappy marriage, her right to a sexually fulfilling relationship, her disappointments, her desires, her complex and individual subjectivity are easily as significant as Joe Lampton's social aspirations; the film is arguably as much 'about' Alice as it is 'about' Joe. Susan Brown's pregnancy is a functional affair in many ways, both in its actual enactment and in its purpose is to secure Joe's social status. In the film Susan describes 'it' as 'wonderful' but confesses that she was reluctant to tell Joe because 'you seemed so strange lately, as if you didn't like me very much'. Succeeding films of the British New Wave revealed more troubled and thoughtful accounts of women and pregnancy. The adaptation of *Look Back in Anger* to film involved the addition of several scenes to Osborne's original play, one of which sees Alison getting confirmation from the Doctor that she is pregnant. Her tentative enquiry about what her options are is swiftly and angrily suppressed by him but the film, if briefly, addresses itself to her misery within marriage, a misery compounded by a lack of agency and lack of choice about her own body. Such misery about loss of control is seen at its most moving and expressive in Brenda's experiences of unwanted pregnancy in the film of *Saturday Night and Sunday Morning*. Where the novel describes her attempt to abort the foetus by drinking gin in a hot bath, the British Board of Film Censors refused permission to replicate this scene or indeed to indicate that the abortion was 'brought off' at all (Sillitoe 2004: 259). Sillitoe (who wrote the screenplay) regarded the film as a watered down version of his book but the adaptation reveals Brenda to be caught in a troubling cultural transition where she wants more than she can have. Arguably, Karel Reisz's film ends up being morally censorious: marital infidelity, at first represented as so pleasurable for both Brenda and Arthur, carries consequences and Brenda is the one who must bear them. Her reluctance to assume responsibility for the raising of another child coupled with her recognition that this entails the loss of her sexual desirability sounds a striking note that jars with her eventual submission to her decent but dull husband. Although British New Wave Cinema readily aligns women with cultural decline and with mass culture as vulgarising and feminising in films like *A Taste of Honey, The Entertainer, A Kind of Loving* and *This Sporting Life,* the issue of women's autonomy nonetheless arises as politically pressing even if is tentatively raised and dropped again. These films visualise and flesh out the narrative descriptions of Hoggart's industrial communities, the railways, back-to-backs and factories. They also confirm Hoggart's unease with mass-produced cultures and explore the threats to more traditional expression of working-class community life in films like *A Kind of Loving* and *Saturday Night and Sunday Morning*. But they also introduce a nascent shift, emphasised by the camera's manipulation of the gaze, in terms of what women might want and what they might not be happy with. If they are cast as the emblems of cultural debasement as we see in figures like Mrs Rothwell in *A Kind of Loving* or Mrs Smith in *The Loneliness of the Long Distance Runner* or as the imperturbable 'our mam', homogenised in Schlesinger's feminine crowd scenes in *A Kind of Loving* and *Billy Liar,* they are also individualised as figures who trouble traditional assumptions about what women want and who they might be both inside and outside of maternal roles.

The sexual politics in *The Uses of Literacy* has been both castigated and defended (Steedman 1986; Owen 2008a) but what seems more compelling in terms of revisiting these cultural landscapes is less to do with whether or not Hoggart is a crude or sensitive delineator of femininity and domesticity, at least for my argument here. Rather, the kinds of critical, literary and cinematic interventions that began to evolve in the late 1950s and early 1960s reveal a shared concern with and development of several issues. *The Uses of Literacy* itself often makes no qualitative distinction between the literary text and society. Fictional characters from the Wife of Bath to Tess of the D'Urbervilles and Jude Fawley share the same illustrative spaces as extra-textual ones; literature, like ethnography, is recognised as expressing 'in its own right a form of distinctive knowledge about society' (Hoggart 1970: 19). At times Hoggart seems to excavate that belief further: when he recalls his grandmother he invokes her whole ontology as one accessible and interpretable through the rhythms and cadences of ancient poetic tradition. Her speech, he tells us, 'had something of the elemental quality of Anglo-Saxon poetry' (Hoggart 1992: 25). Our capacity to have, to speak and indeed to hear such a textural ontology is clearly at risk in parts of the cultural landscape of the late 1950s; where Hoggart celebrates the 'elemental quality' of Anglo-Saxon poetry in his grandmother's speech, Braine recycles the textual impersonality of readily disposable culture and links that to a potentially circular economy of dwindling returns, to what we see and read, with who we are, and with what we are conditioned to want. Such alignments spell out a clear, compelling and urgent reminder about the critical, aesthetic and political responsibilities of a thinking literature to society and in turn of a thoughtful society to its literature. And yet this is not to suggest that these writers entirely consign their culture and its attendant sensibilities to some inexorable decline: the socio-cultural observations of a writer like Braine and a critic like Hoggart are inter-related. That the observations they make were also taken up in film adaptations signals alertness to the potential movements between one kind of text to another and to opening them out in ways that start to tentatively address the sexual politics of the period as crucial to its cultural landscape. At the very moment that they address cultural decline, these writers and filmmakers are, of course, instating cultural renewal in critical, literary and cinematic representation.

Hoggart has described his 'histrionic sense' as 'weak' (Hoggart 1991: 112) and the *Daily Herald*'s description of *The Uses of Literacy* as the work of an 'Angry Young Man' sounds at best like an inaccurate gloss. But it is worth revisiting the description. Read alongside *The Uses of Literacy*, the tenuous 'anger' of the decade gets a clearer definition where emotional affect and political efficacy are fatally compromised, where the working-class consumer of pop music, film, fiction, newspapers, television is treated with 'concealed contempt' (Hoggart 1992: 185). The tendency to characterise texts within an homogenising 'movement', where that characterisation was unsympathetically sneered at by the 'mandarins' of London's literary scene meant that each new articulation of working-class experience or social realism might be treated as symptomatic of the undifferentiated mass-market culture that in reality those writers and their texts, filmmakers and films, interrogated; there are marked differences within the cultural pleasures and expectations of working-class communities as the literary and film culture of these decades affirmed. If Hoggart sensed a cultural theft from the working class, the fiction and film of the period also revealed a serious commitment to putting back and interrogating what was being taken away.

Bibliography
Braine, J. (1989) *Room at the Top* (London: Arrow).
————— Literary Manuscripts, Brotherton Collection MS 20c, University of Leeds.
Brook, S. (2007) *Literature and Cultural Criticism in the 1950s: The Feeling Male Body* (Basingstoke: Palgrave Macmillan).
Carpenter, H. (2002) *The Angry Young Men A Literary Comedy of the 1950s* (London: Penguin).
Clarke, B. '"To think fearlessly": Richard Hoggart and the Politics of the English Language'. In Sue Owen (ed.), *Re-reading Richard Hoggart* (Newcastle: Cambridge Scholars Press), pp. 43-57.
Collini, S. (2008) 'Richard Hoggart: Literary Criticism and Cultural Decline

in Twentieth-Century Britain'. In Sue Owen (ed.), *Richard Hoggart and Cutural Studies* (Basingstoke: Palgrave Macmillan) pp. 35-56.

Hall, S. (2007) 'Richard Hoggart, *The Uses of Literacy* and the Cultural Turn', *International Journal of Cultural Studies*, 10 (1), pp. 39-49.

Hoggart, R. (1970) *Speaking to Each Other, Vol II: About Literature* (London: Chatto and Windus).

———— (1991) *A Sort of Clowning* (Oxford: OUP).

———— (1992) *The Uses of Literacy* (London: Penguin).

Lodge, D. (2007) 'Richard Hoggart: A Personal Appreciation', *International Journal of Cultural Studies*, 10 (1), pp. 29-37.

Long, P. (2008) *Only in the Common People; The Aesthetics of Class in Post-War Britain* (Newcastle: Cambridge Scholars Publishing).

Owen, S. (ed.) (2008a) *Richard Hoggart and Cultural Studies* (Basingstoke: Palgrave Macmillan).

———— (ed.) (2008b) *Re-reading Richard Hoggart* (Newcastle: Cambridge Scholars Publishing).

Osborne, J. (1999) *Looking Back: Never Explain, Never Apologise* (London: Faber and Faber).

Ritchie, H. (1988) *Success Stories: Literature and the Media, 1950-1959* (London: Faber and Faber).

Sillitoe, A. (2004) *Life Without Armour* (London: Robson Books).

Sinyard, N. (2000) *Jack Clayton* (Manchester: Manchester University Press).

Steedman, C. (1986) *Landscape for a Good Woman: A Story of Two Lives* (London: Virago).

Wales, K. (2008) '"The Anxiety of Influence": Hoggart, Liminality and Melvyn Bragg's *Crossing the Lines'*. In Sue Owen (ed.), *Re-Reading Richard Hoggart* (Newcastle: Cambridge Scolars Press), pp. 102-117.

'TRADING ON HUMAN WEAKNESS': RICHARD HOGGART AND HIS ADVERTISING CRITICS IN THE 1960S

Sean Nixon

It is one of the paradoxes of social change in post-war Britain that affluence, as much as austerity, generated enormous anxiety and polarised public debate.[1] Whilst governments increasingly took it for granted that one of their functions was to improve the standards of living of the mass of the population and measures of private sector consumption (like family expenditure surveys and retail prices indices) became routinised within the practices of government, the larger social and cultural implications of expanded private sector consumption troubled many politicians, commentators and critics.[2] Perhaps one of the most celebrated observers of the dilemmas posed by post-war affluence was Richard Hoggart. Hoggart remains an enduringly fascinating and significant figure in understanding the debates about affluence and the expanded field of commercial life that was associated with it. At the heart of this, of course, stands *The Uses of Literacy*, one of the most revered and widely read accounts of the effects of emergent prosperity upon working-class life.[3] The book was notable for the way it read contemporary social change — the world of milk bars, juke box boys and the 'shiny barbarism' of post-war commercial culture — through the lens of cultural decline. If much of the emotional punch of the book stemmed from its evocation of the robust and honest virtues of working-class life in the era before post-war affluence, then the power of this account was heightened by the sense of panic about the social changes of the early 1950s that threatened the world described. As Francis Mulhern has argued, the book tells a story of 'decline already far gone, perhaps irretrievable' (Mulhern 1996: 29). It is also a book shaped by a set of solid moral convictions that owe much, as Stefan Collini has shown, to the residues of a secularised Protestantism (Collini 2008). For Hoggart, hardship is held to encourage 'effort, self-control and social purpose', whilst prosperity brings only 'passivity, indulgence and selfishness' (Collini 2008: 41). Hoggart's moral convictions about post-war prosperity evidently touched a nerve amongst many of his readers. Dennis

---

[1] Britain was not unique in this regard. Similar concerns surfaced in the USA and Continental Europe. See Horowitz (2004) and Ross (1995).
[2] On family expenditure surveys see Majima (2006).
[3] See also Hoggart, 1971a.

Potter, just down from Oxford and his illustrious career as a television playwright ahead of him, produced a scathing commentary on the 1959 General Election that owed much to Hoggart in its assessment of the deleterious effects of advertising and consumerism on popular experience (Potter 1960).[4] Picking up on a prevalent metaphor of the time, Potter railed against 'espresso-bar prosperity' and the way the Labour Party had accommodated itself to consumerism-fuelled apathy (Potter 1960: 10).[5] A large part of the problem, for Potter, was that politics had itself been corroded by the techniques of commercial persuasion. The 1959 election had been the first television election and the debate between the parties had been recast for Potter so that it felt like 'a bitter trade struggle between Nescafé and Maxwell House or Pink Camay and Palmolive' (Potter 1960: 12).

The influence of *The Uses of Literacy* on social commentators like Potter, together with its immediate success amongst a wider reading public, helped to propel Hoggart into the public spotlight in the late 1950s and 60s where he acted as a genuine public intellectual.[6] This included, we should not forget, being called as one of the defence witnesses in the trial of Penguin books over the publication of the paperback edition of *Lady Chatterley's Lover* in 1960. It was Hoggart's disarming defence of the moral and highly virtuous nature of Lawrence's book that did much to undermine the case of the prosecution as they sought to ban the publication on the grounds that it was an obscene publication, 'one you would not want your wife or servant to read', in the memorable words of Mr Griffith-Jones, the prosecuting barrister.[7]

In his thinking and writing, Hoggart returned on a number of occasions to one aspect of the larger transformations associated with post-war affluence. This was the expansion of commercial mass communication. Like many other critics, Hoggart saw advertising — and especially the new form of television advertising — as the most visible manifestation of the increasing commercialisation of post-war British society and the negative drift of social change that flowed from

---

[4] See also Potter's Hoggartesque *The Changing Forest*, Potter (1962).

[5] Richard Hoggart's famous comments in *The Uses of Literacy* about watching youth in a milk bar in Goole, in East Yorkshire, confusingly invoked the interior look of the espresso bars. See Moran (2006: 552-559) for a discussion of the development of milk bars and espresso bars and a comment on the type of establishment Hoggart was referring to.

[6] On the success of *The Uses of Literacy*, see Owen (2008).

[7] For a recent revisionist account of the Chatterley case, see Sandbrook (2005: xv-xxii).

this. Little attention, however, has been given to Hoggart's criticisms of advertising. This is perhaps in part because his thinking appeared to express a more widely held antipathy towards advertising common to both left and right leaning cultural commentators and a wider educated public. In this chapter, however, I want to return to Hoggart's thinking and writing about advertising and commercial persuasion, focusing on his contributions to the Pilkington Committee on broadcasting. In doing so, I want to bring Hoggart's arguments up against the defence mounted by those advertising people who were the subject of his disapprobation.

One of the consequences of Hoggart's public profile in the 1960s is that advertising people read him, sometimes approvingly cite him, and seek to engage with and critique him. In important ways, then, Hoggart's arguments had a generative effect on the defenders of commercial society, pushing them to elaborate a positive account of their practices. More than that, the exchanges between Richard Hoggart and his advertising critics point to larger questions bound up with the social changes the 'affluent society' was ushering in. These concerned competing understandings of the role that commercial persuasion should play in public life, especially within broadcasting, and the consequences that this might have for established cultural hierarchies and forms of cultural authority. Also at work in their exchanges are competing ideas about human motivations and desires, with Hoggart's protestant ideas of self-control and self-improvement rubbing up against the more self-expressive conception of human beings proposed by ad men. These are divisions — between the values of commercial popular culture and legitimate culture and between puritanism and hedonism — that take us to the heart of the debate about the transformations wrought by post-war affluence and the modernising of British society through the 1950s and 60s. For this reason, then, looking at Hoggart's critique of advertising and the intellectual arguments that were mounted by those who were his target throws light on some of the social and cultural issues at stake in advertising's post-war economic and cultural rise in an expanded consumer society.

Hoggart, Pilkington and the case against advertising

Hoggart's growing standing as a public figure and commentator in the late 1950s and 60s drew him to the attention of civil servants and government officials seeking members of 'the great and the good' to participate in parliamentary committees. He was invited to sit on the Macmillan government's broadcasting committee, chaired by Sir Harry Pilkington, in

1960.[8] His name had been suggested by the Minister of Education after what Hoggart himself later described as the usual 'trawl' around the interested ministries (Hoggart 1990: 60). More suspicious minds, like the Director-General of the Independent Television Authority (ITA), claimed that it was an essay that Hoggart had written in *Encounter*, published in January 1960, called 'The Uses of Television', that had led to him being selected. 'The Uses of Television' had given ITV short shrift (Hoggart 1990: 60). Whatever the precise mechanisms of his selection, Hoggart agreed to work on the broadcasting committee and proved to be an influential member.[9] He was joined by, amongst others, the actress Joyce Grenfell, with whom he struck up a notable rapport (Hoggart 1990: 64-5).

The final report of the committee, published in June 1962, was an important but controversial statement on British broadcasting in the era of competition inaugurated by the creation of ITV.[10] While it is true that the Macmillan government resisted some of the report's more radical conclusions, the Pilkington Committee's desire to constrain commercialism within British broadcasting proved influential and it was the BBC that was the main beneficiary of the Tory government's response to the report.[11] A second commercial channel, favoured by the advertising industry and free-market Tories like the Bow Group, was explicitly rejected.[12] It would not be until 1972 that commercial radio was licensed in Britain and 1982 before a second commercial TV channel was established. Whilst it had not been part of the Pilkington Report's recommendations, its generally critical comments on ITV formed part of the context in which the Chancellor, Selwyn Lloyd, levied a new advertising tax on the ITV companies in 1963.

The Pilkington Report was certainly highly critical of ITV and sought to elaborate an updated defence of public service broadcasting. This argued that broadcasters ought properly to be in a 'constant and sensitive relationship to the moral conditions of society' (Report of the Committee on Broadcasting 1961-2: paras 42, 15). Tellingly, it also argued that television needed to resist the temptation to address, only or predominantly, mass audiences and, rather, should seek to cater for

---

[8] Hoggart had already sat on the Albemarle Committee 1958-60, which had investigated the problems of young people and the state provision of youth services.

[9] See Hoggart (1990: 62-66) for his memories of the Pilkington Committee.

[10] See Milland (2001); Freedman (2001); Sandbrook (2005: 391-3); Nixon (2010).

[11] The Report proposed a major reorganization of ITV. This included the proposal that the selling of advertising time should be taken away from the programme companies.

[12] See Jarvis (2005).

overlapping minority audiences. Out of this thinking came its recommendations that a third TV channel should be awarded to the BBC and not ITV and thus was born, in 1964, BBC2. The vision of broadcasting proposed by the Pilkington Report and its specific policy recommendations were the product of collective endeavour on the part of the committee and its expert witnesses. Hoggart's presence, however, is evident at many points in the final report, not least in those sections devoted to TV advertising. The report was troubled by the nature of the appeal made by some advertising. It suggested that advertising 'played on impulses which were discreditable; upon acquisitiveness, snobbery, fear, uncritical conformity and "keeping up with the Joneses"' (Report of the Committee on Broadcasting 1961-2: paras 244-5). Challenging the views of Sir Robert Fraser, the first Chairman of the Independent Television Authority (ITA), who had claimed under cross-examination that the image of life portrayed in TV adverts was a 'pleasing one', the Report chided Sir Robert: 'The charge is not that it is wrong to add to the gaiety or pleasure of life by using this or that product. The criticism is rather that advertising too often implies that unless you buy the product, one will have cause for shame, or loss of self-respect, or cannot hope for happiness'. Such appeals, it claimed, 'trade on human weakness' (Report of the Committee on Broadcasting 1961-2: paras 252-4).

The minutes of the committee proceedings of the report reveal Hoggart to be an important source of these assessments of advertising. When cross-examining members of the Institute of Practitioners in Advertising (IPA), the advertising trade body, Hoggart pressed them firmly on the impact of TV advertising upon viewers, contrasting its power and directness with that of press advertising. Hoggart claimed that, surely, TV advertising had a 'more immediate emotional effect'. He put the following example to Dan Ingman, a member of the IPA's Radio, Television and Cinema committee. Hoggart suggested that in a press advert for a patent medicine the copy had offered the injunction: 'Take so and so's pills, they're hospital tested'. He went on:

> There is a difference between the impact of that appearing in a newspaper and the impact of a 'commercial' in which a man looked out of the screen and said, 'Take so and so's pills', and then in a deep voice full of every foreboding said, 'They're hospital tested'. The statement was thus of an entirely different kind in its impact on a great number of people who are not particularly sophisticated. [13]

[13] Committee on Broadcasting, Notes of a meeting held at Cornwall House, 25 July 1961, PRO HO 244/553, 5.

Hoggart's insistence on the greater communicative power and influence of television relative to the press underpinned his concerns about TV advertising, reaching as it did directly into the home and addressing an audience through the combined medium of sound and vision. Hoggart's written comments to the secretary of the Pilkington Committee during the drafting of the final report also revealed his thinking about TV commercials. Hoggart pressed the committee to recognise the corrupting power of TV adverts and their crass style. As he put it,

> We ought to grasp the nettle about TV advertising as little engaging emotional dramas. Of course, we are back at professional standards — compared with real TV drama writers ... the guys who write these little advertising dramas are like Soho strip joints to Verdi — they have the techniques and tricks, but nothing to say ... all virtuosity and no virtue. [14]

This withering critique, with its overtones of advertising being sleazy and manipulative and a low cultural form, were echoed in other comments Hoggart made during the committee proceedings. When members of the Independent Television Contractors Association (ITCA) appeared before the committee in July 1961, Hoggart, along with other committee members, interrogated them on how the ITCA judged some of the claims made by commercials. Hoggart was less concerned about the use of fantasy in adverts, an issue raised by other committee members in relation to commercials for Camay Soap and Knights Castile (soap), than with the 'ones which try to be nearly real'.[15] In particular Hoggart reflected on commercials made for Fairy Liquid and Persil washing powder. These adverts, he suggested, were socially problematic because they used a range of important human emotions, such as 'mother love' and 'aunty love', and linked these with the use of the product. In the process, the commercials not only hijacked these values but reduced the complexity of human relationships. This was problematic for Hoggart. As he argued,

> Now let us see as many happy homes as we can on TV, [but] always bearing in mind that the happy home has to be worked for very hard by

---

[14] Notes from Mr Hoggart to Draft Chapter VII of the Pilkington Report, p. 4, PRO HO 244/269, 1

[15] ITCA Evidence to the Committee on Broadcasting, 25 July 1961, PRO HO 244/585, 7-9.

the business of living together with one another in a state of tension and mutual needs and desires. [16]

Hoggart's criticisms fed into the final recommendations of the Report and are evident in its concern about the way commercials used 'the excitement of fiction and the compelling reality of the everyday' to persuade viewers (Report of the Committee on Broadcasting, 1961-2:Para 253, 80). Informed by this thinking, the Pilkington Committee recommended that the ITA should develop further effective restraint of television advertising. [17]

Hoggart was also instrumental in the recommendation of the Pilkington Report to ban 'advertising magazines' or 'ad mags'. This was a recommendation eventually implemented by the Conservative Government in 1963. Ad mags were presentations in which a linked series of promotions for different products or services were made. Ad mags — or 'advertising documentaries', as the Independent Television Authority (ITA) called them — were produced by the ITV companies, rather than advertising agencies and used on-screen presenters to introduce the products. Early examples included 'Cooking with the Craddocks' and 'Girl with a Date', though the most celebrated was 'Jim's Inn', first broadcast in 1957 and running for nearly 300 editions. 'Jim's Inn' was set in the fictitious village of Wemblenham and centred upon Jim and Maggie Hanley, the publicans of the eponymous pub. As familiar in its time as 'The Rover's Return', 'Jim's Inn' wove product presentations into its fictional narrative. [18] The format was popular with small regional advertisers given that it cost far less to promote goods on 'ad mags' than it did to buy airtime in the form of a 'spot advert'. Under the terms of the Television Act, however, 'ad mags' did not count as advertising and so were excluded from the amount of advertising per hour that the ITV companies were permitted to broadcast. It was this anomaly and the presentational techniques of 'ad mags' that concerned Hoggart. In a lengthy section in his notes on the draft of chapter vii of the Report, he spelt out his concerns. Arguing that 'ad mags' went against the spirit if not the letter of the TV Act, he suggested that:

---

[16] Hoggart, ITCA Evidence to the Committee on Broadcasting, 25 July 1961, PRO HO 244/585, 18-19. Another member of the committee, the actress Joyce Grenfell, was troubled by an advert for Bluinite Tide (9).

[17] Commenting in the 1990s on the reception of the Pilkington Report, Hoggart argued that it had helped to improve ITV. As he suggested, people tend to remember ITV as 'behaving well from its inception ... but in its first eight or nine years it [ITV] behaved like an Oxford Street barrow boy' (Hoggart 1990: 71).

[18] See Henry (1986); Turnock (2007: 145-6).

the total suggestiveness of these warm little productions [is] designed to capitalise on viewer's loyalty. Worse, they still often retain a meretricious trace of the idea that they should be shopper's guides. These friendly comperes or meres do their best to suggest that they've thought deeply about possible purchases [...] and have settled on this particular one. The whole tone of the script and acting suggest someone wise and nice helping you to make a choice [...] As someone concerned with education, [this is] a very dubious operation; a muddy operation beside which the straight commercials are comparatively clean.[19]

This damming analysis, which also manages to underline his antipathy again towards TV commercials ('comparatively clean', indeed), led Hoggart to propose that 'ad mags' should count towards advertising time, be cut or replaced by 'genuine shopper's guides'. Significantly, his comments on 'ad mags' went against the previously settled views of the Pilkington committee which had collectively agreed to reserve judgement on the mags. Hoggart even considered producing a minority report on them.[20] However, this proved to be unnecessary as he managed to persuade other members of the committee to come around to his position. These included Joyce Grenfell, who expressed her desire for the 'ad mags' to be banned.[21] In the end, as we have seen, the Pilkington Report recommended their prohibition.

Richard Hoggart's concern about the influence of commercial mass persuasion on television was not restricted to his interventions within the Pilkington Committee. Earlier published comments on advertising revealed much about his feelings towards TV advertising. Reviewing the first three years of ITV in *New Left Review* in 1958, Hoggart had balked at the style of TV advertising. There was, on ITV, 'the fever of alternation between "crude spots", "hard" and "soft" sell, jingles, insistent echo chamber repetition, halting infant voices (a particularly nasty form)' (Hoggart 1958: 34). The adverts were 'unpleasant things'. Similar criticisms of the vulgar forms of TV advertising and their manipulative power over viewers was repeated in an essay published in *Advertiser's Weekly*, the trade magazine, a few years after the publication of the Pilkington Report. Originally titled in the paper, 'Advertising — a form of emotional blackmail exploiting human inadequacy', though later published by Hoggart as the more temperate 'The Case Against Advertising', the essay

---

[19] Notes from Mr. Hoggart to draft chapter VII of the Report, PRO HO 244/269, 2.
[20] Notes from Mr. Hoggart to draft chapter VII of the Report, PRO HO 244/269, 2.
[21] Letter from Joyce Grenfell to Dennis Lawrence, April 21 1962, PRO HO 244/269.

condemned advertising as a 'shabby business' that exploited 'human frailty'. This Veblenesque sense of the play on human weakness meant that advertising was, for Hoggart, culpable of 'emotionally abusing its audience'. As he suggested, 'recognising that we all have fears, hopes, anxieties, aspirations, insecurities, advertisers seek not to increase our understanding of them, but use their existence to increase sales' (Hoggart 1970d: 206).

Advertising responds

Hoggart's comments did not go unnoticed or unchallenged by those who were the target of his disapprobation. In the proceedings of the Pilkington committee, on the pages of *Advertiser's Weekly*, in the industry's professional journals and in company documents, advertising people sought to engage with Hoggart. During the appearance by representatives of the IPA before the Pilkington Committee, Sinclair Wood, a former IPA president, was the most forthcoming of the IPA representatives in taking on Hoggart's arguments. Wood offered a firm defence of advertising. Dismissing Hoggart's criticisms, he suggested that advertising had an important social role to play. This sprung from its contribution to the rise in living standards through increased consumer spending. Echoing established thinking within the advertising industry, Wood proceeded to emphasise how mass production had made possible higher standards of living through making many previously luxury goods available to the majority.[22] Mass production, however, required 'mass selling': 'It is in our interests as a nation, both from an exporting point of view and from the raising of the people's standard of living that goods should be sold effectively. If this nation were not allowed to practice [...] salesmanship then we would begin to be materially less effective as a nation'.[23] To this end, modern mass communications 'should be at the service of legitimate

[22] Committee on Broadcasting, Notes of a Meeting Held 25 July 1961, PRO HO 244/553.

[23] *Ibid.*, 8. The Advertising Association produced a pamphlet in 1964 titled the 'Facts about Advertising'. The pamphlet sought to offer guidance to industry speakers on how to challenge its critics. Notable amongst the advice offered to prospective speakers was an emphasis on the business case for advertising. Again, this argued that advertising was an integral part of salesmanship, helping manufacturers to communicate the value of their goods to consumers and also stimulating the production of new and better products. Moreover, by expanding demand for goods, advertising helped to support mass production, which in turn not only stimulated production but also created jobs. The net effect was to encourage an increase in the standard of living (AA, 1964).

commerce and business' and more television airtime should be available to 'commercial mass communication'.[24] Sinclair Wood's arguments offered a justification for the IPA's demand for a second commercial channel and the lengthening of the broadcasting day.

The advertising trade press was less restrained than Wood in its response to the Pilkington Report itself. *Advertiser's Weekly* castigated the report as 'despicable' and 'a waste of public money' and saw it as 'a savage attack on modern marketing methods' and 'an anti-commercial diatribe'. Mocking the members of the Committee, the paper suggested that it had been prepared by a 'bevy of footballers, variety artistes and socio-economic pundits' (*Advertiser's Weekly*, 6/7/1962: 22).[25] On the specific charges made by Hoggart, that TV advertising was manipulative and vulgar, advertising people offered a defence of their industry that conceded some of the force of Hoggart's arguments. This was sometimes strategic. For example, the lengthy response produced in June 1962 by the advertising agency J. Walter Thompson for the Labour Party's advertising commission on which Hoggart was also sitting, defended the fact that advertising made emotional and not strictly rational appeals to the consumer.[26] The agency claimed that not only did consumers expect some emotional pleasure from the goods they bought, but emotional appeals added to the subjective value of the goods. As the JWT submission argued, 'the emotions used to express the subjective value are almost invariably positive ones. They included such emotions as pride, love, security, patriotism [...] in each case they are designed to add to the pleasure in buying and using a product'.[27] JWT did concede, however, that there were certain emotions that advertising should avoid using or stimulating. Approvingly citing chapter eight of *The Uses of Literacy*, they claimed that 'advertising should avoid appealing to inadequacy and avoid invoking fear, loneliness or hate amongst consumers'.[28]

A similar defence was elaborated by Tom Corlett, a senior figure at JWT, in an essay in the industry journal, IPA Forum, published in the late 1960s. The essay directly engaged with Hoggart's *Advertiser's Weekly* piece in

---

[24] *Ibid.* 9.

[25] For other hostile responses to the Pilkington Report, see Hoggart (1970c).

[26] For a discussion of the Labour Party's advertising commission, see Nixon (2010).

[27] Advertising Commission Replies to questionnaire Ref.RD 282/June 1962, J. Walter Thompson Co. Ltd. JWT/HAT Box 255.

[28] Ibid. In 1965, JWT listed Hoggart amongst a list of possible speakers to its 'Creative Lunches' seminar, JWT/HAT Box 238.

particular (Corlett 1968).[29] In almost Leavisite terms, Corlett took apart Hoggart's sweeping claims about the way advertising exploited human inadequacy. He claimed that Hoggart was guilty of conflating rather different human emotions under the umbrella concept of human weakness. Whilst Corlett conceded that it was wrong in any circumstances for advertising to play on fears, anxieties and insecurities, he felt that appeals to hope and aspiration were legitimate so long as the address made was neither false nor misleading (Corlett 1968: vii). Moreover, he felt that critics too quickly dismissed the subjective factors which advertising added to products. As he suggested, 'In a more sophisticated and affluent economy, minor and subjectively perceived differences in convenience of use, aesthetic appeal and so on are surely admissible' (Corlett 1968: ii). Corlett also contended that consumers were selective in what they derived from advertising and acted in more complex ways than critics like Hoggart suggested. Drawing on US mass communications research, Corlett argued that consumers failed to give adverts their full attention most of the time. Competition from other forms of entertainment, friends and their own preoccupations mediated the reception of particular adverts. Moreover, the authority of adverts was filtered through 'nearer and more powerful authorities', such as family, neighbours and their own personal experiences. Adverts, he argued, were selectively read and the ideas in them that did not fit the world view of viewers were rejected.[30]

Conclusion

Corlett's promotion of an active conception of the consumer and their mediated and selective reading of advertising formed part of his up-beat reading of advertising's social effects. Taken alongside his claims about the positive role that advertising could play in enhancing the experience of consumption, Corlett's essay offered a defence of advertising that stood in sharp contrast to Hoggart's withering critique. If intellectual differences separated Hoggart from his critics, these differences were overlaid with moral judgments. The moralism of Hoggart's analysis is clearest. This moralism was both the greatest virtue of his analysis and its greatest shortcoming. Whilst it allowed him to pose important ethical questions to advertising, the moralistic tone prevented a sustained engagement with the

---

[29] The letters page of *Advertiser's Weekly* also featured responses to Hoggart's essay: 8/10/65, 23; 15/10/65, 31; 22/10/65, 23; 29/10/65, 23.
[30] This view came perilously close to suggesting that advertising could be defended on the grounds that it was harmless at the expense of being proved useless! Corlett's essay was printed by the IPA and sent to teacher's organizations to raise discussion of advertising and its place in the economy.

utility and pleasures of goods promoted by advertisers. Moreover, it enabled advertising people in response to float a positive vision of advertising and its role in legitimating consumer's desires for a better life expressed through the world of goods. Such arguments supported a more self-expressive conception of consumers that counter-posed the small pleasures of everyday consumption with the ideal of self-control and restraint defended by Hoggart. In fact, it was the emotional and symbolic dimensions of goods and the way these should properly enter the process of consumer calculation that set the defence of advertising apart from its critics. Through such understandings advertising people pieced together an expanded account of advertising's social and economic role. This kind of intellectual defence was important for key sections of the advertising industry. Whilst they may have over-reacted to the charges of critics like Richard Hoggart, the desire to give legitimacy to advertising as a practice served to strengthen the hand of those 'respectable reformers' within advertising who had long sought to raise the public standing of advertising, especially amongst educated opinion. It was the respectable reformers within bodies like the IPA and urbane agencies like J. Walter Thompson who had most to gain from these arguments and who most readily came forward to take on advertising's critics. But what is also clear is that Hoggart's advertising critics in the 1960s felt that they had the wind of history in their sails, that their vision of the self-expressive possibilities of consumption and its little freedoms was in tune with the movement of history. Rising advertising expenditure and booming private sector consumption gave them the belief that for all the irritation provoked by critics like Hoggart, theirs was the vision that was prevailing. If advertising could tell a compelling story about the world of goods and its freedoms, however, Hoggart reminded them — and us — that working out what the limits of these freedoms might be is an extremely difficult question and requires an act of collective imagination in which a little of Hoggart's acuity, if not his moralism, is still of value.

Bibliography

Advertising Association (1964) *Facts about Advertising* (London: AA).

Cohen, L. (2003) *A Consumer's Republic: the Politics of Mass Consumption in Post-War America* (New York: Knopf).

Collini, S. (2008) 'Richard Hoggart: Literacy Criticism and Cultural Decline in Twentieth Century Britain'. In Sue Owen (ed.) *Richard Hoggart and Cultural Studies* (Basingstoke, Palgrave Macmillan), pp. 33-56

Corlett, T. (1968) 'Advertising – 'Is this the sort of work that an honest man can take pride in?' in *IPA Forum* , 22, May, pp. i-viii.

De Grazia, V. (2005) *Irresistable Empire, America's Advance Through Twentieth*

Century Europe (Harvard: Harvard University Press).

Freedman, D. (2001) 'Modernising the BBC: Wilson's Government and Television 1964-66', *Contemporary British History*, 15 (1), pp. 21-40.

Henry, B. (1986) *British Television Advertising: the First Thirty Years* (London: Ebury Press).

Hoggart, R. (1957) *The Uses of Literacy* (Harmondsworth: Penguin Books).

————— (1958) 'BBC and ITV After Three Years', *New Left Review*, no. 5, pp. 32-6.

————— (1961/1970a) 'Changes in Working Class Life'. In *Speaking to Each Other, Volume 1: About Society* (Harmondsworth, Penguin).

————— (1960/1970b) 'The Uses of Television', in *Speaking to Each Other, Volume 1: About Society* (Harmondsworth, Penguin).

————— (1963/1970c) 'The Difficulties of Democratic Debate, the reception of the Pilkington Report on broadcasting', in *Speaking to Each Other, Volume 1: About Society* (Harmondsworth, Penguin).

————— (1965/1970d) 'The Case Against Advertising', in *Speaking to Each Other, Volume: About Society* (Harmondsworth, Penguin).

————— (1990) *An Imagined Life: Life and Times 1959-1991* (London, Random House).

Home Office Papers (HO), 1960-6, Public Records Office, Kew

Horowitz, D. (2004) *The Anxieties of Affluence: Critiques of American Consumer Culture 1939-79* (Amherst: University of Massachusetts Press).

Jarvis, M. (2005) *Conservative Governments: Morality and Social Change in Affluent Britain, 1957-64* (London: Palgrave Macmillan).

J. Walter Thompson Company Archive, History of Advertising Trust, Norwich.

Majima, S. (2006) 'Affluence and the Dynamics of Spending in Britain 1961-2004', *Contemporary British History*, 22 (4), pp. 573-597.

Milland, J. (2001) 'Courting Malvolio: The Background to the Pilkington Committee on Broadcasting, 1960-2', *Contemporary British History*, 18 (2), pp. 76-102.

Moran, J. (2006) 'Milk Bars, Starbucks and *The Uses of Literacy*', *Cultural Studies*, 20 (66), pp. 552-559.

Mulhern, F. (1996) 'A Welfare Culture? Hoggart and Williams in the Fifties', *Radical Philosophy*, pp. 26-30.

Nixon, S. (2010) '"Salesmen of the Will to Want": Advertising and its Critics in Britain, 1951-67', *Contemporary British History*, 24 (2), pp. 1-21.

Owen, S. (2008) 'Introduction'. In Sue Owen (ed.), *Richard Hoggart and Cultural Studies* (Basingstoke: Palgrave Macmillan), pp. 1-19.

Potter, D. (1960) *The Glittering Coffin* (London: Victor Gollancz).

————— (1962) *The Changing Forest* (London: Secker and Warburg).

Report of the Committee on Broadcasting 1960, 1961-2 Cmnd 1753

(London: HMSO).

Ross, K. (1996) *Fast Cars, Clean Bodies: Decolonization and the Reordering of French Culture* (London: MIT Press).

Sandbrook, D. (2005) *Never Had it so Good: A History of Britain from Suez to The Beatles* (London: Abacus).

Turnock, R. (1997) *Television and Consumer Culture* (London: I.B Tauris).

RICHARD HOGGART
AND THE POLITICS OF AUTOBIOGRAPHY
Ben Clarke

All of Richard Hoggart's work is characterised by a concern with the particular, with the contours of individual lives and texts. It inhabits what he described as the 'British tradition in literary-cultural thinking', which 'has tended to be above all concrete' (Hoggart 1969: 4). This does not mean that it ignores broad social structures and institutions, that it has nothing to say about capitalism or the advertising industry but that it insists upon these as material practices and explores the ways in which they are embodied in individual lives and specific situations. Hoggart represents capitalism, for example, not as a monolithic idea that manifests itself in corporations, stock exchanges, and workforces, but as a necessary abstraction from such phenomena. This does not imply that capitalism does not 'actually' exist, but simply that it does not precede the material relations in which it is realised. His concern with dense texture of individual and communal experience demonstrates that 'political engagement with a material historical reality' which, Lawrence Grossberg argues, 'defines [...] the project of cultural studies' (Grossberg 2007a: 41). This method of analysis demands a constant movement between general and particular if it is to resists, on the one hand, a reductive abstraction that obscures the complex, constantly changing ways in which individuals and groups negotiate specific historical conditions and, on the other, a narrow focus that ignores the broader narratives that connect and define their experience. It is inherently dialectical, encoding an idea of the 'intellectual life' as defined by what Hoggart calls a concern with 'generalization and its relations to particular things' (Hoggart 2005: 65).

Hoggart engages with 'material historical reality' partly through a detailed exploration of his own life, working out from personal experiences to broad cultural structures and back again. The process is central to his critical method, and Stefan Collini argues that his 'best writing has nearly always been his most autobiographical' (Collini 1999: 220). He grounds his interpretations of working-class culture, for example, in his experience of growing up in Hunslet, the area of Leeds where he lived after being orphaned at the age of eight, much as his contemporary Raymond Williams traces his political thought back to the 'distinct working-class way of life [...] I was bred in' (Williams 1989: 8). For both writers, concern with the detail and ambiguities of their own lives is integral to their exploration of a section of society often dismissed as a homogeneous mass, and their insistence on the intricacy, diversity, and value of its culture and history.

This direct investment in working-class life informed the development of the field both helped shape. As Grant Farred argues, '[m]ore than anything, Cultural Studies was a project intent upon making working-class culture an object of serious study, granting it an institutional and broader social recognition' (Farred 1996: 10), and it often drew strength from the complex relations between researchers and the communities they wrote about. The critical use of individual histories not only questioned the notion that academic work is defined by its separation from the personal, but provided a foundation for the field's diversification. The continual transformation of its methods and concerns reflects, in part, the entrance of previously excluded groups into the academy, and indeed into public discourse.

From its foundation, cultural studies has explored the ways in which critics are invested in the social structures and institutions they analyse, and the implications of such investment. This involves a recognition that the cultural locations from which such figures emerge and write not only shape their intellectual concerns but their assumptions and methodologies. Autobiographical writing is one method of examining this process, a way, as Hoggart describes it, to 'look-at-our-own-ways-of-looking, our own hidden agendas' (Hoggart 2002a: 14). His exploration of his own life does not simply construct it as material for analysis but is a reflexive process that recognises the ways in which social systems and values informed his intellectual development and therefore critical practice. It exposes his cultural analyses as situated works with particular histories. To argue this is not to suggest that the essential meaning of Hoggart's text can be found in a life external to them or that his writing is simply a function of the conditions within which it was produced. It provides a critical response to the historical moments and social spaces he inhabited rather than a passive reflection of them. It is, though, to insist that his texts function within the structures that they analyse, that they are cultural acts rather than detached studies of such acts. They are, in short, always political, interested contributions to evolving debates.

The use of autobiography to 'look-at-our-own-ways-of-looking' is complicated by the conventions of the form itself. It is not an unmediated truth telling, free of the assumptions and values that define other varieties of writing, but a genre that encourages the reproduction of certain narrative structures and patterns of emphasis. In the first place, it tends to construct an image of a coherent self with an exemplary value, whether in the sense of demonstrating some particular excellence or of encapsulating a common experience. Whilst the latter quality is valuable insofar as it emphasises the ways in which specific lives can illuminate broader social narratives and systems, it risks, as Hoggart observes, suggesting 'the idea of a model, to some extent to be admired' (Hoggart 1990: 206). In both senses, then, the notion of an exemplary life can lead to evasions that simplify the individual described in order to celebrate them, whether in themselves or as an archetype. In addition, autobiographical tradition provides a series of ready-made forms that distort experience, rather than enabling an engagement with its complexities. Hoggart argues that 'much modern English autobiographical writing', for example, is 'folksy, winning, rampantly poeticised, ripely humane, falsely naïve', full of '[e]pithets [...] used for their likely effect on the reader, not to catch the nature of what is being described' and stories that 'have no reverberations outside themselves' (Hoggart 1990: 205). Its structures are determined by a network of conventions that provide, as Hoggart insists, only a 'phoney shape' (Hoggart 1990: 218), and therefore only generic interpretations of the experiences described. This does not imply that an authentic, transparent form is available elsewhere, but rather that the organisation of the text is part of a process by which meaning is produced, by which a writer engages with the specific contours of their material.

Hoggart addresses these problems of autobiographical writing by continuously reflecting on both the genre and his own process of composition. This undermines the notion that there is a 'natural' way of representing a given variety of experience, that any working-class childhood or process of intellectual development can be described and interpreted within the terms of an inherited form. It also emphasises the political implications of decisions, conscious or otherwise, about the selection and organisation of material and the development of a narrative voice. The 'folksy' character of the texts described above, for example, constructs 'a world in which every day is Christmas, in which almost everything — even grief — is seen in a retrospective glow' (Hoggart 1990: 205). This results in a celebration of the past on aesthetic rather than rational grounds that obscure questions of suffering, inequality and injustice. The fact that Hoggart has often been accused of this kind of nostalgia, despite his explicit resistance to it, suggests that the interpretation of his work has often been defined as much by preconceptions about the narration of working-class life as by his texts themselves. His accounts of his childhood in Hunslet respond to the evasions and constraints of this '[h]iccupingly anecdotal' (Hoggart 1990: 205) tradition, as they do to middle-class accounts of the poor as brutal and ignorant. This practice of critical engagement is repeated throughout his life writing, which both exposes the formal tradition within which it operates and seeks to extend its possibilities. Hoggart does not claim to juxtapose his cultural criticism with a neutral, objective account of its foundations, as though he could somehow evade the problems of representation, but uses one genre to reflect upon another.

As this suggests, Hoggart's autobiographical writing cannot be separated from his scholarship, as though it were a diversion from more rigorous cultural analysis. Indeed, his work undermines the notion that there is a stable division between academic writing and more literary or personal forms that is enacted in the style as well as the content of texts. It actively resists dominant academic conventions and indeed any simple classification, drawing upon multiple genres and linguistic registers, often within individual texts. This is illustrated, for example, by *The Uses of Literacy*. As Raymond Williams observed, although the book is 'primarily a critical work, the analysis of documents is cut across by [...] sketches of "allegorical figures" in the cultural situation; wry accounts of personal feeling; parodies and generalised comments' (Williams 1957: 423). It also incorporates what Bill Hughes describes as a 'Bakhtinian multiplicity of voices' (Hughes 2008: 220), juxtaposing dialect phrases from Hoggart's childhood with a critical idiom shaped by the Leavises and *Scrutiny*. A similar use of use of personal experience, and openness to multiple genres and linguistic registers persists in late works such as *Everyday Language and Everyday Life*, which not only grounds its analyses of idiomatic phrases in the 'known, felt [...] daily life of the Northern English working class from the 1930s onwards' (Hoggart 2003: xiii), but uses the words of this community, employing 'demotic rather than "educated" language when [...] fitting; and [...] some local as well as public forms' (Hoggart 2003: xv) This quality of his writing implicitly critiques professional discourses and methodologies, refusing what Hoggart describes as the 'shield of an academic discipline's formal approaches' (Hoggart 1972: 32). It insists upon the need to communicate with a broader audience, to incorporate forms of knowledge conventionally dismissed as subjective, and to make sense of experiences often regarded as trivial or inconsequential. Hoggart does not reduce the practices, ideas, and language of those he represents to raw material that is significant only insofar as it is transformed through scholarly analysis, but insists upon their inherent value and complexity. His work therefore engages in a dialogue with his subjects, and indeed allows their voices and perspectives to permeate his texts. This process focuses attention on his own location within culture, on the positions from which he writes, issues often obscured by notions of proper scholarly detachment.

Hoggart's ideas about relations between author, subject, and audience are not simply described in texts but enacted in his style, in his use of personal examples and asides, and in what Melissa Gregg describes as his 'voice' (Gregg 2006). His sophisticated, democratic prose is indebted as much to a tradition of autobiographers, essayists, and novelists as to the conventions of university departments. Collini insists that his work demonstrates 'the presence of a strong writerly urge that has only found partial fulfilment in conventional academic genres' (Collini 1999: 220), and Gregg observes that, as a consequence, he often ventures outside such forms and 'doesn't choose academic work as his sole means of intervening in the public sphere, nor even his preferred mode' (Gregg 2006: 31-2). F. R. Leavis famously remarked, after reading *The Uses of Literacy*, 'that it had some value but "he should have written a novel"' (Hoggart 1990: 206). This is an ambiguous compliment at best, but concisely emphasises the difficulty of classifying the text. Hoggart draws upon a range of forms, often concentrating on varieties of creative non-fiction that use personal experience to illuminate broader historical structures. His decision to subtitle his memoirs a 'Life and Times', which he describes as the 'least unsatisfactory' (Hoggart 1990: 206) label available, emphasises this approach, and in his preface to the first volume he argues that the work 'is an attempt to make, out of a personal story, a sense rather more than personal' (Hoggart 1988: xi). As Sue Owen (2008: 73) observes, this movement from 'the personal to the general' characterises his work as a whole. An effective analysis of his life writing must look beyond a narrowly defined model of autobiography and explore other closely related genres, including what Collini, in his analysis of *Townscape with Figures*, describes as that 'tradition of unclassifiable and personal writing', the 'Condition-of-England book' (Collini 1999: 222). It must also consider all these as literary genres, in the sense discussed above, ways of writing and therefore of understanding. Though Simon Hoggart observes that his father 'always wanted to be a novelist' and sometimes felt that he had 'missed his way' (Hoggart 2008: xiv), Richard Hoggart does employ and indeed contribute to a number of well-established if neglected literary traditions. This enables him to explore and extend the conventions that shape academic texts, exposing them as rhetorical structures that concentrate on particular subjects and varieties of knowledge whilst obscuring others. The value of his work comes in part from its ability to work across established generic boundaries, and indeed to question the function of such divisions.

Hoggart's use of autobiographical writing is not simply a way of mining his life for historical information but of incorporating literary knowledge and analysis into his cultural criticism. It is about form as well as content. It depends upon the idea that literature explores the ways in which individual actions are performed within an intricate network of social, economic and intellectual forces. In 'Literature and Society' he insists that:

Good literature re-creates the immediacy of life — that life was and is all these things, all these different orders of things, *all at once*. It embodies the sense of human life developing in a historical and moral context. (Hoggart 1970a: 20-21)

Indeed, he argues that literature, and art more generally, is important partly for this reason, as '[o]nly art recreates life in all its dimensions — so that a particular choice is bound up with space, people and habits' (Hoggart 1970b: 249). In this, it contrasts with other forms of writing, such as philosophy and sociology, which, for Hoggart, focus on general, abstract structures. Literature, on the other hand, both enacts and explores the experiential complexity of life, refusing to narrow its focus, insisting upon the place, and therefore importance, of the seemingly trivial as well as the obviously significant. This distinction is clearly indebted to F. R. Leavis' (1952) division between the 'abstract' and 'concrete' in essays such as 'Literary Criticism and Philosophy', although Hoggart shows a far greater willingness than Leavis to analyse the significance and implications of these terms and, thereby, the foundations of his own critical judgements. He does, however, retain the idea that literature is concerned with the specific, with the detailed texture of life as it is experienced. Hoggart argues that, at its best, literature helps us to 'know better what it must have meant to live and make decisions in that time and place, to have smelled roast beef, been troubled by falling hair and wondered what we were making of our lives' (Hoggart 1970a: 21). It not only traces the multiple pressures and sensations within the context of which individuals act, but the relations between them, the ways in which each modifies the others.

This does not mean that literature is confined to the individual. Although it 'starts in absorbed attention to the detail of experience, in immersion in "the destructive element", in "the foul rag and bone shop of the heart"', it is 'driven by a desire to find the revelatory instance, the tiny gesture that opens a whole field of meaning and consequence' (Hoggart 1970b: 248). It communicates the intricacies of individual lives that operate at the intersection of shifting narratives and relations of power, transforming the personal into a common resource, an object of debate. Literature, Hoggart argues, 'can help recreate, inwardly, that shared sense of being human without which our world would truly be a wilderness, a chaos' (Hoggart 2002b: 131). Indeed, the purpose of writing 'is to reach others' (Hoggart 1972: 41), to make the particular available to all. This is as true of autobiographical texts as of novels. Exploring question of how 'one's personal experience can ever have more than a personal meaning', Hoggart remarks that when:

[w]e look at our own lives, we find ourselves returning to some occasions in them because they seem to be what Virginia Woolf called 'moments',

to have a symbolic force, to be telling incidents. We feel also that they probably tell something about other people's lives, in this kind of society, here and now. And so we begin to move, gingerly, to make contact across the gaps. (Hoggart 1972: 39)

The reference to Woolf implies that fiction and autobiography share a foundational objective, that both attempt to see a social significance even in the seemingly incidental details of individual experience. Despite their obvious differences, there are parallels between modernist novels, with their emphasis upon the 'symbolic force' of the 'moments' that structure a given life, and a text like *The Uses of Literacy*, which uses Hoggart's memories of growing up in Hunslet to explore northern working-class communities, something Collini recognises when he describes Hoggart's text as, in part, 'a prose version of *Sons and Lovers*' (Collini 2008: 53).

Hoggart's use of autobiographical writing enables him to integrate literary knowledge and academic scholarship, or perhaps rather to explore the tense, ambiguous boundary between them, a process that exposes both to scrutiny. In particular, it uses the forms of 'qualitative' analysis he associates with literature and literary criticism to explore individual lives, identifying tensions, complexities, and values that he argues 'quantitative' methodologies too often ignore. Textual scholarship provides tools for examining such lives, just as literature offers a way of representing them. The resulting insights can be used to modify established cultural models, to develop a more complex and nuanced understanding of social structures and the ways in which they shape experience. Hoggart's objection is not to abstraction, or even 'theory', but to what Grossberg (2007b), following Blake, terms the 'single vision' that some abstract systems of interpretation sustain, which reduces the diversity and ambiguities of social practices to a uniform, if intricate, narrative. Hoggart's emphasis upon the particular is not driven simply by the need to consider new subjects and problems, important though this is, but also to incorporate new forms of understanding, not least those of groups who have historically been excluded from scholarly, and indeed public debate.

In the remainder of this paper, I will briefly explore three specific ways in which Hoggart uses life writing to extend dominant social and academic discourses. In the first place, he contributes to a tradition of working-class autobiography that challenges the concept of the 'masses', insisting on the intricacies and specific value of working-class life. Secondly, his use of his experience in cultural analyses posits a broader idea of knowledge that includes, for example, both poetry and intuition. Finally, his constant reflection on the intellectual and experiential basis of his criticism emphasises the author as a social actor, or even activist. In all these instances, life writing provides a critical resource, offering perspectives not available from more conventional academic methods of analysis.

In his anonymous 1902 work, *From the Abyss*, C. F. G. Masterman argued that '[n]o future historical novelist will be able to reconstitute from contemporary documents the inner life of Pentonville and Camberwell' (Masterman 1902: 26). These areas, the text suggests, are inhabited by an inarticulate multitude defined solely by its 'overwhelming inconceivable number' (Masterman 1902: 26) which is such that 'it seems incredible that each individual should count for anything at all in the sight of man or of God' (Masterman 1902: 26). The statements equate being inarticulate with a lack of differentiation and value, principally through what John Carey describes as the 'metaphor of the mass', which denies others 'the individuality which we ascribe to ourselves and to people we know' (Carey 1992: 21). Being unable to represent an 'inner life' is the same as not having one. In this context, working-class writing is inherently radical, a way of insisting upon difference, upon a complex social landscape in which solidarities are founded, not upon essential equivalence, but upon moral and political choices. Autobiography, with its explicit focus on individual lives, provides the ideal medium for such a challenge, something which explains its importance to working-class authors, as to other groups, such as women and colonial peoples, who have traditionally had little access to the means of communication and whose personal identities have been subsumed under general categories. As Jonathan Rose argues in *The Intellectual Life of the British Working Classes*, the study of such texts enables a new understanding and appreciation of 'the history of what were once called "the inarticulate masses" — who, as it turns out, had a great deal to say' (Rose 2002: 3). His book reveals a rich history of literary production and consumption that contradicts pervasive images of the poor as uniformly ignorant, apathetic, and silent.

Hoggart's autobiographical writing is not, then, an isolated phenomenon but a contribution to an established and evolving tradition. In particular, he repeatedly emphasises the importance of the literary and political culture of the 1930s to his intellectual development, tracing the formative influence of representations of working-class life such as the 'documentaries on coalminers, fishermen and other dramatic labourers' (Hoggart 2002c: 305). These were part of an attempt to represent previously marginalised communities and forms of labour that also produced a generation of autobiographical writers. The period saw the publication of collections such as Margaret Llewelyn Davies' *Life as We Have Known It, by Co-operative Working Women* (1931) and Jack Common's *Seven Shifts* (1938), as well as individual works such as B. L. Coombes' *These Poor Hands* (1939) and Jack Hilton's innovative *Caliban Shrieks* (1935). The mere existence of such texts challenges Masterman's image of an inarticulate and homogeneous working-class. Much of Hoggart's writing on his childhood and family evokes and contributes to this tradition. It emphasises the complexity and value of working-class lives and social networks, the fact that, as Hoggart argues in *The Uses of Literacy*, to 'live in the working-classes is even now to belong to an all-pervading culture, one in some ways as formal and stylised as any that is attributed to, say, the upper-classes' (Hoggart 1957: 31). It also insists that such cultures both merit and repay careful analysis, and demonstrates that voices do emerge from them, albeit with difficulty, and are worth listening to.

Hoggart does not simply write from a position within the working-class communities, however. He may still retain some of their habits and perspectives, still find the tinned 'red middle-cut' of salmon 'far "tastier" than fresh salmon' (Hoggart 1957: 36), but, as a successful academic and writer, a former Assistant Director-General of UNESCO and Warden of Goldsmiths College, he is also separated from them by education, profession and, indeed, income, as he himself recognises. Writing of the 'daily life of the Northern working class' in *Everyday Language and Every Life*, he describes it as 'where I began; but did not remain' (Hoggart 2003: xiii), and as early as *The Uses of Literacy* he observes that although he is 'from the working-classes' he feels 'both close to them and apart from them' (Hoggart 1957: 18). His work exploits this critical distance, which enables him to both analyse and sympathise with members of working-class communities. This is, again, illustrated most directly in his autobiographical writing. His studies of his relatives, from his fiery aunt Ethel to his stoical Grandma, are characterised by an attempt to see them simultaneously as individuals and representative figures. They do this primarily by an intuitive working out from particular scenes and phrases, a practice that enables Hoggart to draw general conclusions without reducing those he describes to symbols. His description of Ethel's desire to escape Hunslet and 'those shabby streets among those "common" people' for a 'dreams of semis, of colourful curtains which pulled across rather than lace curtains which stayed permanently in place across the bottom half of the sash window and a plain roller blind for the evening; and an inside "toilet" with a matching U-shaped rug and cover over the seat, a bathroom, some garden at front and rear and nicely spoken neighbours' (Hoggart 1988: 18), illustrates the ways in which working-class aspirations were often both contained and commodified by middle-class notions of refinement. However, Ethel is not simply used to illustrate a critical point but is represented as a multifaceted, contradictory character, whose experience is interesting in its own right. Hoggart insists upon the need to avoid simplifying her life, for example by choosing to 'make her a figure of grotesque fun; or to sentimentalise her' (Hoggart 1988: 26). She is not a blank space within which petit-bourgeois narratives are inscribed, and even her desire for gentility is more complex than it might initially appear. There is a 'baffled poetry' in the ideal of 'England and of "nice" English life' (Hoggart 1988: 67), that shapes her retirement with Ida in Morecambe, and Hoggart argues that '[h]ers is not in itself an ignoble dream' (Hoggart 1988: 18). Hoggart's account of her reveals the limitations of dominant images of working-class 'respectability', their failure to do justice to its ambiguities and contradictions. More broadly, it illustrates his use of individual lives to explore the ways in which social narratives are enacted and transformed within specific contexts.

This critical process, which depends upon a close, sympathetic engagement with particular experiences, parallels Hoggart's method of interpreting literature, which he argues is characterised by its 'poetic, metaphoric, intuitive understanding'. Literature offers 'a form of knowledge', but one that 'cannot be objectively measured' (Hoggart 1970a: 22-23). His interpretations of both literary and social texts depend on these forms of understanding, demonstrating an ability to recognise the symbolic importance of specific words or acts and willingness to consider what cannot be determined in the dominant, 'scientific' sense. This strategy is not without risk. The conclusions it generates cannot easily be challenged with reference to an agreed system of proof in the way that, for example, the solution of a mathematical equation or a problem in analytical philosophy can, and as a result can appear ungrounded or purely individual. As Sean Matthews argues, the kind of literary criticism Hoggart practices is often represented as 'impressionistic and imprecise', particularly in comparison to the 'rigorous scientism of Theory' (Matthews 2008: 94), and his social analyses have been described and marginalised in similar terms. However, his work does not represent its own use of direct observation, personal experience and 'intuitive leaps' (Hoggart 1995: 194) as an alternative to more systematic scholarship, but as a way of questioning its boundaries and extending what qualifies as legitimate knowledge.

Hoggart's emphasis upon the importance of 'intuitive leaps' is interwoven with an interest in what he describes as the 'self-acquired imaginative wisdom' of those like his grandmother and a willingness to consider the insights this might produce (Hoggart 2003: 126). He insists, for example, that 'working-class people have considerable sensitiveness in reaching conclusions on some things' (Hoggart 1957: 89) and repeatedly emphasises the ways in which 'people without an intellectual bent' may be 'wise in their own way' (Hoggart 1957: 276). There are, he famously argues, 'other ways of being in the truth' (Hoggart 1957: 276) than those which shape academic scholarship, and his work continually contests what Lawrence Grossberg calls 'the assumption that there is only one valid way of knowing, defined by the epistemology of the formal sciences' (Grossberg 2007b: 128).

Autobiographical writing, then, provides a means of exploring groups, experiences and forms of knowledge that are largely excluded from academic discourse. It also offers a way of situating the critic within culture, alongside the texts and practices he or she examines. By insisting on critics as individuals with specific histories, who intervene in particular debates, in particular ways, from particular cultural positions, autobiography undermines the notion of scholars as detached or objective observers. This need not mean accepting in its entirety John Carey's argument that:

> all books of social commentary should carry up-to-date information about the author's income and property-holdings. This would save the reader a lot of time, since he would know from the start how much of the book's contents he could automatically discount. (Carey 1987: x)

Nor need it involve fetishising the writer as a point of origin or final meaning, as though to understand their consciousness was to resolve the text, to reveal what Barthes terms the 'single "theological" meaning' of a work, the '"message" of the Author-God' (Barthes 1977: 146). It is rather one technique of exploring the material and intellectual spaces from which the text speaks, the narratives from which it is constructed and to which it contributes. Autobiography need not represent the author as an autonomous, inspired creator or interpreter, but can expose writing as historically-specific form of production. Hoggart's exploration of his own material and intellectual formation identifies his work as a series of interested acts, as interventions in evolving debates, in short, as political. This does not undermine, or indeed affect, its claims to scholarly rigour or truth. It does, however, suggest that it has a function, that it is a way of acting in the world, and that it is produced and operates within a complex network of economic, political, moral and intellectual forces.

Hoggart's autobiographical writing is integral to his critical work. His reflections on his own experience enable him to question and extend not merely the objects but the form of academic discourse. Though his life writing is not theoretical in any straightforward sense of the word, it fulfils some of the same functions, destabilising comfortable, received ideas and methodologies, and insisting on a broader, more complex view of culture and interpretation. Above all, it demonstrates that social analysis is not just a matter of collecting, sifting and interpreting a safely distanced body of material using a neutral, accepted set of techniques, but a more active, engaged, essentially political process. Hoggart's work is important not only because it dedicates serious critical attention to previously neglected cultural practices, but because it insists that such analysis demands a flexible, open, and self-aware mode of writing. It rejects the 'shield of an academic discipline's formal approaches', which would enable it to evade the question of its own form, and separate its language and analytical practices from the individuals and communities it interprets. Instead, it insists upon criticism as a situated practice, in dialogue with, rather than detached from both those it analyses, a process that demands constant revision of its methodologies and form. Autobiographical writing is central to this process, as it recognises the critic as a figure speaking to others, responsible to language, to the diversity of knowledge, and to the specific complexities of the places and historical moments they represent.

Bibliography

Barthes, R. (1977) 'Death of the Author'. *Image Music Text* (trans. Stephen Heath). (London: Fontana), pp. 142-8.

Carey, J. (1987) *Original Copy: Selected Reviews and Journalism 1969-1986* (London: Faber).

————— (1992) *The Intellectuals and the Masses: Pride and Prejudice among the Literary Intelligentsia, 1880-1939* (London: Faber).

Collini, S. (1999) 'Critical Minds: Raymond Williams and Richard Hoggart'. In *English Pasts: Essays in History and Culture* (Oxford: Oxford University Press), pp. 210-230.

————— (2008) 'Richard Hoggart: Literary Criticism and Cultural Decline in Twentieth-Century Britain'. In Sue Owen (ed.), *Richard Hoggart and Cultural Studies* (Houndmills: Palgrave), pp. 33-56.

Farred, G. (1996) 'Leavisite Cool: The Organic Links Between Cultural Studies and *Scrutiny*', *dispositio/n: American Journal of Cultural Histories and Theories*, 21(48), pp. 1-19.

Gregg, M. (2006) *Cultural Studies' Affective Voices* (Houndmills: Palgrave).

Grossberg, L. (2007a) 'Introduction: CCCS and the detour through theory'. In Ann Gray, Jan Campbell, Mark Erickson, Stuart Hanson and Helen Wood (eds.), *CCCS Selected Working Papers: Volume 1* (London and New York: Routledge), pp. 33-47.

————— (2007b) 'Rereading the past from the future'. *International Journal of Cultural Studies*, 10 (1), pp. 125-33.

Hoggart, R. (1957) *The Uses of Literacy: Aspects of Working-Class Life* (London: Chatto and Windus).

————— (1969) *Contemporary Cultural Studies: An Approach to the Study of Literature and Society* (Birmingham: University of Birmingham, Centre for

Contemporary Cultural Studies).

———— (1970a) 'Literature and Society'. *Speaking to Each Other, Volume 1: About Literature* (New York: Oxford University Press), pp. 19-39.

———— (1970b) 'Schools of English and Contemporary Society'. *Speaking to Each Other, Volume 2: About Literature* (New York: Oxford University Press), pp. 246-259.

———— (1972) *Only Connect: On Culture and Communication* (London: Chatto and Windus).

———— (1988) *A Local Habitation: Life and Times, 1918-1940* (London: Chatto and Windus).

———— (1990) *A Sort of Clowning: Life and Times, Volume 2; 1940-59* (London: Chatto and Windus).

———— (1994) *Townscape with Figures: Farnham – Portrait of an English Town* (London: Chatto and Windus).

———— (1995/1998) *The Tyranny of Relativism: Culture and Politics in Contemporary English Society* (New Brunswick: Transaction).

———— (2002a). 'Are Museums Political?', *Between Two Worlds: Politics, Anti-Politics, and the Unpolitical* (New Brunswick: Transaction), pp. 9-17.

———— (2002b) 'Freedom to Publish: Even Hateful Stuff', *Between Two Worlds: Politics, Anti-Politics, and the Unpolitical* (New Brunswick: Transaction), pp. 121-131.

———— (2002c) 'Looking Back: An Interview with Nicholas Tredell', *Between Two Worlds: Politics, Anti-Politics, and the Unpolitical* (New Brunswick: Transaction), pp. 301-313.

———— (2003) *Everyday Language and Everyday Life* (New Brunswick: Transaction).

———— (2005) *Promises to Keep: Thoughts in Old Age* (London: Continuum).

Hoggart, S. (2008) 'Foreword'. In Sue Owen (ed.), *Re-reading Richard Hoggart: Life, Literature, Language, Education* (Newcastle: Cambridge Scholars), pp. x-xv.

Hughes, B. (2008) 'The Uses and Values of Literacy: Richard Hoggart, Aesthetic Standards, and the Commodification of Working-Class Culture'. In Sue Owen (ed.), *Richard Hoggart and Cultural Studies* (Houndmills: Palgrave), pp. 213-226.

Leavis, F. R. (1952/1962) 'Literary Criticism and Philosophy'. In *The Common Pursuit* (Harmondsworth: Penguin), pp. 211-222.

Matthews, S. (2008) 'The Uses of D. H. Lawrence'. In Sue Owen (ed.), *Re-reading Richard Hoggart: Life, Literature, Language, Education* (Newcastle: Cambridge Scholars), pp. 85-101.

Masterman, C. F. G. (1902) *From the Abyss: of its Inhabitants by One of them* (London: R. Brimley Johnson).

Owen, S. (2008) 'Richard Hoggart and Literature'. In Sue Owen (ed.), *Re-reading Richard Hoggart: Life, Literature, Language, Education* (Newcastle: Cambridge Scholars), pp. 58-84.

Rose, J. (2001/2002) *The Intellectual Life of the British Working Classes* (New Haven and London: Yale Nota Bene).

Williams, R. (1957) 'Fiction and the Writing Public'. *Essays in Criticism*, 7(4), pp. 422-428.

———— (1989) 'Culture is Ordinary'. In *Resources of Hope: Culture, Democracy, Socialism* (London and New York: Verso), pp. 3-18.

RICHARD HOGGART
AND THE IDEA OF DEMOCRATIC EDUCATION
Nick Stevenson

The idea of a democratic education has long been connected (although not exclusively) to a democratic socialist tradition of thinking. This tradition is deeply concerned about the ability of the capitalist system to subjugate human needs for education to its own requirements for consumers with an ever expanding sense of their wants, competitive individualism, relevant skills for the work place (most notably vocationalism) and of course massive social inequalities that erode a sense of solidarity and common citizenship. The democratic socialist tradition has become progressively sidelined in a capitalist driven culture where education has become a commodity whose ethos more generally is defined by the needs of the market. As education's ability to be able to communicate a liberal culture of curiosity and inquiry for the many rather than the few has diminished, the wider society has witnessed increasing inequalities between rich and the poor and the triumph of the values of hyper-consumerism with an increasing attack upon genuine public spaces where citizens are able to meet and explore alternative ideas and social agendas. At this point it is important to defend a genuinely democratic education for everyone based upon dialogic encounter, the ability of students to formulate their own questions, have an appreciation of the complexity of arguments, be mixed in with other communities and status groups, and be able to participate meaningfully within wider publics. It has of course long been the argument of democratic socialists that only a community based upon equality and democratic participation that will be able to live up to this particular vision. We also need to remember that historically democratic socialists did not call for a revolutionary movement to end capitalism. Instead the argument was for an economy and society that had become progressively civilised in order to take account of democratic values and human needs. As we shall see the idea of education was central to this way of thinking precisely because of the argument that working people were not simply bodies who labored but were complex beings who should be at liberty to develop themselves.

Here I explore the contribution of Richard Hoggart to this debate. My argumentative strategy is that the wider tradition of democratic socialism should be returned to after the failures of 10 years of New Labour in the British context. As I write, there is gathering evidence that the new Conservative-Liberal Alliance government are to go even further in abandoning comprehensive forms of education. The democratic socialist tradition in this regard is not represented by the watered down social democracy of the Blair and Brown government but also steers clear of some of the more dogmatic features often associated with certain strains of Marxism. Here the argument is that if a counter-cultural Left is to survive the neoliberal assault then it will need to become the democratic Left. The ability of the Left to be able to uphold democratic ideas and to develop the common ground for democratic citizenship will be a key testing ground in respect of its future relevance. Here as I have indicated there is no need for those interested in developing a democratic education for future democratic citizens to reinvent the wheel. There is already a rich tradition for such debates to draw upon of which Richard Hoggart's contribution in the British context remains central. Under the assault of neoliberalism, Richard Hoggart's contribution to our thinking about the public assumes a renewed level of importance often missed by many within cultural studies. As Henry Giroux (2004) argues, democratic educators need to defend participatory public spaces by both defending liberal freedoms and redistributing resources.

Democratic education: the case of Richard Hoggart

Richard Hoggart (1995) provides a forceful defence of the public value of education in an age that is increasingly dominated by market values and relativism. Since the 1980s along with the growth of a genuinely mass society and new communications technologies, the collective values of the old industrial working class and notions of public service have been increasingly assaulted by the ideologies and practices of free market capitalism. While some of these changes have allowed ordinary working-class people to shake off the yoke of deference in respect of the hierarchies of social class, Hoggart describes the emergence of a society that is both 'more horizontal and diffused' (Hoggart 1995: 6). The undermining of cultural hierarchies has not introduced a more genuinely democratic public sphere but has witnessed instead the growing dominance of the market over other social and cultural spheres. If the market has diminished the social standing of the educated middle classes it has simultaneously provided new opportunities for the cultural products of large corporations. In this respect, Hoggart accuses many on the cultural Left of adopting a form of market friendly relativism for fear of being seen to disrespect the cultural practices of ordinary people. If there exists a plurality of lifestyle and tastes whose 'superiority' is a matter of easily punctured snobbery, then nothing seemingly stands in the way of the commodifying logic of the dominant consumer society. The dominant hegemony of an age that refuses to admit a hierarchy of cultural tastes and preferences becomes 'stay as sweet as you are' (Hoggart 1995: 9). In this the ethos of the public becomes replaced by progressive privatisation, atomism and the decline in the idea that we have a civic duty to the community. Cultural worth is no longer measured by questions of quality and value, but is more likely to be determined by the ability to either make a profit or in the new technocratic logic of public services to satisfy 'performance indicators' and produce 'measurable outcomes'. The increasing dominance of neoliberal capitalism has produced a dominant hegemony of the 'puritan and prim' and the 'intensely money-conscious' replacing more social democratic concerns for the common good and the urban poor (Hoggart 1995: 13). The displacement of the ethic of community where I am 'my brother's keeper' has seen the public sector caught in a vicious pincer movement where it both adopts the language and management styles of the private sector while being forced into a constant battle over scarce resources.

These social and cultural changes, as we shall see, have particular implications for the value of education. In the mid-1990s Hoggart reports that the collapse in the public value of education and the persistence of entrenched hierarchies of social class meant 'vocationalism' had gained a new respectability in debates concerning education. This not only reflects the dominance of the market in the governance of education but also is an expression of a class-based society that increasingly aims to teach young working-class people practical skills. If the lives of the underclass are marked by illiteracy and narrow horizons those at the top of the social hierarchy are still able to buy educational success through access to elite private schools (Hoggart 2004). The divisions of class prepare some children for a life of success and achievement and others either for exclusion or for a world of mostly dead-end employment. For Hoggart the 'right' to choose a private education is actually the 'right' to choose a competitive advantage over others. Education here is not being viewed as a public good, but as a passport to success in the labour market. The concept of market choice when applied to education ends up reinforcing class divisions, however unintentionally. Hoggart's argument is that the increasing penetration of the market into education further reinforces existing class relations that in turn enhance elitist assumptions that working-class children are incapable of handling difficult works of literature and abstract concepts. These arguments, we might summarise, are not only a matter of class prejudice but also act as a form of political control.

The history of democratic socialism is marked by the idea that working people should be enabled to expand their intellectual capacities beyond those required for the functioning of the labour market. Hoggart's argument is that the dominance of the market over educational values and perspectives requires relativism. If capitalist driven democracies require a compliant population willing to unquestioningly fit into the requirements of flexible and market orientated lifestyles, it is not surprising that knowledge is no longer valued in terms of its capacity to open up repressed questions. A democratic rather than a capitalist driven education system and society is dependent upon the 'the belief in the worthwhileness of the pursuit of knowledge for its own sake, and the respect due to those who seek it' (Hoggart 1995: 302). The capacity of modern societies to offer its young people equal forms of educational provision and critical forms of inquiry beyond the narrow confines of 'vocationalism' are then necessary requirements for democracy. Such arguments seek to break with the elitist traditions of education (public schools for the elite and vocationalism for the masses) and seek to foster genuinely critical forms of inquiry demanded in a society that is able to hold in check the colonising logic of capitalism.

Hoggart's writing needs to be seen in a democratic socialist tradition that was committed to the values of self-development, community and solidarity with the poor and dispossessed. For most of the twentieth century, social democracy adopted a genuinely parliamentary road to socialism while seeking to maintain a fair distribution of wealth, mixed economy, the building of a welfare state and the empowerment of trade unions. European social democratic parties sought to establish alternative public spheres that acted as a counter-weight to the dominant capitalist ethos of market competition. We might remember that, despite the internal variety of European social democratic parties, they were more than election winning machines and were directly involved in the ideological and cultural organisation of the working class (Moschonas 2002). For the most part, the culture of social democracy was built upon an alliance between the educated middle class and the organised working class. Both these groups historically found a common cause in seeking to mediate the more destructive tendencies of capitalism.

Richard Hoggart's classic work *The Uses of Literacy* (1957) captures some of the essential features that democratic socialism had to grapple with during this period. As Hoggart so memorably argues, there are deep dangers to democracy when social progress and cultural development become defined in terms of the accumulation of material possessions. Hoggart has, however, been rightly criticised for his overly moralistic reaction to the arrival of commercial culture and its corrupting effect upon the working class. Here Hoggart stands accused of the view that culture can be uproblematically assigned into categories of 'good' and 'bad' (Hebdige 1979). The struggle for an emancipated society becomes entangled in a binary logic that opposes democratic forms of education to that of the market that has the consequence of producing a form of condescension in respect of the cultures of the working class. Further, the feminist historian Carolyn Steedman (1986) argues that Hoggart's study fails to recover more subsumed stories that do not conform to working-class Labour values. Yet what later work offering more contested accounts of culture than Hoggart's own displace is his social democratic concern with a shared civic culture. The problem Hoggart identified was the erosion of a class based culture by 'mass opinion, the mass recreational product, and the generalised emotional response' (Hoggart 1957: 343). Further there is also a deeper concern that the promise of mass culture would fail to develop the critical potential evident within the scholarship boy who is 'earnest for self-improvement' (Hoggart 1957: 303). In other words, what is missing from some of the later cultural studies literature is an engagement with Richard Hoggart's central narrative which concerns the educated development of people that industrial civilisation had relegated to the status of labouring people.

Richard Hoggart and critique

In this and other respects Hoggart's work bears a family resemblance to what his contemporary Raymond Williams (1965) called 'the long revolution' that was an attempt to link economic, social and political issues to cultural questions. Here Williams problematises the development of standardised cultural products, a paternalistic state and a capitalist economic system that had stalled the possibility of a more participatory and genuinely diverse popular culture. Raymond Williams suggested an alternative democratic framework where a radically decentralised communications system would be open to a diverse republic of voices (Williams 1962). The idea at heart was that in the context of the labour movement there existed the potential for an alliance between radical educationalists, politically committed artists and organised labour. All had interests in curtailing the power of the market and the establishment of a genuinely democratic and inclusive public sphere. However the growth of a synthetic popular culture, the continued existence of class divisions and cultural elitism prevented the possibility of the development of what Williams (1989) termed a 'culture in common'. A culture in common did not mean the construction of a common culture, but could be said to more accurately describe the possibility of cultural dialogue and exchange and a shared civil status.

Both Williams and Hoggart were acutely aware that coming from working-class families meant that their initial experience of 'culture' was one of inequality. Culture was primarily experienced through a sense of being excluded from high culture (Williams 1968). Raymond Willliams most acutely explores these features through his first two novels, *Border Country* (1960) and *Second Generation* (1964). Here rather than simply resting on the argument that education needs to develop critical forms of understanding, Williams explores the tensions within subjective experiences involved in the moving across borders including social class. Similarly, Hoggart (1957) explores the anxieties of the 'scholarship boy' who displaces his own sense of personal inadequacy onto his family and class background while seeking to improve himself. Notably Hoggart and Williams refuse to either romanticise or denigrate their shared if regionally distinct working-class backgrounds. In particular Hoggart (1982) argued that a genuinely critical education is best fostered through the development of a searching dialogue between students and teachers. In this regard, Hoggart was critical of the working-class deprivation thesis that presumes that students are simply 'blank slates' waiting to be written over with the complexities of high culture. However, he is equally critical of educational debates that deny any language of 'improvement' or 'development'. Hoggart argues that a culturally relativist approach that merely seeks to reaffirm working-class identities may be well meaning but unintentionally reinforces the rule of the market and corporate capitalism given its dominance in shaping the aspirations of the young. For Hoggart education does not have a neutral value but instead needs to be protected from the market so that it can become a place of critical engagement, diversity and transformation.

In this respect, Hoggart (2001a) argues that education should not be confined to basic literacy, but should also encompass questions of critical literacy. If critical literacy is about being able to decode the relations of dominance that are part of the everyday world of consumer capitalism, it is also the ability to be able to understand complex ideas and associations. Similarly, Martha Nussbaum (1995) argues that an education driven by utilitarian sentiment reduces the complexities and meaningfulness of our lives to simple forms of calculation. In this respect, Richard Hoggart's (1970a) persists with the argument that the study of literature is central to any democratic vision of education. A complex appreciation of literary culture is crucial because of its ability to offer new ways of seeing, new experiences and complex moral and cultural vocabularies. Both Nussbaum and Hoggart are rejecting an education that deals merely with that which is 'objective' or can be scientifically verified by focusing upon the need to develop the poetic and the imaginative potential of citizens. Many writing in cultural studies have been suspicious of this move thinking that it automatically led to a denigration of popular culture. Yet Hoggart (Hoggart 1970a: 38) also argues that popular culture is worthy of detailed study even if it is unlikely to attain the level of complexity of good literature. This assumption, which has been endlessly deconstructed by postmodernism, is perhaps no longer helpful, but the defence of cultural complexity against more utilitarian calculations is still well worth making. More recently Martin Ryle and Kate Soper (2002: 199) have defended the ability of complex cultural texts to promote learning and self-reflection in an age dominated by a capitalist based rationality. It is perhaps this view, rather than the intrinsic superiority of literature over other cultural forms, that is worth defending today. Here I would agree with Nick Couldry that 'what is urgent now is not defending the full range of cultural production and consumption from elitist judgment, but defending the possibility of any shared site (whether or not overlapping with specialised spheres of cultural production) for an emergent democratic politics' (Couldry 2004: 10).

Hoggart and democratic socialism

For Williams and Hoggart then democractic socialism is caught up with the capacity of citizens to learn both through the education system and democratised public spheres. Of course their views are not interchangeable. Later Williams, who was to adopt a more overtly Marxist stance in his work than Hoggart, described socialism as 'not only the general "recovery" of specifically alienated human capacities, but also, and much more decisively, the necessary institution of new and very complex communicative capacities and relationships' (Williams 1980: 62). For Williams only a socialist transformation of society would enable the institution of an inclusive democratic and educated public culture. As Paul Jones (1994) argues the more cautious ideas of 'service' evident within Hoggart can be contrasted to Williams's more radical insistence on the need to press for the transformation of capitalism. However, before we begin to oppose the Marxist Williams to the social democratic Hoggart it should be remembered that much of Williams's political writing refuses any easy separation between these different traditions. Indeed with hindsight it is perhaps more useful to assimilate them both to overlapping traditions of democratic socialism.

The rise of neoliberalism saw a much harsher version of market capitalism develop during the 1980s that politically defeated the democratic form of socialism proposed by Hoggart. Since this period there also emerged a new kind of social democracy (usually referred to as the 'third way') that has increasingly sought to adapt itself to the demands of the global market. If old style social democracy depended upon an unequal balance of forces between capital and labour, it at least validated working-class organisations at an institutional level. Educational institutions were to play a key role in this process providing universal forms of education necessary for the maintenance of full employment.

However despite Tony Blair's (1994) claim that education was central to the New Labour project it is surprisingly marginal in much 'third way' thinking. Anthony Giddens (1998, 2003) argues over a number of high profile publications for the need for social democracy to reinvent itself in order to create the possibility for the twenty-first century becoming the progressive century. As a leading sociologist it is not surprising that Giddens locates the need for a rethinking of social democracy in the context of radical social change. 'Third way' politics not only seeks to break with old style statist social democracy and neoliberalism, but also offers a new politics of citizenship that presses 'no rights without responsibilities' (Giddens 1998: 65). By this Giddens is concerned that old style social democracy often stressed the unlimited expansion of rights in such a way that is not sustainable in a competitive and increasingly individualised world. The key question in the context of the decline of tradition and the rise of life-style politics becomes 'What are our duties in a fast moving and increasingly global world?' Giddens argues that in the modern world the central questions are no longer about social justice but how we should live in the context of the decline of tradition. These features, as many will be aware, refer back to Giddens's (1994) earlier work on the relative decline of emancipatory politics and the rise of a reflexive politics of lifestyle.

Despite the development of new political initiatives, risks and opportunities the nation state remains central to the 'third way'. However Giddens argues that we need to radically rethink the relationship between the state and civil society in order to help foster a deeper involvement in the political process by community and local initiatives. Whereas neoliberals wish to shrink the state, the 'third way' is all about a reconstructed national state. Here the state should engage in processes that seek what Giddens calls the 'democratizing of democracy' (Giddens 1998: 72). This involves constitutional reform, the expansion of the public sphere, the devolution of power, citizens' juries and more flexible decision structures. Yet when it comes to education the 'third way' offers only the most culturally impoverished agenda. Gone is the need to develop the critical sensibilities of democratic citizens and scepticism in respect of what markets can deliver. Instead the 'third way' becomes complicit with the New Right's attempt to rearticulate the politics of education around standardised tests, the expansion of 'choice', league tables and the needs of the labour market. Here Giddens (2003) argues for the expansion of 'quality' education for all without ever saying how this might be defined or in whose interests it is shaped.

Stuart Hall (2003) has demonstrated how 'third way' political parties like New Labour have consistently combined economic neoliberalism with more social democratic concerns. New Labour is best thought of as a hybrid regime that combines a dominant neo-liberal strand with a more subordinate social democratic strand. Viewing the 'third way' in these terms allows us to understand how New Labour has been able to balance modest forms of redistribution while progressively marketising and privatising the public sector. The role of the welfare state is no longer to support the least fortunate but to help individuals provide for themselves (where they can) and to target means tested aid for the rest. Neoliberalism is not simply about the 'external' operation of markets but is explicitly concerned to instill certain behavioral norms. Under neoliberalism it becomes the civic duty of citizens not to become overly reliant upon the state and to become self-reliant. In these terms Jürgen Habermas emphasises that the 'third way' seeks to foster a society of individualised risk takers who embark upon 'a kind of fitness training' seeking to foster 'positive' lifestyles and attitudes attuned to the demands of the global market place (Habermas 1999: 6). In this respect, we could argue more critically that the 'third way' cancels the historic project of democratic socialism to confront the generation of systematic inequalities and exclusions that are the outcome of the increasing dominance of global capitalism (Mouffe 2005). What is missing from the 'third way' in the context of the arguments I outlined earlier is how questions of social justice and an ethic of educational development can be pursued in a world that preserves genuinely public values. Before I seek to answer this question however I want to look at how the ideas and practices of neoliberalism can be said to be progressively reconstructing education.

Neoliberalism, New Labour and education

Here I seek to outline some of the broad ways in which neoliberalism is seeking to convert the education system into a competitive market. Implicit in new Labour and the 'third way' strategy in respect of education has been having the appropriate attitude. Poor educational performance can no longer rely upon the 'excuse' of wider patterns of social and cultural inequality, but such features are to be overcome by the upgrading of expectations (Power and Whitty 1999). The disciplinary mechanisms through which new Labour has sought to implement this change in behaviour, as is well known, has been through the development of targets and league tables that enable the performance of individual schools to be judged. Further ideas of market choice have lead to the rejection of 'one size fits all' comprehensive schools in favour of the increased development of 'specialist schools' or academies. Whereas comprehensives are viewed negatively as being rigidly egalitarian the development of 'specialist schools' or academies are valued through their ability to provide 'choice'.

The context of market and consumer driven choice has meant that schools are increasingly seeking to attract parents with children who are judged to be both 'able' and 'motivated'. Schools are able to enhance their position in the context of local competition by 'improving' the 'quality' of their intake. According to Michael Apple these features institute a crucial change in focus 'from student needs to student performance and from what the school does for the student to what the student does for the school' (Apple 2001: 413) The argument here is that enhanced forms of competition between educational establishments ends with an increased emphasis upon marketing and public relations and the exclusion of students who are either working-class or who are perceived to have 'special needs'. Indeed the expansion of choice (as is widely recognised in many public political debates on these questions) is most likely to favour the parents who have the cultural capital and flexible lifestyles that can locate the 'better' schools. Indeed such a situation could be said to reward both the entrepreneurial attitudes on the part of parents while encouraging enhanced forms of competition amongst children. The marketisation of education not only privileges higher status families who are best able to exercise 'choice' thereby encouraging a 'third way' style entrepreneurialism, but also enables the privileged to 'exit' comprehensive schools that are seen to be failing. This is evident in recent educational reforms suggested by the Labour government promoting consumer choice, the end of the 'bog standard' comprehensive, more specialist schools, the weakening of local education authorities and enhanced forms of selection. The most likely casualties of such changes, as many commentators have pointed out, are those deemed unfit to compete (Benn and Millar 2006; Tomlinson 2006).

If comprehensive forms of education ensure a reasonably educated labour force and egalitarian values, the marketisation of education is likely to result in enhanced forms of social inequality and deprivation. In such a situation it would seem that the most vulnerable and excluded children are the ones most likely to suffer. In particular as Richard Hoggart remarked we should 'feel more strongly about' the educational prospects of the underclass (Hoggart 2001b: 2). Poverty researcher Ruth Lister (2008) reports that in Britain the top 20% of earners have 44 per cent of the wealth with the bottom 20% having access to only 6%. It is in this context that New Labour adopted the language of 'opportunity Britain' as a means of responding to the knowledge revolution and 'positive' thinking about globalisation. As Lister points out, New Labour has focused almost exclusively upon the responsibility of the poor while failing to mention the unsustainability of many rich people's life styles and evidence of tax evasion. Further New Labour have consistently sought to deny the link between poverty, under-funded schools and poor educational attainment. In the poorest areas fewer than 1 in 4 British students achieve 5 good GCSE's; further, while 44% of the richest 20% go to university, only 10% of the poorest 20% make this journey. Polly Toynbee and David Walker (2008) make the case that despite some modest success New Labour has failed to make substantive inroads into the persistence of child poverty with 20% of children living in poverty. This means children growing up with no access to a home computer, holidays and birthday parties in a celebrity culture that increasingly celebrates wealth (Hoggart 2004). At the other end of the scale it has been estimated that tax avoidance costs Britain £25 billion annually with only £3.4 billion required to half child poverty by 2010 (Toynbee and Walker 2008: 16). If we add this to a context where the top rate of tax since 1979 has been progressively reduced from 83% to 40% and recent cuts in inheritance tax implemented, then it is not surprising that many are becoming increasingly concerned about the effects of class inequality.

If the provision of comprehensive education represented the ethic of solidarity this social contract has been progressively broken up where the needs of the poor are progressively ditched in the attempt to provide more 'choice'. If the poor and excluded are not to be converted into a new 'Other' then we need to quickly return to the democratic socialist ethics of solidarity with the least advantaged while recovering the educational ideal of self-development for all social classes. It is notable for example in recent class based talk about so called 'chavs' (basically middle-class forms of revulsion in respect of working-class 'bad taste') that the need to provide a counter-hegemonic alternative to neoliberalism is more pressing than ever. Beverley Skeggs (2004) similarly argues that dominant representations of working-class people within popular culture are of the 'Other' of middle-class values of good sense and respectability. In this context, many working-class people are seen as 'beyond' the reach of educational institutions and progressive initiatives. Yet with the coming to the end of the New Labour project there is an opportunity at the current juncture to rethink what a genuinely democratic education might become in a reformulated social democracy. If New Labour is dead in the water how might a new and more substantial project be reimagined in the context of the twenty-first century?

Education, respect and democracy

If the New Labour experiment in a market driven society is now coming to an end then something more substantial needs to take its place. As with the social democracy represented by Richard Hoggart such a project would only make sense if it were able to suggest a new way of linking questions of morality, culture and economics. If for Hoggart's generation there was a desire to link ideas of educated self-improvement, democratic participation and a social state this needs to be reimagined in the twenty-first century. As I have indicated ideas of the 'third way' had very little to contribute to our understanding of education which it saw in mostly instrumental terms while abandoning the social democratic project of fostering a more egalitarian and less market driven society. In this respect, what is actually required is less a critique of social democracy and more of a return to some of its more positive features. The 'third way' argument that social democracy was overly 'rights' based is difficult to square with its intellectual history. For instance, R. H. Tawney (1961) who is often thought to be a classic social democrat author argues that it is capitalist individualism that places emphasis on the right to ownership and consumption rather than duty to the community. Neal Lawson (2008), chair of the social democratic orientated pressure group Compass, has argued that if New Labour delivered the market state then a revitalised social democracy needs to develop a democratic state. If the idea of the Left is to survive the coming decades it needs to become a democratising Left. This would mean, as Lawson suggests, a radical curtailment of the power of the market in terms of people's everyday lives (this might include publicly owned railways, a ban on advertising to children, the democratisation of parliament and radical measures to reverse the rampant inequality of the New Labour years) but also surely the development of a genuinely democratic education system and pedagogic ethos. This is inevitably a tall task and yet if we are to build on Richard Hoggart's arguments for a dignified society for all of its citizens it is precisely these features that need to be developed. However the idea of a democratic society and state is unlikely to progress very far unless it able to decisively reject the dominance of neoliberalism.

In this context, we are currently witnessing the arrival of a new politics that Zygmunt Bauman calls 'mixophilia' to describe the reluctance of citizens to come together in urban places across class boundaries (Bauman 2007: 90). If the global elite are increasingly placeless as they move through rather than interact with localities then the poor have much thicker ties to the local. Concerns about personal safety and security become translated into adopting a lifestyle that keeps the poor at a distance. Urban politics on this reading is subject to a class-driven attempt to occupy spaces and places that seek to keep questions of difference at an arm's length. The fostering of communities of sameness is not simply a way of keeping out otherness but is also deeply undemocratic. As Bauman recognises, if citizens in their daily encounter with public spaces are not called upon to negotiate understandings and meanings they are likely to become frightened by that what they don't recognise (Bauman 2007: 88). The politics of fear in this setting both minimises the possibility of unexpected encounters and also closes the possibility of constructing hospitable public spaces where meanings and experiences require artful negotiation. In this respect, a democratic culture requires what Hoggart calls a common culture (Hoggart 1970b: 132). This is a culture that can ordinarily call into question divisions of status and class by promoting a debate and discussion based upon the idea of the equal worth of citizens. This is also a culture that provides a genuinely common ground offering space to 'minorities' thereby fostering a platform for a genuinely inclusive culture. A common culture is less a homogeneous culture but is produced through democratic institutions and practices seeking to debate shared questions and concerns. As Ruth Lister (2007) points out, if the inclusive potential of citizenship depends upon marginalised communities finding a multiplicity of voices in the policy process then the recent abandonment of the idea of multi-culturalism is a cause of considerable concern especially given some of the successes in these areas in respect of schooling. A radical and democratic Left then would not only need to defend the idea of public spaces against neoliberal attempts to foster a nation of competitive entrepreneurs but also give voice to the multicultural and diverse place that Britain has become. This does not mean (as many seem to think) abandoning the idea of a common culture but of it becoming more explicitly connected to a democratic ethos.

Our best guide in seeking to uphold the idea of a democratic culture remains the democratic socialist tradition to which Richard Hoggart is, of course, such an important part. Rather than retreating into a dogmatic Marxism or simply tinkering with the legacy of New Labour, it is this tradition that urgently needs to be rediscovered if the Left is to recover arguments for democratic citizenship. In doing this, the Left would need to recognise how entrenched class hierarchies are built on feelings of disrespect and hierarchy. Here we would need not only to address questions of wealth distribution but of cultural respect and recognition (Stevenson 2003). Richard Wilkinson (2006) argues that the levels of inequality promoted by neoliberal social policies undermine the common life of the community promoting increasingly individualistic forms of competition. Increasing competition for status, employment, houses and consumer goods promotes a stressful society where many people feel vulnerable to being considered inferior. If social integration is good for citizen's sense of well being then competitive individualistic market cultures promotes a sense of being a disrespected second-class citizenship. A sense of a lack of status leads not only to poor personal health but also to a general lack of self-worth and confidence more generally. Further class-divided societies also promote feelings of superiority and self-satisfied privilege amongst the better off. This was dramatised by the comments made by Chris Woodhead (former head of Ofsted, the body charged with inspecting schools) who argued that middle-class children simply have superior genes and it is this that determines their success (Curtis 2009). This argument is used to legitimise a return to grammar schools, selection and of course voucher systems. It is worth noting that when considering the failures of new Labour they have consistently used the language of equal opportunity for all in such a way that has held in check a return to the unashamed cultures of class privilege. This language has no room for Hoggart's social democratic acceptance that, of course, middle-class children begin their educational careers with a number of class specific advantages (Hoggart 1970b: 77). This would include not only an ability to pay for education equipment, space within the home but also a closer association with the dominant culture of learning and education. It is only a democratic education that can give all children an equal chance to develop themselves. However, we should note that the cultures of disrespect in terms of the working classes would be difficult to root out even by the most progressive and democratic of educators. As bell hooks (2000) reminds us, one of the strategies that poor have at their disposal for dealing with their sense of shame is by identifying with the celebrity endorsed culture of hyper-consumption.

Capitalistic cultures of greed and excess can only be countered by developing common cultures of democracy where what is important is not what you own but your ability to ask questions, live ethically and develop a sense of compassion for others. Democratic cultures are necessarily egalitarian cultures that promote a sense of equal worth and respect that can really only become lived once the excesses of free market capitalism have been curbed. There is, then, no simple 'return to' Hoggart given the need to recognise the multicultural plurality of modern citizens in a way that is absent from much of his writing. Here the emphasis of the 'third way' on questions of individualisation and the radical pluralisation of the public sphere remain important. However, Richard Hoggart remains a central figure in the attempt to reimagine democratic socialism given his emphasis upon questions of public service, responsibility and helping build a democratic culture of educated dialogue. As Richard Hoggart (1982) understood, a democratic educator (or simply a good teacher) would need to recognise the responsibility of the educator to develop the curiosity and autonomous development of the individual within a communal setting. It is precisely this ethos that recognises the virtues of developing inquiring minds that is less about the communication of doctrines, and more about the tolerance of dissent while developing the capacity to speak in your own voice that best communicates a democratic education. The socialist aspect of this tradition is to argue that such an education is not only for an elite but should be owned by the wider community.

Bibliography

Apple, M. (2001) 'Comparing Neo-liberal Projects and Inequality in Education', *Comparative Education*, 37 (4), pp. 409-423.

Bauman, Z. (2007) *Liquid Times* (Cambridge: Polity Press).

Benn, M. and Millar, F. (2006) *A Comprehensive Future: Quality and Education for all our Children* (London: Compass Pamphlet).

Blair, T. (1994) *The 'third way': New Politics for the New Century* (Fabian Society Pamphlet).

Couldry, N. (2004) 'In the Place of a Common Culture, What?', *The Review of Education, Pedagogy and Cultural* Studies, 26 (3), pp. 3-21.

Curtis, P. (2009) 'Don't say I was wrong', the *Education Guardian* newspaper, Tuesday 12.05.09.

Giddens, A. (1994) *Beyond Left and Right* (Cambridge, Polity Press).

————— (1998) *The 'third way': The Renewal of Social Democracy* (Cambridge, Polity Press).

————— (2003) 'Neoprogressivism. A New Agenda for Social Democracy', in Anthony Giddens (ed.) *The Progressive Manifesto* (Cambridge: Polity Press).

Giroux, H.A. (2004) The Terror of Neoliberalism (London: Paradigm Publishers).

Hall, S. (2003) 'New Labour's Double-Shuffle', *Soundings* 24, pp. 10-24.

Habermas, J. (1999) 'The European Nation-State and the Pressures of Globalization', *New Left Review* 235, pp. 1-12.

Hebdige, D. (1979) *Subculture: The Meaning of Style* (London: Methuen).

Hoggart, R. (1957) *The Uses of Literacy: Aspects of Working-Class Life* (London: Chatto and Windus).

————— (1970a) *Speaking to Each Other, Vol II: About Literature* (London: Chatto and Windus).

————— (1970b) *Speaking to Each Other, Vol I: About Society* (London: Chatto and Windus).

————— (1982) *An English Temper: Essays on Education, Culture and Communications* (London: Chatto and Windus).

————— (1995) *The Way We Live Now* (London: Pimlico).

————— (2001a) *Between Two Worlds* (London, Aurum Press).

————— (2001b) 'Adult Education: The legacy and the future', **www. gla.ac.uk/adulteducation/lastestnews/RichardHoggart.html**.

————— (2004) *Mass Media in a Mass Society* (London: Continuum).

hooks, b. (2000) *Where We Stand: Class Matters* (London: Routledge).

Jones, P. (1994) 'The Myth of "Raymond Hoggart": On "Founding Fathers" and Cultural Policy', *Cultural Studies*, 8 (3), pp. 394-416.

Lawson, N. (2008) 'The End of new Labour', *New Statesman*, 28 August 2008.

Moschonas, G. (2002) *In The Name of Social Democracy: The Great Transformation: 1945 to the Present* (London: Verso).

Mouffe, C. (2005) *On the Political* (London: Routledge).

Nussbaum, M. (1995) *Poetic Justice: The Literary Imagination and Public Life* (Boston: Beacon Press).

Power, S. and Whitty, G. (1999) 'New Labour's Educational Policy: First, Second or 'third way'?', *Journal of Educational Policy*, 14 (5), pp. 535-546.

Ryle, M. and Soper, K. (2002) *To Relish the Sublime? Culture and Self-Realization in Postmodern Times* (London: Verso).

Skeggs, B. (2004) *Class, Self and Culture* (London: Routledge).

Steedman, C. (1986) *Landscape for a Good Woman: A Story of Two Lives* (London: Virago).

Stevenson, N. (2003) *Cultural Citizenship: Cosmopolitan Questions* (Maidenshead: Open University Press).

Tawney, R. H. (1961) *The Acquisitive Society* (London: Fontana).

Tomlinson, S. (2006) *Education in a Post-Welfare Society* (Maidenshead: Open University Press).

Wilkinson, R. (2006) 'The Impact of Inequality', *Social Research*, 73 (2), pp. 711-732.

Williams, R. (1960) *Border County* (London: Chatto and Windus).

———— (1962) *Communications* (London: Penguin).

———— (1964) *Second Generation* (London: Chatto and Windus).

———— (1965) *The Long Revolution* (Harmondsworth: Penguin).

———— (1968) 'Culture and Revolution: A Comment' in Eagleton, T. and Wicker, B. (eds) *From Culture to Revolution* (London: Steed and Ward), pp. 22-34.

———— (1980) *Problems in Materialism and Culture* (London: Verso).

———— (1989) 'The Idea of a Common Culture', *Resources of Hope* (London: Verso).

RECOILING THE SPRINGS OF ACTION:
THE USES OF LITERACY AND HAMISH HENDERSON'S CONCEPTUALISATION OF SCOTTISH FOLK-SONG REVIVALISM
Corey Gibson

Richard Hoggart's *The Uses of Literacy* (1958) shares many of its most distinctive theoretical and methodological qualities with contemporary writings that sought to defend and promote the Scottish folk-song revival. Superficially, the critical agendas set out by these two sources appear to be unrelated: the former exploring the interplay of the effects of mass literacy and the development of a 'mass culture' in the North of England and the latter orchestrating and theorising a popular reinvestment in 'traditional' culture in Scotland. However, an exploration of the extent to which these discourses intersect, reveals deep running parallels that can contribute to our understanding of both Hoggart's text and the cultural-political programme of folk revivalism in Scotland. Hamish Henderson was one of the most visible champions of the folk-song revival and though he never produced a major critical or theoretical work, his writings — published in various journals, magazines and newspapers — have contributed to his reputation as the 'principal strategist' of this cultural movement (Henderson 2004: xi). As such, Henderson can be seen to conceive of folk-song in cultural-political terms that reflect the structures and processes of Hoggart's *The Uses of Literacy*. The parallels between these figures' works can be recognised in respect to their methodologies, in the terms of their understanding of 'cultures', and finally, in the dialectical tensions that their works represent. By studying the hitherto unrealised affinity between the project of folk revivalism in Scotland and *The Uses of Literacy*, we can hope to extend the revived critical investment in Hoggart's work represented by volumes like *Richard Hoggart and Cultural Studies* (2008), to include the study of contemporary cultural and political movements.

Between November 1959 and January 1960, and later throughout most of 1964, Henderson engaged in a series of public exchanges in the opinion columns of the *Scotsman* newspaper concerning folk-song revivalism in Scotland and its relationship with developments in the national literary culture. Henderson's main opponent in these debates was Hugh MacDiarmid, the celebrated Scottish poet and proponent of the Scottish

Literary Renaissance. These debates, or 'flytings',[1] took place in the context of the growing visibility of the folk revival movement.[2] With the establishment of folk-clubs across the country, the broadcast of commercial folk performances by the BBC, and the work of Henderson and others at the School of Scottish Studies at the University of Edinburgh, the redistribution and re-contextualisation of folk-song was an unavoidable cultural presence at the time of these public discussions. The disputes came out of a disagreement over the prescription of artistic value in contemporary Scottish literary culture. However, the seemingly irreconcilable cultural-politics of MacDiarmid and Henderson came to inform a dialogue that had implications reaching further than its apparent concern with the worthiness of folk-song's popularity.

During the 'flytings' of 1959, MacDiarmid described one of his opponent's contributions as a mere 'gamin's cry' (the inarticulate cry of the street urchin) (in Henderson 1996: 91). In his response to MacDiarmid's letter, Henderson condemned the 'razory epigrammatic derision' of common folk-culture that he felt was implicit in the term (Henderson 1996: 93). As an extension of this retort he then turned his attention to contemporary developments in cultural and political theory:

> Of late, a new school of Socialist thinking has grown up around *Universities and Left Review*, *The New Reasoner*, Hoggart's *The Uses of Literacy* and Raymond Williams's *Culture and Society*, a school which is not afraid of sociological revaluations, and goes out into the streets to hear not only the 'gamin cry', but the voice and song of the people ... It is strange to find the author of 'A Seamless Garment' and *Second Hymn to Lenin* officially enrolled not among the sponsors of *New Left Review* but among the British representatives of what is now, in the Western world, a withered and archaic political spent force.[3]

---

[1] 'Flyting' is a poetic genre - a formalised bardic contest, distinguished by its show of virtuoso versification and powerful invective. The most celebrated examples of 'flyting' date from sixteenth-century Scotland, and include *The Flyting of Dunbar and Kennedy* (c.1503) and *The Flyting of Montgomerie and Polwart* (c.1585).

[2] See Ailie Munro, (1996) Chapter III. 'The Story of the Revival: Developments in Scotland', *The Democratic Muse: Folk Music Revival in Scotland*. Aberdeen: Scottish Cultural Press. For a broader history see Michael Brocken, (2003). *The British Folk Revival: 1944-2002*. Hants: Ashgate.

[3] Henderson 1996: 93. 'A Seamless Garment' (1931) and *Second Hymn to Lenin* (1932) are among MacDiarmid's most explicitly political works, and both make close reference to the relevance of Marxist thought to 'the man in the street'. See MacDiarmid (1993: 311-314, 320-328).

The exchanges in this so-called 'flyting' are characterised by their rhetorical flair as part of a public performance. Nevertheless, it is significant that part of Henderson's strategy is to align himself with the publications of the early New Left and to condemn MacDiarmid, his opponent, to a seemingly ageing and immobile Marxist orthodoxy. This feeds into a broader effort on Henderson's part to portray MacDiarmid as 'the apostle of a kind of spiritual apartheid' manifest in the intellectual elitism and 'acrid anti-humanist flavour' of some of his writings (Henderson 1996: 131-132). By calling upon the thinkers of the New Left to proffer an alternative leftist perspective, Henderson infers democratic, humanist values that match his own and that alienate those of MacDiarmid.

For Henderson, the distinguishing virtue of the New Left, and, by implication, of Hoggart's *The Uses of Literacy*, was the effort 'to go out into the streets to hear the voice and song of the people' (Henderson 1996: 93). This statement speaks not only of the intended content of such studies, but of the methodological principles that informed their practice. This practice is manifest in *The Uses of Literacy* in its two-part structure with the contextual function of the first part of the book aiming to set the second, more analytical section, into a 'landscape of solid earth and rock and water' (Hoggart 1958: 324). As Stuart Hall has recognised, Hoggart attempted to provide a complex answer to the questions he had set himself, and this required an expansive conception of 'culture' as 'lived experience', whereby no individual cultural practice, such as reading romance novels or club-singing, can be understood in isolation, but only as part of the complex fabric of 'everyday life' (Hall 2007: 43; Hoggart 1958: 324). On this basis Hoggart 'tried to see beyond the habits to what the habits stand for ... to detect the differing pressures of emotion behind idiomatic phrases and ritualistic observances' (1958: 17).

Henderson sought to understand folk-song on similar terms, though his methodology was less self-consciously constructed. Indeed, for Henderson, it seems that the compulsion to set his folkloristic findings in their social-historical contexts was a wholly natural and necessary response to the character of folk-song itself. As part of a living-tradition, any given folk-song was bound inextricably to the lives of its carriers, 'living on the lips of the people' (Henderson 1955: 45). Henderson considered the role of the song-collector to be 'deeply humanistic' (1964: x), and recordings and transcriptions of his collection-tours are testament to this approach, as source-singers are routinely engaged not only on the subject of a particular song's social-historical lineage, but on the details of their lives and livelihoods. The lives of people, and of communities, form the landscape that is inhabited by the 'carrying stream' of folk-culture (Henderson 1958: 20). One of Henderson's early field-interviews, recorded for the School of Scottish Studies archives, offers a good example of this process. Through his exchanges with Jock Ainslie, a Stirlingshire Horseman, Henderson gently guides the conversation from the first hearing of a particular song, towards Ainslie's personal experiences as a ploughman in the Stirlingshire area; from impromptu ceilidhs and singing-sessions, to the demographic of the work-force on the farms, their relationship with the farmers who employed them, and the details of their living conditions (Henderson 1991: 51-58). In this way the narrative discourses of Henderson's study of folk-song and of oral history overlap to such an extent as to become part of the same process. 'Culture', for Henderson as for Hoggart, was to be analysed as 'lived experience'.[4] For both figures, resources like folk-song and trends in literary tastes have the potential to be elevated as vital expressions of a community's cultural, social and political identities.

In light of this common methodological principle, it can be seen that Henderson and Hoggart also employ comparable strategies in realising their cultural studies. For example, Hoggart's extensive use of working-class aphorisms in *The Uses of Literacy* is remarkably similar to Henderson's interpretative approach to folk-culture. For instance, Hoggart illustrates his assertions about working-class cynicism with regard to the dominance of the cash-nexus in society by citing commonly heard phrases such as 'they're all on the fiddle' and 'everybody's out for number one' (Hoggart 1958: 279). Similarly, Henderson substantiates his claim that source-singers are conscious of the heritage of their songs among countless 'singer ancestors' who reshaped and passed on the material by calling upon the type of typical remark made after a given interpretation of a song: 'It's a real pity ye couldna hae listened tae auld Andra' (Henderson 1995: 429). Furthermore, Henderson reads the folk songs themselves as indicative of a community's sense of its local history and therefore of its identity. He recognises for example that the popular old folk-song 'The Haughs of Crumdel' resulted in a general acceptance across the North of Scotland that the battle fought on the Haughs of Cromdale in the late seventeenth century was a famous victory for the clans; in fact the Highlanders were brutally defeated (Henderson 1956: 29). In respect to common aphorisms and folk-songs, Hoggart and Henderson ascribe depths of meaning that

---

[4] The methodological and theoretical implications of this view of culture as 'lived experience' was developed by Raymond Williams in *The Long Revolution* (1961) with regard to his concept of the *structure of feeling*. Richard Johnson later identified those methodological premises common among 'cultural Marxists' such as Hoggart, Williams and Thompson (1979a, 1979b), and it is in the context of this cultural turn that I compare Henderson's theory and practice with Hoggart's.

are not immediately obvious but, once elaborated, serve to support their respective conceptions of working-class culture and folk-culture.

Another important aspect of Hoggart's methodology is his recognition of the effects of his own agency on the landscape of working-class culture that he presents. Rather than excluding his personal experiences of working-class life as a potentially corrupting influence on a scholarly piece of work, Hoggart indulges in vivid impressions of the working-class community based on his own life. Perhaps most importantly, he acknowledges his dualistic perspective - of proximity to, and distance from, majority working-class attitudes (Hoggart 1958: 17). The autobiographical vein running through *The Uses of Literacy* is especially evident in the account of the '"Older" Order' of Hoggart's childhood, and in the figure of the uprooted 'scholarship boy' at the 'friction-point of two cultures' (Hoggart 1958: 292). Furthermore, Hoggart calls upon personal reminiscences to illustrate points about working-class attitudes, such as the single mother from his neighbourhood who worked as a prostitute, and the widow charwoman who refused to alter her lifestyle under the gaze of those who disapproved of it (Hoggart 1958: 97-98, 141-143). The open recognition of his own close connections to the subject of his study allowed him to weave his own memories and experiences into the discourse of *The Uses of Literacy*. Hoggart's style speaks of a perspective of participant observation, allowing him access to 'the differing pressures of emotion behind idiomatic phrases and ritualistic observances' (Hoggart 1958: 17).

Henderson also wrote extensively of his own personal and professional relationship with the subject of his studies. As with *The Uses of Literacy*, Henderson's writing is scattered with his own personal reminiscences, employed to add colour and depth to his arguments, and to substantiate his theses by way of illustrative examples. In various articles Henderson narrates his song-collecting efforts, or else develops an argument on some aspect of the nature of folk-song out of a chance encounter or conversation.[5] As a songwriter and poet, Henderson invested, in a creative capacity, in the processes that he studied. This has its equivalent in Hoggart's work also. There are passages in *The Uses of Literacy* where Hoggart replicates the traits and techniques of the sensationalist, mass-produced novel. By offering up his own examples of the 'modern popular publication' and later, of the 'gangster-novelette' (Hoggart 1958: 235, 266-267, 271), Hoggart presents us not only with a 'manner of writing' but, through his critical interpretation, he also reveals the world-view of these

---

[5] See 'Folk-singing in Auld Reekie' (1965: 5-15), 'The Underground of Song' (1963: 31-36), 'The Midnight Ceilidh in the Sun Lounge of the Angus' (date not specified: 95-96), and 'Folk-song from a Tile' (1961: 104-109) for examples.

texts, condemning their brashness and their moral simplicity (Hoggart 1958: 235). For both Henderson and Hoggart, this aspect of creative investment speaks of a close understanding of the mechanisms of the creative arts that they studied, and of a level of involvement that suggests a genuine, experiential absorption in those arts.

Shared methodological principles and practices cannot be isolated from the more theoretical parallels between Hoggart and Henderson. For both figures the symbiotic relationship of theory and practice determines that their cultural-political projects share more than the recognition of culture as 'lived experience' and the desire to involve themselves in the cultural processes they study. The precise nature of their common structural conceptions, however, needs careful qualification. In his writings on folk-song in modern Scotland,, Henderson warns against the incursions of 'Tin Pan Alley', of kitsch distortions of 'traditional' song, and of the commercialisation of popular folk music more generally.[6] However, these observations do not, in and of themselves, represent the same degree of sophistication that characterises Hoggart's exploration of the mass entertainments industry, its appeals, its processes and its consumption. The unifying principle of much of Henderson's writings is instead concerned with the vitality of the folk-song revival, as he sought to stimulate a more expansive definition of folk-song — in a Scottish context — as a politically liberating process of interpersonal transmission.[7] In this sense, Henderson actively promoted a cultural-political programme in his writings, one that was based in the folk revival, and aimed towards a new, 'genuine people's culture' (Henderson 1985: 1). Despite their ostensible differences, Hoggart's portrayal of working-class culture in *The Uses of Literacy*, and Henderson's explorations of folk-culture, rely on similar theoretical constructions.

One of Hoggart's most fundamental assertions in *The Uses of Literacy* is that the reason for the gradual nature of change in working-class culture

---

[6] Henderson's views on commercialisation and folk-culture are set out with uncompromising vigour in his article 'Enemies of Folk-song' originally published in the *Saltire Review* (1955: 45-50). Here he explains his understanding of the role of the 'mandarins of official taste' and the 'culture of the élite' in conspiring to 'purvey a diluted spirit [of folk-song] to the public' (45). In a later piece for the *Folk Scene* magazine in 1965, Henderson laments that 'the "cash-nexus" [had] begun to take the modern folk-song revival by the throat' (11) and shows his support for other folklorists' recognition of the 'fatty degeneration of the commercialised folk scene' (15) (1965: 10-15).

[7] The article 'Enemies of Folk-song' is again a useful document in tracing the over-arching cultural-political aims that Henderson worked towards. Also, see 'Freedom Becomes People' (1985).

is the interminable resilience and adaptability of that culture. This is reflected in Henderson's work on folk-culture. Henderson acknowledged the historical precedent of song collectors who perceived folk-song as an ill-fated mode bound to extinction in the face of modernising socio-political conditilons, that needed to be collected if only to be rescued as museum pieces (Henderson 1958: 19-20). Henderson rather envisaged folk-song as a 'a permanent aspect of human culture, which will go on persisting whatever social and technological changes take place, and will certainly adapt itself, as it has always done, to changing circumstances' (Henderson 1958: 19-20). The strength and flexibility of folk-song for Henderson was rooted in its oral transmission, which has been able to adapt to print culture, through broadsheets and chapbooks, and to mass communications like LP recordings, radio, and even (though he promotes this idea quite tentatively) television (Henderson 1958: 22). Indeed Hoggart also attributes the resilience of working-class culture, at least in part, to the residual strength of the 'oral tradition' (Hoggart 1958: 31). However, just as Hoggart went on to construct a notion of working-class culture whereby its strengths are also the basis of its vulnerability when faced with the spectre of a manipulative 'mass culture' (Hoggart 1958: 170), Henderson too conceded that folk-song, as a process, was susceptible to exploitation by outside influences seeking to commodify and emasculate the medium (Henderson 1955: 45).

Hoggart's assertions about the resilience of working-class culture are dependent to some extent on the constructions of 'otherness' that separate it from alternative prevalent 'cultures'. This aspect is detailed in Hoggart's exploration of the notion of "'Them" and "Us'" (Hoggart 1958: 72-101), which is developed to account for the 'group-sense' of the working classes, and their conceptualisation of 'Them', that is, the 'composite dramatic figure' that represents the world of the 'bosses' and 'public officials', and those that are generally not known by the working classes as individuals (Hoggart 1958: 72). Henderson conceives of folk-culture on similar terms - in respect of its separation from other 'cultures'. He referred to folk-culture as 'a kind of anti-culture', 'embodying ideas, predilections and values which are not those of learned culture' (Henderson 1963: 34). In this sense, folk-song is the domain of Hoggart's 'Us', in that it speaks with a collective and anonymous voice, and is therefore capable of the kind of sincerity that can, as Hoggart explains, never be attributed to the products of the mass culture industries, descending as they do, from the world of 'Them' (Hoggart 1958: 273-276). As Hoggart writes '... these attitudes [of cynicism and suspicion] are at present still employed mainly for contact with the world outside, with those who are not "Us'" (Hoggart 1958: 275). The products of mass culture are then subject to a healthy strain of cynicism and suspicion according to Hoggart, and are contrasted by the perceived directness and sincerity of the working classes (Hoggart 1958: 276-278, 106). The freedom afforded by the views of the working classes, has its equivalent in Henderson's work, as part of the viral appeal of the 'rebel underground' of folk-song having 'no use for the conventional hypocrisies and taboos of respectable society … it handles the joys, miseries, and above all the comedy of sex with medieval directness' (Henderson 1963: 35). This freedom from hypocrisy in regard to sex, is also something Hoggart attributes to the working classes in light of their regard for the qualities of directness and honesty (Hoggart 1958: 91, 97-101).

These constructions, of 'Them' and 'Us', and of 'culture' and the 'anti-culture' of folk-song, offer an example of the structural affinity between Hoggart's and Henderson's respective conceptions of working-class culture, and folk-culture. However, Henderson's and Hoggart's cultural politics seem to engage most directly in terms of the common dialectical tensions that characterise their discourses. To explain this shared element, it is first necessary to elaborate briefly on the major formative theoretical influences on Henderson's thought. Hugh MacDiarmid and Antonio Gramsci represent two of the most pervasive influences on Henderson's various writings; his relationship with their world-views instilled significant tensions in his understanding of folk-culture and its political potential. Henderson spent the years following his demobilisation after the war translating Gramsci's *Prison Letters*, and, though his familiarity with the Italian philosopher's work gave his fledgling conceptions of folk-culture and its political potentialities a great resolve and confidence, it also fostered an important dilemma that was later to characterise his writing on the subject.[8] Henderson found in Gramsci a paradoxical vision of folk-culture. He wrote that 'on the one hand he [Gramsci] elevates folklore to the status of a world-view which demands serious study, and on the other hand he defines it as an incoherent heap of detritus which must be swept away by the class-conscious broom of a future working-class hegemonic culture' (Henderson 1988: 353). It is essentially this same opposition that is explored in Henderson and MacDiarmid's public debates. Where Henderson seeks to 'elevate' the world-view of folk-song, MacDiarmid dismisses it in favour of a more radically politicised, and less populist, literary art form. The central issues in the 'flytings', when disentangled from the polemics of the debates, are: firstly, the problem of the prescription of literary 'value' and the role of the 'popular' in determining

---

[8] Although Henderson translated Gramsci's prison letters between 1949 and 1951, they were not published in full until 1974 when the *New Edinburgh Review* produced three special issues on Gramsci.

this value; secondly, the disputed dichotomy of the 'high' and 'low' arts; and finally the contestation of the guiding principles of the 'individual' and the 'communal' in the pursuit of a politically progressive literature.[9] These issues can be traced in Henderson's later writings as he consistently anticipated the kinds of attacks that MacDiarmid made real in the *Scotsman* debates. Henderson (e.g.1994a: 381-404; 1994b: 405-426; 1995: 427-435) returned again and again to the 'flytings' in his later writings, redressing the debates and fine-tuning his arguments after the event.

Gramsci's seemingly contradictory views on folk-culture, and the dialogical opposition of Henderson and MacDiarmid in their disputes, are both representative of a forum of debate on the nature of popular culture that is also embodied by Hoggart's *The Uses of Literacy*. The process can be understood as dialectic in the sense that it is an investigation of truth through discursive practice. In Hoggart's work the characteristics of the 'older order' of working-class culture engage with those of the new 'mass culture' in this dialectical process, whereby each absorbs and responds to the claims of the other. In this way, working-class culture is explored through the dialogue of contending forces that are, regardless of their ostensible opposition, in fact co-dependant in the context of Hoggart's thesis. The respective halves of Hoggart's text present us, in effect, with the two sides of this dialectical narrative: 'An "Older" Order' and 'Yielding Place to New' offer an account which is artificially divided into the two parts of the text, yet as the study shows, each bleeds endlessly into the other. Although the thesis is clearly set in a particular temporal and geographical setting, it clearly represents a process that is, in its essence, supposed to be more broadly apparent. Commentators have recognised the 'unresolved tension' of the two kinds of writing embodied by the respective halves of the study, and the tension has furthermore been formulated in terms of the relationship between the 'literary' character of the first part, and the 'literary-critical' nature of the second (Hall: 40; Owen: 87).

The critical analysis typical of the second part of *The Uses of Literacy*, and its treatment of the threat of cultural classlessness, evokes many of the same arguments purported by MacDiarmid in his public clashes with Henderson. MacDiarmid, inhabiting the role of the intellectual and cultural elitist that he had created for himself in the debates, called out: 'the philistinism I oppose is that which attacks literature and the arts for not appealing to the big public, but does not expect science to do anything

---

[9] The 'flytings', including not only Henderson's contributions, but also those of his allies and opponents, are published in *The Armstrong Nose: Selected letters of Hamish Henderson* (1996: 79-100, 117-141).

of the sort' (MacDiarmid in Henderson 1996: 94). In another contribution he asserted that 'those who insist that the level of utterance should be that of popular understanding are part of a parasitical "interpreting class"… who are the enemies of the people, because what their attitude amounts to is "keeping the people in their place", stereotyping their stupidity' (MacDiarmid in Henderson 1996: 127). The sentiment behind these passages lies very much in line with Hoggart's exploration of the implications of mass culture:

> … the new manners include a variety of 'democratic' tones of voice and are decided by the urge for gaiety and slickness at all costs; the main assumptions are over-weening egalitarianism, freedom, tolerance, progress, hedonism, and the cult of youth. Liberty equals license to provide what will best increase sales; tolerance is equated with the lack of any standards other than those which are so trite and vague as to be almost wholly incantatory and of little practical use; any defence of any value is an instance of authoritarianism and hypocrisy… (Hoggart 1958: 241)

These are the forces behind what Hoggart calls the 'noiseless unbending of the springs of action' (Hoggart 1958: 196). The comparison with MacDiarmid's attacks on the folk revival dwell in Hoggart's claims that the development of these ideas creates an environment where freedom becomes 'freedom not to "be" anything at all' (Hoggart 1958: 177); where there is a pervasive 'refusal to admit that anyone can be judged for anything' (Hoggart 1958: 177); where 'egalitarianism' becomes 'a refusal to recognise any sort of differentiation' (Hoggart 1958: 180); where an 'embattled lowbrow tone' cultivates a widespread inverted snobbery (Hoggart 1958: 184); and where 'indifferentism' renders everything meaningless (Hoggart 1958: 194). These 'dangerous comforts of unreason' (Hoggart 1958: 187) are, for MacDiarmid, extended to the realm of the folk-song revival as a 'regression to simple outpourings of illiterates and backward peasants' and indicative of a dangerous 'indifference to the peaks of human achievement' (MacDiarmid in Henderson 1996: 127). In this sense both Hoggart and MacDiarmid rally against popularising values that they conceive to be erosive of the capacity for critical or creative thought, values that, for Hoggart, mean that 'good writing cannot be popular today, and popular writing cannot genuinely explore experience' (Hoggart 1958: 180-181), and that for MacDiarmid, threaten to 'reduce all arts to the level of mere entertainment' (MacDiarmid in Henderson 1996: 100).

While Hoggart and MacDiarmid lament the spread of popular, self-confident philistinism, Henderson, in his formulation of folk-song revivalism, sought out a unifying cultural project to overcome these problems. At one point in their public debates, Henderson calls upon a line from MacDiarmid's own poetry: 'our concern is with human wholeness'.[10] He then insists that 'the communally shared and developed folk-arts' could be a valuable aspect of this 'wholeness' (Henderson 1996: 132). This drive for 'human wholeness', shared by Henderson and MacDiarmid, though interpreted in different ways, is also apparent in Hoggart's text. While Hoggart's thesis diagnoses the 'enjoyment of "fragmentation"' which is part of the malaise of working-class cultural tastes (Hoggart 1958: 202), it also counterpoints this perceived degeneration with the shared group experience of 'deep emotions about personal experiences' as manifest in popular song, and group singing (Hoggart 1958: 154-156). In this sense Hoggart's work holds within it the strains and tensions of Henderson's folk revival project, complete with a tentative optimism with which to address MacDiarmid's criticisms.

There are more obvious parallels between Hoggart's *Uses of Literacy*, and the broader discourses of the Scottish folk-song revival, to which I have not referred. Indeed, some of Hoggart's passages on club-singing and commercial popular songs show a nuanced understanding of the societal and cultural role of song that would fit comfortably in Henderson's conceptualisation of folk-song. For example, Hoggart recognises the need for a song to 'meet certain general requirements of melody and sentiment' and to express something of the 'feeling heart' (Hoggart 1958: 159,166) before gaining entry to the repertoire of the working classes. This echoes Henderson's insistence that the 'only test worth a docken' in judging whether a song constitutes a 'folk-song' is that 'the people have taken it, possessed themselves of it, gloried in it, recreated it, loved it' (Henderson 1955: 50).

Nevertheless, it is in regard to methodological strategy and the dialectical discourses of popular and working-class culture, rather than in their ideas of 'song' that Hoggart's thesis and Henderson's ideas of folk-culture can be seen to engage most directly. In the concluding pages of *The Uses of Literacy*, Hoggart writes that, 'it is easier for a few to improve the material conditions of many than for a few to waken a great many from the hypnosis of immature emotional satisfactions' (Hoggart 1958: 323). Hoggart emphasised the fact that the problem with mass culture was not that it was not 'highbrow' but that it was not 'truly concrete and personal' (Hoggart 1958: 339). In doing so he mediated between the aspects that brought about tensions in Henderson's cultural-political project. The programme for a genuine popular culture had to negotiate with the

---

[10] This line is adapted from MacDiarmid's 'Third Hymn to Lenin' (1993: 900), the original line reads: 'Our concern is human wholeness'.

demands of intellectual elitism of the type MacDiarmid represented in the public debates, whilst also avoiding the debased populism, and the debilitating effect, of commercial mass culture. Henderson envisaged a revived folk-culture, as part of the solution to the cultural malaise that Hoggart presents in *The Uses of Literacy*. This folk-culture was to be inclusive and communal in character, flexible and absorbent in its approach to the changes of modern society, and most importantly, open to an alliance with the literary and political vanguard of contemporary Scotland. In conclusion, Henderson's conception of folk-song revivalism is, in its intentions, akin to Hoggart's desire for a popular art that might make its audience or readership more likely to 'arrive at a wisdom derived from an inner, felt discrimination in their sense of people and their attitude to experience' (Hoggart 1958: 339). In short, Henderson sought to recoil the springs of action that had been so quietly bent out of shape by the surreptitious incursions of 'mass culture'.

Bibliography

Brocken, M. (2003) *The British Folk Revival: 1944-2002* (Hants: Ashgate).

Fleming, M. (1967) 'Seumas Mór'.*Chapbook*, 3 (6).

Gramsci, A. (1996) *Prison Letters* (translated and introduced by Hamish Henderson) (London: Pluto Press).

Hall, S. (2007) 'Richard Hoggart, *The Uses of Literacy* and the Cultural Turn', *International Journal of Cultural Studies*, 10(1), pp. 39-49.

Henderson, H. (1955) 'Enemies of Folk-song', reproduced in (2004) *Alias MacAlias: Writings on Songs, Folk and Literature*, 2nd ed. (Edinburgh: Polygon), pp. 45-50.

——— (1956) 'Come Gie's a Sang', reproduced in (2004) *Alias MacAlias: Writings on Songs, Folk and Literature*, 2nd ed. (Edinburgh: Polygon), pp. 28-30.

——— (1958) 'Rock and Reel', reproduced in (2004) *Alias MacAlias: Writings on Songs, Folk and Literature*, 2nd ed. (Edinburgh: Polygon), pp. 19-22.

——— (1961) 'Folk-song from a Tile', reproduced in (2004) *Alias MacAlias: Writings on Songs, Folk and Literature*, 2nd ed. (Edinburgh: Polygon), pp. 104-109.

——— (1963) 'The Underground of Song', reproduced in (2004) *Alias MacAlias: Writings on Songs, Folk and Literature*, 2nd ed. (Edinburgh: Polygon), pp. 31-36.

——— (1964) Preface. Goldstein, K. S. *A Guide for Field Workers in Folklore* (London: Herbert Jenkins).

——— (1965) 'Folk-singing in Auld Reekie', reproduced in (2004) *Alias MacAlias: Writings on Songs, Folk and Literature*, 2nd ed. (Edinburgh: Polygon), pp. 5-15.

————— (1985) 'Freedom Becomes People' (1968). *Chapman 42*, 8 (5), 1.

————— (1988) 'Introduction to *Prison Letters* of Antonio Gramsci (translated by Hamish Henderson)', reproduced in (2004) *Alias MacAlias: Writings on Songs, Folk and Literature*, 2nd ed. (Edinburgh: Polygon), pp. 345-364.

————— (1991) 'Jock Ainslie: A Stirlingshire Horseman' (recorded in 1957), *Tocher: Tales, Songs, Tradition*, 43, pp. 51-58.

————— (1994a) 'Tangling with the Langholm Byspale', reproduced in (2004) *Alias MacAlias: Writings on Songs, Folk and Literature*, 2nd ed. (Edinburgh: Polygon), pp. 381-404.

————— (1994b) 'Flytings Galore: MacDiarmid v. The Folkies', reproduced in (2004) *Alias MacAlias: Writings on Songs, Folk and Literature*, 2nd ed. (Edinburgh: Polygon), pp. 405-426.

————— (1995) 'Zeus as Curly Snake: The Chthonian Image', reproduced in (2004) *Alias MacAlias: Writings on Songs, Folk and Literature*, 2nd ed. edition (Edinburgh: Polygon), pp. 427-435.

————— (1996) *The Armstrong Nose: Selected letters of Hamish Henderson* (Edinburgh: Polygon).

————— (2004) *Alias MacAlias: Writing on Songs, Folk and Literature*, 2nd edition (Edinburgh: Polygon).

————— (date not specified). 'The Midnight Ceilidh in the Sun Lounge of the Angus', reproduced in (2004) *Alias MacAlias: Writings on Songs, Folk and Literature*, 2nd ed. (Edinburgh: Polygon), pp. 95-96.

Hoggart, R. (1958) *The Uses of Literacy* (Harmondsworth: Penguin).

Johnson, R. (1979a) 'Culture and the Historians', *Working Class Culture: Studies in History and Theory* (London: Hutchinson), pp. 41-71.

Johnson, R. (1979b) 'Three Problematics: Elements of a Theory of Working-Class Culture', *Working Class Culture: Studies in History and Theory* (London: Hutchinson), pp. 201-237.

Lloyd, A. L. (1967) *Folk Song in England* (London: Workers' Music Association).

MacDiarmid, H. (1993-1994) *Complete Poems*. 2 Vols. (Manchester: Carcanet).

Munro, A. (1996) *The Democratic Muse: Folk Music Revival in Scotland*, 2nd ed. Aberdeen: Scottish Cultural Press).

Owen, S. (2007) 'Richard Hoggart as Literary Critic', *International Journal of Cultural Studies*, 10 (1), pp. 85-94.

————— (ed.) (2008) *Richard Hoggart and Cultural Studies* (Basingstoke: Palgrave Macmillan).

Williams, R. (1961) *The Long Revolution* (London: Chatto and Windus).

JOHN, PAUL, GEORGE AND RICHARD: THE BEATLES' USES OF LITERACY

James McGrath

Richard Hoggart's most substantial comments on The Beatles occur when his 1971 Reith Lectures address cultural relativism:

'The Beatles are as good as Beethoven' is the quickest shorthand for that attitude. It would be daft to beat The Beatles about the head because they are not Beethoven. In a way which did not seem possible ten or twelve years ago, they caught some aspects of the culture of young people; they are far ahead of the popular songwriters who came before them. (Hoggart 1972: 83)

Hoggart's mention of 'a way which did not seem possible ten or twelve years ago' loosely suggests how The Beatles demonstrated possibilities within commercial popular music unforeseen in his seminal study *The Uses of Literacy* (1957). Hoggart's *The Way We Live Now* (1995), reiterating many of the 1957 book's concerns, lists song lyrics which he takes to be of the highest calibre (Hoggart 1995: 112). Only two post-date *The Uses of Literacy*: The Beatles' 'Eleanor Rigby' (1966) and 'Hey Jude' (1968). Nonetheless, The Beatles do not escape Hoggart's cautionary 1971 distinction:

To claim that 'they're both authentic' may say something about The Beatles and Beethoven, but is not the last word. To imply from it that the two are, in all important senses, as good as each other is to give up thinking. (Hoggart 1972: 83-4)

I argue that to consider The Beatles' contribution to twentieth-century culture in Britain especially, it is most insightful to compare their work not with that of Beethoven — nor that of W. H. Auden, subject of Hoggart's first monograph (1951) — but with *The Uses of Literacy*. My contention is that for understanding The Beatles' social roots in relation to their work as a group and as solo artists, *The Uses of Literacy* is more valuable than most studies nominally concerning the band. Although Hoggart (1971) refers to The Beatles in terms of 'the culture of young people', this essay concentrates on a dimension of their career unacknowledged by Hoggart: its relationship to *working-class* culture.

Although much can be said of Beatles drummer Ringo Starr's work and persona in relation to working-class culture, I focus here on songwriting, thus prioritising the legacy of John Lennon (1940-80), Paul McCartney

(1942-) and George Harrison (1943-2001), identifying key phases in the work of each. In doing so, I seek to demonstrate how — despite Hoggart's ambivalence to 'theory' (Hoggart 1995: 173) — his 1957 terms and arguments, if read critically, can be constructively employed as theory to illuminate texts, including aspects of working-class life itself. Here, I explore Hoggart's discussions of 'uprooting', 'personalisation', working class 'baroque' and 'primary religion'. The chapter concludes that correspondences and occasional contradictions between The Beatles' career and Hoggart's commentaries on working-class culture are mutually insightful, revealing under-explored facets of the legacies of Hoggart and The Beatles.

The Uses of Literacy is invaluable when studying post-war authors of broadly working-class origin whose work recreates such environs. Most obviously useful are Hoggart's reflections on attitudes and routines integral to working-class life as he experienced it. Equally incisive however is his discussion of 'uprooting' (Hoggart 1957: 262-87), affecting those who no longer belong to 'Us' (the working-classes) yet remain uneasily self-conscious of their roots in the social milieu of 'Them' (those wielding power over 'Us'). Hoggart refers predominantly to changes affecting the individual working-class 'scholarship boy'. The 1944 Butler Act enabled children from less privileged families to attend grammar-schools. Hoggart was writing as the first generation of such individuals entered adulthood. Before relating this to The Beatles, it is worth noting the transferability of Hoggart's notion of uprooting in terms of being levered out of the working-classes but without assuredly belonging to the middle classes: '[in] one sense, it is true, no one is ever "declassed"; and it is interesting to see how this occasionally obtrudes' (Hoggart 1957: 264).

Hoggart's model of uprooting parallels his emphasis on the imaginative if not the political grip of working-class roots upon those who become socially distanced from this group. The most dramatic instance of uprooting in The Beatles' biography is their 1963 move from Liverpool to London. By 1965, they were millionaires and awarded MBEs. Yet The Beatles' 1962-70 recording career marks a trajectory in which working-class culture as outlined by Hoggart becomes *increasingly* prominent in their work. The final track on The Beatles' last album *Let It Be* (1970) implores: 'Get back to where you once belonged'. Alongside preoccupation with return is the suggestion of its impossibility: you 'once' belonged. Before considering notions of class within The Beatles' work, it is instructive to consider how, in Hoggart's original sense, uprooting was implicit in their origins.

Terry Eagleton emphasises two ways in which The Beatles indicate a cultural shift in English popular music. Firstly, their performing of their own compositions; secondly, the grammar-school backgrounds of

Lennon, McCartney and Harrison. Eagleton notes how in Beatles songs, relationships 'never exist at an intense level' and concludes that this apparent slackening of tension in popular music marks a 'movement away from the disturbed secondary modern world' (Eagleton 1964: 176-8). Yet Lennon, McCartney and Harrison's pursuit of popular music — for almost five years between sitting O-levels and acquiring a recording contract (1962) — *rejected* typical grammar-school ideals. Precipitating the 1944 Act, the Board of Education reported that grammar-school normally produced individuals who entered 'learned professions' or 'higher administrative posts' (1943: 2). Lennon's 1956 fifth-form report warned: 'He has too many of the wrong ambitions' (Henke 2003: 8). He had started a band, the Quarrymen. By the time they became The Beatles (1960), the group had five O-levels and one A-level between them, all belonging to McCartney. He comments: 'I nearly did very well at grammar-school' but 'Elvis started to pull me away from the academic path' (Miles 1997: 19). As I have discussed elsewhere (McGrath 2008: 116-21), Lennon and McCartney's family backgrounds were far from unambiguously working-class. Yet unlike these and indeed unlike their grammar-school education, their careers in popular music — a form traditionally associated with the working-classes, not least by Hoggart — represented a *choice*.

Although Hoggart's commentary on uprooting foregrounds the plight of the individual, *The Uses of Literacy* also addresses broader implications for the working-classes. Hoggart's sixth chapter, concerning mass art's effects on the working classes, is titled 'Unbending the springs of action'. The tenth, 'Unbent springs: A note on the uprooted and the anxious', implies neutralisation of the potential radicalism of working-class individuals uprooted via grammar-school. Hoggart suggests that the selection process is:

> likely to cause the working-classes now to lose many of the critical tentacles which they would have retained years ago [...] at a time when many who seek the money and favour of working-people approach them constantly along the lines to which they are most receptive. (Hoggart 1957: 306)

The uprooted are effectively caught between serving 'Us' and serving 'Them'. The Beatles' work demonstrates this dilemma. Closer to the culture of 'Us', popular music was a form which sought 'the money and favour of working-people'. It is useful here to compare Hoggart's somewhat disparate 1957 distinctions between older 'working-class' art and newer 'mass art'. Working-class art was produced by a greater number of publishers but for smaller, specifically working-class audiences.

Centralised mass art is produced by fewer but larger magnates for wider consumption. Although the target 'mass' audience exceeds the working-classes, producers of mass art must have the working-class majority as its target, to achieve maximum sales. Hoggart foresees two consequences. Firstly, the working classes are deprived of art closely relating to their lives. Secondly, mass art spreads cultural subordination beyond the working classes. Thus, 'the great majority of us are being merged into one class', defined by passivity (Hoggart 1957: 310).

Hoggart's 1957 critique of 'commercial', mass-produced popular music indicates how The Beatles' lyrics approach a predominantly working-class audience along 'lines to which they are most receptive'. His discussion of 'personalisation' typifies his valuable yet incompletely defined provision of critical terms in *The Uses of Literacy*. It therefore exemplifies the potential of such terms to be adopted, adapted and applied as micro-theoretical models decades later, to texts which his commentary predated.

In evaluating personalisation in mass media, it is useful to differentiate two approaches in which Hoggart critiques personalisation: *narrative* and *thematic* personalisation (my terms). Most directly — leading to its greater acknowledgement elsewhere — Hoggart scrutinises narrative personalisation in publications which, though produced for a mass audience, appeal to 'you' (Hoggart 1957: 171-6).[1] Thematic personalisation, meanwhile, implies social proximity between author and reader, as evident in what Hoggart calls the corollary of personalisation, simplification: '[t]he reader must feel intimately at one with the dream that is being presented' (Hoggart 1957: 176). Thematic personalisation foregrounds — at the expense of wider socio-political considerations — what Hoggart constructs as core, 'personal' working-class values: home, love and friendship (Hoggart 1957: 22). He examines these themes in older working-class songs (communally sung in working-men's clubs) before criticising how such concerns are trivialised in newer commercial songs, consumed less by the group in the club than the individual at home, via radio (Hoggart 1957: 129-44; 197-206). The result of personalisation for a mass audience, Hoggart conjectures, is 'subjection'; pressure 'not to look outwards and upwards' (Hoggart 1957: 217). Both forms of personalisation mark The Beatles' 1962-4 recordings.

Of narrative personalisation in commercial songs, Hoggart comments: '[t]he singer is reaching millions but pretends that he is reaching only "you"' (Hoggart 1957: 202). The Beatles' first six singles included 'Love Me Do', 'She Loves You' and most tellingly, 'From Me To You'.

---

[1] Cited in, for example, Marcuse's *One-Dimensional Man* (1964: 95).

McCartney comments that he and Lennon wrote 'for our market', phrasing lyrics as if addressing 'you', the individual fan: 'Personal pronouns, we always used to do that [...] always something personal' (quoted in Lewisohn 1988: 9). 'Love' in The Beatles' lyrics exemplifies thematic personalisation. Complicit with his contention that the working classes most value the personal, Hoggart discusses how in older songs, love is elevated as 'compensation' for lack of worldly goods; love is 'better than money' (Hoggart 1957: 140). The Beatles' 'Can't Buy Me Love' (March 1964) esteems love as priceless and money, without value. The timing is significant. They recorded the song on 29 January 1964. Over the previous year, The Beatles dominated British record sales; days earlier, they topped the US charts. As their fame and wealth increased, 'Can't buy me love' intimated that The Beatles still belonged to 'Us'. Personalisation denies The Beatles' uprooting as wrought by commercial success. The Beatles' early singles demonstrate Hoggart's accuracy in identifying, half a decade earlier, the emergence of personalisation as a defining lyrical characteristic. Yet while these songs were fundamental to the band's initial success across English-speaking nations, Beatles lyrics — owing first to Lennon — soon grew more complex.

Although Hoggart can highlight how The Beatles relied on standard traits of mass art, the group's fuller career renders questionable his main generalisation between 'serious' and 'popular' writers. Discussing fiction, Hoggart asserts that popular writers' work does not progress through 'phases' — which 'in a serious writer mark developments in his experience and consequent changes in his manner of expression' (Hoggart 1957: 184). Hoggart's original manuscript — more pointedly titled *The Abuse of Literacy* — conjectures the equivalent in popular music:

> Vera Lynn has a shrewd idea of the elements she must stress to acquire her characteristic effect [...] These are what her listeners want, so that the songs shall call up their special kind of dream world. (Hoggart 2001: 7-4; cf 1957: 185)

Thus, Hoggart stresses the necessity of familiarity in popular music. However, though narrative and thematic personalisation would remain integral to The Beatles' work, both approaches develop in ways which, in retrospect, mark phases in their work. A pivotal song is Lennon's 'A Hard Day's Night' (July 1964). No longer offering a personalised approach to the listener, this, complicit with Lennon's 1964 lifestyle, casts the other as a spouse.

While 'A Hard Day's Night' recalls Hoggart's identification of older song traditions in celebrating home and love, these conflict with awareness of an aspect of working-class life conspicuously under-represented by Hoggart: labour. The song indicates how working-conditions dominate home-life; awareness of work persists ('I should be sleeping like a log'; 'I work all day/ To get you money'). Marking a maturation in The Beatles' lyrical style, this song opposes Hoggart's earlier summary that working-class songs elevate home and love while insisting 'that money does not matter' (Hoggart 1957: 67). Nonetheless, a decisive pattern of thematic personalisation in The Beatles' work emerges. Though home and work are invoked, the singer's wealth is obscured. Despite The Beatles' uprooting, it is their relatively ordinary lifestyles as left behind in Liverpool that their work usually suggests.

While it remains important to relate Hoggart's 1957 depiction of the working-classes to his *concern* for this group, his portrayal of the majority as passively apolitical is problematic for Marxist critics such as Colin Sparks (1974). Although Hoggart explains that he focuses on 'the majority who take their lives as they find them' because they are the target of his nemeses, mass publicists (Hoggart 1957: 11-12), Sparks attacks Hoggart's inattention to labouring conditions and especially to Trade Unions, which relied on the supposedly apolitical working-classes for support. Furthermore, although Hoggart's concern is the working-classes' *cultural* rather than economic subordination, in addressing this, *The Uses of Literacy* also depicts the working classes as resilient but ultimately passive. Yet the content and popularity of The Beatles' 1965-7 work necessitates — and rewards — reconsideration of Hoggart's conjectures regarding popular musicians' reliance on familiar, 'characteristic' effects, and of what a mass audience 'wants' in relation to this.

Particularly valuable here is Hoggart's critique of working-class 'baroque', a term he uses 'without necessarily implying an historical link' (Hoggart 1957: 123). Hoggart's outline of working-class baroque suggests how this group defines its own traditions amidst subordination. 'Baroque' is Hoggart's adjective for the expression of an attitude which the working classes bring to all that marks a break from regulated routine. Working-class baroque is an 'allegorical and brief statement of a better, a fuller life' (Hoggart 1957: 128). What Hoggart's commentary implies without significantly addressing is mass openness to otherness.

Amidst the increasing prominence of working-class signifiers through The Beatles' career, working-class baroque is pivotal. This constitutes an uprooting of a working-class cultural language, presenting it to a mass audience beyond the working classes. Yet the tradition as evident in The Beatles' work is crucial to the expansion of cultural and indeed spiritual literacy that the group offered to an audience which must have the working-classes as its core target. In The Beatles' 1965-7 output, baroque traditions affirm the band's working-class roots in various ways. A tradition of interest in the world beyond the known and immediate, working-class baroque 'loves the East', imagined as 'exotic and elaborate' (Hoggart 1957: 123). Summarising this, Hoggart effectively suggests working-class variants of Orientalism — a cultural tradition which Said's influential 1978 study discusses predominantly in upper- and middle-class Western imaginings of the East.[2]

By 1966, Indian musical traditions were informing The Beatles' work. In this, they were led by Harrison who that year began studying Vedic culture as part of his formal sitar instruction from Ravi Shankar. However, in the first Beatles recording to feature Harrison's sitar-playing, one year earlier — Lennon and McCartney's joint-composition 'Norwegian Wood (This Bird Has Flown)' (*Rubber Soul*, 1965) — the Indian instrument is less a signifier of 'the East' than of working-class baroque itself. Alongside this, the sitar flatters a narrative of uprooting. Uniquely — and contrasting especially with 'home' in 'A Hard Day's Night' — this Beatles song suggests the affluent environs into which they had entered.

'Norwegian Wood' narrates the singer's night with an enigmatically sophisticated girl at her home. Details convey that he does not belong here. Quoting the lines 'Isn't it good/ Norwegian wood', two social histories cite the lyric to illustrate English class division. Bicât contrasts its 'poor boy' and 'sophisticated career girl' (Bicât 1970: 330). Rose summarises the authors as 'working-class poets', uneasy in bohemia (Rose 2001: 459). Yet these readings ignore the musical arrangement. Instructed by Lennon, Harrison paralleled the former's guitar refrain for 'Norwegian Wood' on the sitar — an instrument seldom heard before in Western popular music. However, as Mellers notes, the sitar is used here merely as 'an exotic guitar' (Mellers 1973: 59). Working-class baroque embraces 'splendour which may be Eastern or European, but is never shy' (Hoggart 1957: 123). In The Beatles' 1965 song, the Indian instrument and 'Norwegian' wood invoke less the East or Europe than an England divided by class and consequently, culture.

The second verse's Kerouac-like imagery of a night spent talking, sitting on the floor drinking wine notably corresponds with McCartney's descriptions of 'avant-garde London' (Miles 1997: 211-67), suggesting the culturally-elite homes in which he is keen (retrospectively) to outline his presence. Yet 'Norwegian Wood', narrating an (unconsummated) one-night stand, suggests a passing, baroque encounter with a more elite class, rather than an uprooting into — or just outside of — such environs.

---

[2] Reck (2008) discusses Orientalism across the Beatles' work via Said's terms.

Baroque living and uprooting both transgress regular working-class experience but while the former is temporary, the latter is irreversible. The baroque narrative of 'Norwegian Wood', enhanced significantly by the sitar, personalises the singer as one of 'Us' by conveying the otherness of the setting in which he is placed.

Since the 1980s, McCartney has emphasised how, in 1960s 'avant-garde' London, he became enamoured with works by German electronic composer Karlheinz Stockhausen (Green 1988: 79). His narrative of socialising with writers (Burroughs), artists (Warhol) and film-makers (Antonioni) suggest 'the precarious tenancy in several near-intellectual worlds' of the uprooted (Hoggart 1957: 280). In retrospect, Sir Paul McCartney appears the most aspirational Beatle. However, this should not be equated with betrayal of working-class audiences. McCartney's idiosyncratic combining of populism with experimentalism renders much of The Beatles' most innovative and continually popular work decidedly inclusive. As their musical arrangements grew increasingly experimental in the mid-sixties, McCartney was quoted commenting: 'We can make a bridge [...] between us and Indian music, or us and electronic music, and therefore we can take people with us' (Reck 2008: 67).

It has become commonplace for studies to suggest that by 1967, popular music was undergoing a middle-class takeover. Moore (1997: 79) and Gendron (2002: 193-4) cite The Beatles' McCartney-led *Sgt Pepper's Lonely Hearts Club Band* (1967) as pivotal in the pattern. Negus more discerningly surmises that an 'ideology of rock' was being codified by a new generation of writers: '[c]rucial to *Sgt Pepper*'s mediation [...] were young educated middle-classes of Europe and North America [who] had discovered and then claimed rock music in their own terms' (Negus 1996: 154-5). Negus contends that though responses to *Sgt Pepper* privilege specific meanings for young middle-class audiences, the album also appeals to children and old people (Negus 1996: 159). Yet he does not consider the album's working-class consumers — the basis of a mass audience. It remains overlooked that this most experimental Beatles LP is rooted in working-class traditions — an ignorance which suggests a silent class prejudice in Beatles literature, if not in Popular Music Studies at large. In the case of *Sgt Pepper*, the re-codification, as Negus contends, is more the work of critics than the artists.

While *Sgt Pepper's Lonely Hearts Club Band* redefines The Beatles' characteristic image, personalisation yields an emphatically inclusive approach to a mass audience. Reflecting their influences, the cover depicts The Beatles surrounded by images of Liverpool footballers and comedians (Albert Stubbins; Tommy Handley) along with avant-garde figureheads (Stockhausen; Burroughs). Yet the primary influence that McCartney emphasises for the sleeve's concept (which he proposed to pop artist Peter Blake) is 'northern working-class life', reflecting 'what we were, where we were from'; McCartney describes its inspiration from floral clocks in the 'very municipal' parks of Lancashire and Yorkshire (Miles 1997: 305).

Inglis comments that 'extravagance and complexity' on *Sgt Pepper*'s sleeve reflect the music (Inglis 2001: 87). The cover also reflects the music as a statement of The Beatles' roots. While the opening track employs an emblem of Northern working-class culture, a brass band, imitations of live performance (after The Beatles had ceased touring) revitalise narrative personalisation. McCartney plays master of ceremonies, inviting 'you all to sing along', before 'With A Little Help From My Friends' invokes (again) staple working-class song themes, 'friends' and 'love'. The third such theme as discussed by Hoggart, 'home', shapes McCartney's 'Fixing A Hole' and 'When I'm Sixty-Four', Lennon's 'Good Morning, Good Morning', and the Lennon-McCartney collaboration 'A Day In The Life'. Most intriguing however is the McCartney-led 'She's Leaving Home', inspired by a newspaper report about a seventeen-year-old who confounded her parents by abruptly forsaking college and her affluent home (*Daily Mirror* 1967). Although the article describes the girl leaving her car, fur-coat and (uncompleted) A-levels, the lyric references none of these, personalising this narrative of dropping-out by suggesting a more working-class family; Melly imagines the house as a 'two-up, two-down terrace' (Melly 1970: 128).

Although working-class baroque anchors The Beatles' most innovative work to Northern traditions, this baroque, Hoggart notes, is frequently excessive and sometimes grotesque (Hoggart 1957: 124) — characteristics suffusing The Beatles' most experimental and also most high-profile offering to a mass audience, their self-directed 1967 TV film *Magical Mystery Tour*. Broadcast on Boxing Day, this McCartney-led venture merged working-class baroque with contemporary avant-garde film-making. Though filmed in Southern England, the setting (flattered by The Beatles' Lancastrian accents, here broadened) is Northern, 'on the Dewsbury road'. Intriguingly, the song performed by guest-stars the Bonzo Dog Band is 'Death-Cab For Cutie' — also a fictitious 'sex-and-violence' novel title listed by Hoggart (Hoggart 1957: 231). However, the film's primary link with working-class culture — and only point of consistency — is its basis in a 'chara' coach-trip: the epitome of working-class baroque (Hoggart 1957: 125-8). *Magical Mystery Tour* parallels Hoggart's discussion of the chara-trip as an occasion defined by working-class people through their own sub-traditions, for example, beer drinking and communal singing — the main events of one lengthy scene. Hoggart discusses journey and destination as equal components of the chara-trip.

In the film, the latter remains a 'mystery'. Influenced by French *nouvelle vague*, this largely unscripted movie's erratic scene shifts defy notions of linear plotting. *The Daily Express* called it 'contemptuous of the public' (1967: 4). McCartney responded: 'We thought we would not underestimate people' and 'do something new' (Badman 2000: 333).

Following *Magical Mystery Tour*'s critical failure, McCartney's work began its trajectory 'back' towards more traditional working-class song themes of home and love (anticipating his solo work). The Beatles' next single, 'Lady Madonna' (1968) foregrounds routine existence, narrating days of the week as experienced by a mother. Saturday however, is missing. No break from regulated existence is suggested; the baroque element is hereon largely absent from McCartney's work. Lady Madonna resembles the working-class mother as depicted by Hoggart. Home 'is practically the whole of her world'; life runs 'week-by-week' (Hoggart 1957: 29-32).[3] Like 'Ob-la-di, Ob-la-da' (1968) and 'Another Day' (1971), 'Lady Madonna' exemplifies how McCartney's lyrics prioritise the personal and concrete — Hoggart's 'core' working-class values (1957: 22). Restriction of consciousness to the spatially and temporally immediate in such lyrics illustrates how McCartney's work — more overtly than Lennon's or Harrison's — is rooted in working-class perspectives. In general, writes Hoggart, 'most working-people are non-political and non-metaphysical in their outlook' (Hoggart 1957: 86). The conceptual bases of Lennon's later lyrics — for example, 'Isolation' (1970), 'Imagine' (1971) and 'Intuition' (1973) — are prefigured in the abstract nouns of 'A Hard Day's Night' ('home', 'work', 'money'). In McCartney's songs, such concerns usually remain implicit; evoked, rather than named. Yet McCartney's lyrics, presenting labour as central to working-class life — with greater emphasis, ironically, than *The Uses of Literacy* — illustrate an obviousness suggested throughout Hoggart's narrative but never overtly stated. In a life dominated by externally-regulated routine, the personal and concrete *are* the political and metaphysical.

MacDonald briefly considers how The Beatles' Northern English roots inform their later years as a group. His interpretation of this in McCartney's 'populist anti-elitism' overlooks the significance of working-class baroque in The Beatles' work. However, MacDonald's suggestion that Harrison's following of Indian religion, 'with its distrust of worldliness and stress on the simple things in life' substitutes a 'stock-in-trade' of Northern English culture is convincing (MacDonald 1994: 202).

---

[3] Steedman (1986) provides a substantially different commentary on post-war working-class mothers.

Hoggart's discussions of the personal and concrete are again pertinent. 'Lady Madonna' was backed with Harrison's 'The Inner Light' (1968). For this composition — prompted by communication with Cambridge University-based Sanskrit scholar Juan Mascaró — Harrison adapted a passage called from Lao Tzu's *Tao Te Ching*, translated by Mascaró (see Harrison 1980: 117-9). Harrison sings: 'Without going out of my door/ I can know all things on earth'. This illuminates further implications of the personal and concrete as political and metaphysical. The song — designed for home-consumption — marks, in ostensible intent, a broadening of what Hoggart calls 'primary religion', in which, despite declining church attendance rates, liberal Christian outlooks continue for individuals in private (Hoggart 1957: 94-101). 'The Inner Light' reflects how elevation of the personal and concrete to the political and metaphysical can entail political passivity: 'Do all without doing', Harrison's Taoist lyric concludes. Yet to interpret this most symbolic of Harrison's lyrics literally would be absurd, as his later work proves.

Hoggart emphasises that most working-class people view religion in terms of duties, not doctrines, quoting maxims including 'we're 'ere to 'elp one another' (Hoggart 1957: 99). Mass media — perpetuating, Hoggart argues, mass passivity — was, in Harrison's work, the essential point of contact with the 'inner light' of individual listeners. Harrison's 1971 single 'Bangla Desh' narrated his response to learning of mass casualties following the 1970 Bhola cyclone and the Bangladesh Liberation War. Harrison — who never visited Bangladesh — sings 'Although I couldn't feel the pain/ I knew I had to try', later commenting: 'the reluctance of the press to report the full details created the need to bring attention to it' (Harrison 1980: 220). Harrison's continued avowals of adherence to Krishna are complemented by elevation of compassion in the here and now, the personal and concrete; his 1973 album was titled *Living In The Material World*. The fund and awareness-raising New York concerts which, at Shankar's suggestion, Harrison organised, recorded and filmed in aid of the people of Bangladesh in 1971 became templates for mass media events including Live Aid (1985) and London's Free Nelson Mandela Concert (1988).

Harrison's final recordings, made during his affliction with cancer, repeatedly suggest the imaginative grip of his working-class Liverpool roots. On *Brainwashed* (released 2002), the 'ex-Catholic' Harrison describes 'Smoke signals from the brewery/ Like someone in there found the latest pope' and reflects 'I never got any GCEs' but instead embraced knowledge 'from inner space'. Harrison's connection to his origins is affirmed in characteristically spiritual terms: 'I'm a Pisces fish and the river runs through my soul'. Debunking celebrity-life as an 'avenue of sinners' where he 'was near-destroyed', Harrison muses 'it's only a show, I'll confess [...]

in my concrete tuxedo'. As in Lennon and McCartney's 'Norwegian Wood' in 1965, elite social environs are represented with otherness.

Despite having received extraordinary media attention as a Beatle and then utilised this to charitable ends, Harrison ultimately pontificates on how mass media creates a mass society. 'Brainwashed', the eponymous finale of his last album, contemplates how 'they' brainwash 'us' by 'military', 'media', 'computer' and 'mobile-phones'. Not unlike Hoggart, Harrison does not envisage an alternative society but critiques patterns in an existing one. His final songs, however, maintain hope, appealing to a 'Lord' and 'god'; Harrison dedicated *Brainwashed* to Krishna.

Simon Hoggart's 2009 foreword to *The Uses of Literacy*, after noting the 'Death-Cab for Cutie' link between his father and The Beatles, reveals: '[t]he late Derek Taylor, The Beatles' PR, once told me that George Harrison had admired Dad's work' (Hoggart 1957: vi). Simon Hoggart, answering my email request for him to provide more detail, kindly explains how, 'decades ago', Taylor had been 'very happy to pass the information on' to him that:

he had been round at George Harrison's house a few days before and my Dad had appeared on TV. They had watched and Harrison had said something like 'that bloke talks a lot of sense', or 'I agree with all that'. (Simon Hoggart, email to the present author, 13 October 2009)

Distant admiration appears to have been mutual between Richard Hoggart and George Harrison. Reflecting on responses to Harrison's death (2001), Hoggart offered his own thoughts:

many people had been moved by his songs and, perhaps even more, by what they saw as his integrity, and especially his search for the good and proper life [...]. His public achievement and his inner character appeared to suggest to many who had never met him a kind of admirable consonance. (Hoggart 2004: 70)

While McCartney and Harrison in different ways continued and developed working-class traditions noted by Hoggart, Lennon's work, via narrative and thematic personalisation, most starkly confronts a mass audience with its own subordination. Lennon's solo track 'Working Class Hero' (1970) is the most pertinent song here in relation to *The Uses of Literacy*. It corresponds less with Hoggart's critique of lyrical traditions than with his broader commentaries on working-class life itself in an age of mass media. Lennon described 'Working Class Hero' as 'for the people like me who are working-class, who are supposed to be processed into the middle classes, or into the machinery' (Wenner 1971: 93). These are, effectively, the uprooted. Harker scorns how this song casts Lennon as a 'victim' (Harker 1980: 213-5). Harker overlooks that the victim in Lennon's lyric is 'you', oppressed by a composite Them:

They hurt you at home and they hit you at school
They hate you if you're clever and they despise the fool
Till you're so fucking crazy you can't follow their rules

Lennon's repetitious A/G guitar chord-sequence conveys relentless oppression. This is enhanced though the lyric's half-rhymes ('They hurt you'; 'they hate you'), alliteration ('you can't really function you're so full of fear') and triple end-rhymes ('still', 'kill', 'hill'). Education especially is here an agent of Them: 'they've tortured and scared you for twenty-odd years/ Then they expect you to pick a career'.

However, 'Working Class Hero' suggests the victim being oppressed to the point of rebellion ('Till you're so fucking crazy you can't follow their rules'). Lennon's lyric enhances such potency by mocking listeners:

Keep you doped with religion and sex and TV
And you think you're so clever and classless and free
But you're still fucking peasants as far as I can see

Illusions of being 'classless' and 'free' are central to Hoggart's closing 1957 statement:

even if substantial inner freedom were lost, the great new classless class would be unlikely to know it: its members would still regard themselves as free and still be told that they were free. (Hoggart 1957: 314)

Before stating that 'Working Class Hero' was for people 'processed' into the middle classes, Lennon commented: 'I hope it's for workers' (Wenner 1971: 93). Conveying no sense of contradiction, he suggests awareness of a mass audience in Hoggart's terms — the great majority of us being merged into one class. However, in 'Working Class Hero', notions of craziness ultimately suggests less the anxiety of the uprooted than revolutionary anger, in which (to adapt Hoggart's metaphor), springs of action are not unbent but pressed down to a point where their stored power is unleashed. Lennon ends by hinting at some alternative notion of Us: 'If you want to be a hero, well just follow me'. Lennon's 'Power To The People' (1971) implores: 'Get on your feet, into the street/ Singing power to the people'.

Harrison's body of work, through its spiritual contemplation, is more sustainedly focused than Lennon or McCartney's. Lennon's socialist phase, like McCartney's baroque excursions into the avant-garde, proved transient. Nevertheless, political, aesthetic and spiritual concerns far beyond what Hoggart (1957) viewed as the limits of mass art remain integral to Lennon, McCartney and Harrison's legacies and potential influence. In these ways, they prove Hoggart's amendment to his study's title fortuitous: from *The Abuse of Literacy* to *The Uses of Literacy*.

When, in 2003, I began planning the project that became my Ph.D (from which parts of this paper draw), I emailed Richard Hoggart, asking if he would like to add to his remarks on The Beatles by commenting on how he felt their work engaged with working-class life. He courteously replied that other writing commitments prevented him from entering into detailed correspondence regarding my questions; I still felt privileged to receive his message of good luck. As my thesis progressed, I realised that effectively, in *The Uses of Literacy*, Hoggart had already answered my question, half a decade before The Beatles' first release.

Bibliography

Badman, K. (2000) *The Beatles: Off the Record* (London: Omnibus).

Beatles, The. (1964) *A Hard Day's Night* (UK: Parlophone).

———— (1965) *Rubber Soul* (UK: Parlophone).

———— (1967a) *Sgt Pepper's Lonely Hearts Club Band* (UK: Parlophone).

———— (1967b/1997) *Magical Mystery Tour* (UK: MPI/Apple DVD).

———— (1968) *Lady Madonna / The Inner Light* (UK: Parlophone).

———— (1970) *Let It Be* (UK: Apple).

Bicât, A. (1970) 'Fifties Children: Sixties People'. In V. Bogdanor and R. Skidelsky (eds.), *The Age of Affluence, 1951-1964* (London: Macmillan).

Board of Education, The. (1943) *Curriculum and Examination in Schools Report* (London: HMSO).

Daily Express. (1967) 'Magic Leaves Beatles with Mighty Flop!' p. 4 (December 27).

Daily Mirror. (1967) 'Missing — the Girl who "has Everything"' p. 4 (February 27).

Eagleton, T. (1964) 'New Bearings: The Beatles.' *Blackfriars*, 45 (April) 175-8.

Gendron, B. (2002) *Between Montmartre and the Mudd Club: Popular Music and the Avant-Garde* (London: University of Chicago Press).

Green, J. (1988) *Days in the Life: Voices from the English Underground 1961-1971* (London: Pimlico).

Harker, D. (1980) *One for the Money: Politics and Popular Song* (London: Hutchinson).

Harrison, G. (1971) *Bangla Desh / Deep Blue* (UK: Apple).

————— (1980) *I Me Mine*, 2nd ed. (London: Phoenix).

————— (2002) *Brainwashed* (UK: Dark Horse).

Henke, J. (2003) *Lennon Legend: An Illustrated Life of John Lennon* (London: Weidenfeld and Nicholson).

Hoggart, R. (1957/2009) *The Uses of Literacy: Aspects of Working-Class Life* (London: Penguin Modern Classics).

————— (1972) *Only Connect: On Culture and Communication* (London: Chatto and Windus).

————— (1995) *The Way We Live Now* (London: Pimlico).

————— (2001) *The Abuse of Literacy* The Richard Hoggart Archive, University of Sheffield (reference 3/2/1).

————— (2004) *Mass Media in a Mass Society: Myth and Reality*, 2nd ed. (London: Continuum).

Inglis, I. (2001) 'Nothing You Can See That Isn't Shown: The Album Covers of the Beatles', *Popular Music*, 20 (1), pp. 83-97.

Lennon, J. (1970). *John Lennon/Plastic Ono Band* (UK: Apple).

Lennon, J. and Ono, Y. (1971) *Power To The People / Open Your Box* (UK: Apple).

Lewisohn, M. (1988) *The Complete Beatles Recording Sessions: The Official Story of the Abbey Road Years* (London: Hamlyn).

Marcuse, H. (1964) *One-Dimensional Man*, 2nd ed. (Abingdon: Routledge).

MacDonald, I. (1994) *Revolution in the Head: The Beatles' Records and the Sixties* (London: Pimlico).

McGrath, J. (2008) 'Imagine all the Lonely People: Belonging and Isolation in the Songs of John Lennon and Paul McCartney'. In R. Ganis, (ed), *Displacement and Belonging in the Modern World* (Salford: University of Salford / European Studies Research Institute), pp. 113-28.

Mellers, W. (1973) *Twilight of the Gods: The Beatles in Retrospect*, 2nd ed. (London: Faber and Faber).

Melly, G. (1970) *Revolt into Style: The Pop Arts in the 50s and 60s*, 2nd ed. (Oxford: Oxford University Press).

Miles, B. (1997) *Paul McCartney: Many Years from Now* (London: Secker and Warburg).

Moore, A. F. (1997) *The Beatles: Sgt Pepper's Lonely Hearts Club Band* (Cambridge: Cambridge University Press).

Negus, K. (1996) *Popular Music in Theory: An Introduction* (Cambridge: Polity).

Reck, D. (2008) 'The Beatles and Indian music'. In O. Julien (ed.), *Sgt Pepper and the Beatles: It Was Forty Years Ago Today* (Aldershot: Ashgate).

Rose, J. (2001) *The Intellectual Life of the British Working Classes* (London: Yale University Press).

Said, E. (1978) *Orientalism*, 3rd ed. (Harmondsworth: Penguin).

Sparks, C. (1974) 'The Abuses of Literacy'. In Centre for Contemporary Cultural Studies, *Cultural Studies 6: Cultural Studies and Theory* (Birmingham: University of Birmingham), pp. 7-23.

Steedman, C. (1986) *Landscape for a Good Woman*, 2nd ed. (London: Virago).

Wenner, J. S. (1971) *Lennon Remembers*, 2nd ed. (London: Verso).

RICHARD HOGGART AND UNESCO
Yudhishthir Raj Isar

Introduction

I was Richard Hoggart's Personal Assistant at the United Nations Educational, Scientific and Cultural Organization (UNESCO) from January 1974 till the moment he left it in May 1975. Although this was not a long period, it was a formative one. He was my first real 'boss'.[1] Such people do not necessarily make a deep or lasting impact on one's professional ethos, but he did on mine: during the twenty-eight years I continued to serve the organisation after his departure I was often guided by the example he set or by the analyses he subsequently made, notably in his 1978 book *An Idea and its Servants: UNESCO from Within*, as well as in his later writings. Like several colleagues similarly marked, I believed in and was sustained by Hoggart's firm and tightly reasoned commitment to a certain idea — alas, never fully realised — of what UNESCO ought to be and of what it could one day become. And its corollary, a deontological vision of what we as international civil servants ought to be, and too often were not or were not allowed to be. Hoggart came into the 'big world' of UNESCO from the undoubtedly 'small world' of the British provincial university, but during and after his time there, he formulated a resolutely 'big' vision of the significance of international organisation in today's world. He recognised that such a vision would be very difficult to realise. It has not yet and probably never will be. Yet his 'sober idealism' has nevertheless appeared to me and others the best of possible orientations to work by. The nature of the lessons taught by 'Professor Hoggart' is what I shall attempt to set out here.[2]

At UNESCO he was the very senior official — Assistant Director-General was the official title — in charge of a department (known within the organisation as a 'Sector') that, as he put it, covered 'some of the most politically hot and intellectually tricky issues ... work in philosophy (a

---

[1] This needs a small qualification. In point of fact, on 1 October, 1973 I took up a junior position of 'Policy Analyst' in the Policy Reports Branch of the International Labour Office in Geneva, but just two weeks later received a call from UNESCO telling me of the position for which Hoggart was recruiting. So I too had the experience of the Auden line on 'the telephone call from long distance which defines one's future' that Hoggart referred to in his book about UNESCO (Hoggart, 1978: 15).

[2] The use of academic titles is not part of the UNESCO culture. Although at the beginning he was referred to as 'Professor', by the time I joined his staff this recognition of academic prestige has been dropped from Secretariat usage.

remarkably divisive subject), the social sciences, 'culture' in both the Arts Council and the Ancient Monuments senses, the environment, human rights, racism, 'Peace', population and drugs' (Hoggart 1978: 21).[3] By the time of his arrival, the organisation 'had a variety of well-established methods for executing its projects: publications, seminars missions for experts, establishing international or regional institutes, pilot studies in the field, contracts with Member nations or individuals, and so on' (Hoggart: 20). It is striking, however, that his account makes no mention of specific projects or programmes that he himself devised or initiated during his tenure. My questioning of contemporaries who also served with him confirms that there were none. This is not a reflection on Hoggart, but a consequence of UNESCO's own workings, for the true power of initiating new projects in the organisation tends to be located lower down in the hierarchy. It is directors of division, if not their immediate subordinates, known as chiefs of section, rather than Assistant Director-Generals who design the programmes. The role of the latter is rather more supervisory; they can ask for shifts in broad orientations, or shape programme execution.

It might nevertheless be expected that I would have revealing insights to share with the reader on Hoggart's contribution to *specific* debates of ideas within UNESCO. This cannot be the case, for I was but an ex-graduate student in social anthropology at the *Ecole des Hautes Etudes en Sciences Sociales* in Paris, with scant experience of professional life and only slight acquaintance with the topics for which my mentor was responsible. Such debates probably took place, but I was not a party to them. This no doubt handicaps my present piecing together of now distant memories (I kept no diary at the time) and is clearly a lacuna, given the purpose of the volume to complement or shed light on the positions Hoggart has taken as a public intellectual and commentator in Britain. That being said, in the perspective of the long passage of my own professional life within UNESCO until 2002 and beyond it since, I can share with the reader some of Hoggart's deontological positions that have become reference points for many colleagues in my generation of international officials.[4] I shall therefore explore three sets of principles I see him as having inculcated: principles regarding the use of language, the intellectual debate, and the

---

[3] These together formed the Sector for Social Sciences, Humanities and Culture. After Hoggart's departure a separate Sector for Social Sciences was created.

[4] Although I continued on in UNESCO after Hoggart's departure for twenty-eight years, as an international civil servant I was as 'atypical' as he was during his four, although for rather different reasons. Hence my assessment of his significance deviates from the standard official vision. Nor is it that of an independent external observer.

'fine fictions' that underlie the corporate ideology of the organisation. Then, somewhat riskily perhaps, I shall extrapolate from my memories of these positions to imagine how Hoggart might address certain issues that are much debated in the cultural policy field today. Before doing so, however, some further introductory remarks on a more personal note.

A personal story with broader implications

Hoggart's choice of an untried Indian student to share the relative intimacy of his professional life was 'telling' in itself — to use a term that appears often in his writings. His previous Personal Assistant, with him from the time he began as ADG in January 1970, was a highly intelligent, tough and upwardly mobile German woman in her late thirties who had risen through the ranks and was apparently seen as a bit of an *éminence grise* by the Sector's directors and other senior staff and who was prone to throwing her weight about a bit in his name — a well-known syndrome in all bureaucracies. As befitted her ambitions, in late 1973, with Hoggart's blessing, the woman in question moved on promotion to a more senior post in UNESCO's central forward planning unit. To replace her, Hoggart apparently told his Administrative Officer he wanted not a woman but a man, not a European but somebody from the 'Third World', not a mature (and hence potentially pushy) person but a young (hence probably inoffensive) one. Some intellectual edge was nevertheless required; happily for me, I had given him an inkling of that. Some months earlier, I had been invited to attend an 'international meeting of experts' — on 'the contestation of established culture among young people' (as befitted the post-1968 preoccupations, particularly in France) — that had been organised by his Sector. I was there as an 'observer', hence not supposed to speak. But I found the entire discussion highly Eurocentric and was bold enough to say so. This went down badly with the officials organising the meeting, but Hoggart himself came up to me during the coffee break to inquire who I was, adding that he had found my comments rather sensible. When the PA post needed to be filled, his Administrative Officer mentioned my name and Hoggart asked that I be informed and called for interview if I chose to apply. Having concluded after an interview that I would fit the bill, Hoggart formally recommended, out of a characteristic (British?) spirit of fair play, that because of my young age (25) and lack of experience I should be appointed at entry level — in other word's one grade lower than that of the post — and be promoted to the true grade after a successful probationary period. The ADG in charge of administrative matters, however, a Russian hostile to Hoggart because of his refusal to condone Soviet ideological humbug — and after all, aren't the non-communist Leftists the first in line to be shot when the dictatorship of the proletariat begins? — rejected this solution and insisted that if I was truly the properly qualified candidate I had to be appointed at the grade advertised. And so it was decided.

Hoggart had hardly wanted to jump-start an international civil service career in this way. Yet, behind his choice of an unknown Indian perhaps lay far more than the mentoring impulse of the pedagogue. Perhaps there was an implicit echo there of his having learned at UNESCO 'about the world outside parochial Europe ... the vast and varied spaces of that outer world, its different way of interpreting human experience, its complex and shifting physical and mental landscapes, its beauties of sorts we never knew as we walked in the Lake District or West Country' (Hoggart 1993: 149). This full openness to difference in the world was striking in one whose previous experience had been so narrowly circumscribed within the confines of his own country. Everything I heard him say then and read in his writings afterwards testified to the fact that he was not one to entertain the usual stereotyped expectations of the non-western 'Other'. As a 'postcolonial' thinker was to write much later:

But what if an Indian, or a Nigerian, wanted to be at home in Elizabethan or Romantic literature? Would such a choice be lacking in historical density or urgency? ... The very fact that *what* the postcolonial scholar teaches, rather than *how* or with what critical perspective she teaches, has taken on an almost fetishistic significance in the academy is ample testimony to the reality of the ongoing psychological and internal impact of colonialism. For if one were truly postcolonial, it would not matter what one taught or thought about: Shakespeare, Jane Austen, Chinua Achebe, or Bessie Head. (Radhakrishnan 1996, xv-xvi)

This *cri de coeur* resonates with Hoggart's own comment on one of the reactions to his book about UNESCO, where he says 'two of the English reviewers began favourable notices by showing surprise that I had chosen an international subject. *He* writes about English working-class life, surely? There was half a suggestion I should not have stepped outside my bailiwick' (Hoggart, 1993: 14). But Hoggart knew how to do just that, to be 'truly postcolonial' — before the fact, since that particular trope had not yet been invented. 'We all tend to think,' he wrote, 'we know much about cultural differences from our reading, especially in literature, and in some irreplaceable ways we do. Yet there is bound to be a difference in kind between that and the knowledge which comes from meeting those differences day by day, decision by decision (Hoggart 1993: 158). Consequently, he showed little difficulty, as a Western European, in adapting to a world moving in increasingly unpredictable directions, and whose imaginings, aspirations and workings are so clearly escaping Western control, drawing on other memories and loyalties. Understanding the West as but *one element* in world society, among others, was not default position among senior Western officials at the time, with all their paternalistic good intentions about 'Third World development'. In Hoggart there was definitely none of the supercilious of the British upper classes. But there was also an 'in-between-ness', that made him transcend, as Michael Bailey and Mary Eagleton put it, 'some of the more rarefied ideas, customs and habits of the class to which he nominally belonged as a child, and the professional class he was to later join as an adult' (Bailey and Eagleton 2011: 13). In this he was already a twenty-first century cosmopolitan, displaying the kind of 'dialogic imagination' to which Ulrich Beck (2002) invites us, or the 'hospitality' that Seyla Benhabib sees as 'a right that belongs to all human beings insofar as we view them as potential participants in a world republic' (Benhabib, 2006: 22). Again, in Hoggart's own words:

> When you work with people from many different cultures you are being invited all the time to recognise that there are many more and subtler ways of being a good worker than you had ever realised. Insights from other cultures repeatedly throw a critical light on much you have always taken for granted. Then you realise how easily you have been tempted to settle for a routine exemplification of your own, hitherto secure and unquestionable, cultural styles. (Hoggart, 1978: 134)

It must be said that as far as his new recruit was concerned, Hoggart was unaware that I had not been educated in Britain: all my studies had been in India and France. I sometimes wondered whether he would have been so eager to recruit me had he known. In the light of the preceding paragraph, no doubt he would have. But thereby also hangs another small but telling tale. To be sure, he was somewhat surprised to discover, during a conversation we had a few months after I joined him, my lack of a suitable British pedigree. Perhaps he was even rather intrigued. Emboldened by his curiosity, I volunteered the information that my father, however, had been at Balliol College Oxford in the 1930s. I opined that since he had been an ardent Leftist there (Richard Crossman was among his tutors) and had even joined the Communist Party, no doubt they would have known some of the same people. At this point Hoggart drew himself up slightly in the manner he was wont to adopt when about to say something significant and informed me in dead seriousness: 'I would never have known anybody at Oxford.' What a telling reaction that was, both with respect to the British class system in general and Hoggart's own location with regard to his class origins. Our relations, however, did not suffer and of course I learned something about class in British society!

Key professional principles

Clear thinking and the clear use of language, the primacy of the 'life of the mind', a deontology of committed realism in the face of the 'fine fictions' upon which UNESCO's corporate ideology was based — these were three sets of working principles upheld and transmitted by Richard Hoggart.

As regards the first point, pathological uses of language reign in most bureaucratic organisations, in the double-speak they practice. This was, and still is, acute at UNESCO, reaching near-Orwellian proportions. Hoggart has been ever-sensitive to the different registers of circumlocution. In March 1970, a couple of months after having taken up his ADG position, he sent out a memorandum to all his colleagues expressing his concern 'about the language used in some of our documents; in particular, about the tendency to use jargon of various types' (Hoggart, 1970). He asked the Sector's English language editor to produce an example of this use of jargon and then to produce a translation in clear and simple English.[5] Here is the third paragraph of the 'awful example':

As two-thirds of the world's population are lagging behind in the fight to secure their efficient co-operation towards possible social, economic and cultural welfare targets, the paramount importance of the human factor in the development of these countries and its promotion in all possible ways in being increasingly recognised as a primary goal in Unesco action in favour of education, science and culture.[6]

The alternate version he proposed for that sentence was the following:

The Unesco programme must pay a great deal more attention to the human factor if two-thirds of the world's population are really to be helped to achieve their social, economic and cultural objectives. (UNESCO 1970: 7)

Writing about this effort later as a 'deliberately a comic exaggeration for therapeutic purposes', Hoggart commented on how he 'found that some colleagues reacted miserably, as though I had torn holes in their professional linguistic carapaces. Again, without identifying individuals, I tried to show how one bad practice led to more and more. But some people could not change their methods; they were designed specifically to

---

[5] This incident has also been recounted by Malcolm Hadley (2008), who attributes to Richard Hoggart a greater degree of indulgence for woolliness of language than I observed at first hand.

[6] Although it figures in Hoggart, 1978 as 'UNESCO', the organisation's acronym was officially 'Unesco' until the arrival in 1987 of the eighth Director-General, the Catalan Federico Mayor, who insisted on the capitalized usage.

prevent them from toppling into the outer world again' (Hoggart 1993: 163). There has been some improvement since then, for beginning in the late 1980s with Federico Mayor, the top leadership at UNESCO began to give special heed to the language used to communicate with and for the 'outer world'. Much Secretariat internal drafting continues to be as opaque and euphemistic as it was back then, however — for how else would mutual intelligibility be maintained within this closed system? Yet some texts produced for the organisation's governing bodies, particularly those dealing with planning and budgeting, have gradually taken on aspects of normal English or French, as opposed to the laboured version of Franglais UNESCO favours. At the time, however, although some of us, having taken Hoggart's point, would have liked to write a completely different kind of institutional prose, the need to remain within the confines of a coded language won out.

A second Hoggartian legacy was his unwavering commitment to intellectual debate of high quality. Others have come in to UNESCO from academia to take up senior positions, including that of ADG, but as organic intellectuals fulfilling technical and organisational needs few have given such clear primacy to the 'life of the mind'. Hoggart felt the need to shoulder a particular responsibility on this account, although he was fully aware of the institutional limits set on free inquiry and open debate in any intergovernmental organisation. Thus, referring to the many international meetings it organises, he describes UNESCO as:

> a great market for the traffic of knowledge ... I was tempted to say 'for the intellectual life', but that would be claiming too much. Such meetings tend to succeed best where they can be given a functional character; intelligence — very high intelligence, often — thrives in them rather than intellectuality, speculation. (1978: 36)

What was unique in Hoggart's way of working was the close compensatory attention he gave to that missing 'intellectuality', to the nuances — or ambiguities — behind the conception and articulation of projects and programmes. This was often manifested in long and carefully crafted memos he sent to his directors and other senior staff, often consigned to a dictating machine at his home in late evenings or the wee hours of the morning. The machine came in with him every morning and a junior secretary was in fact employed primarily in his office to transcribe these long disquisitions.[7]

---

[7] Most of these were confidential and were thus transmitted directly to their destinees.

Finally, the 'fine fictions' in the ethos of UNESCO. Fundamental to any organisation's sense of itself, hence in turn of its employees' senses of themselves, is the power of its 'bannerhead phrases' as Hoggart put it. In UNESCO's case the original bannerhead phrase was the resonant opening sentence of its Constitution: 'Since wars begin in the minds of men, it is in the minds of men that the defences of peace must be constructed.'[8] Hoggart thought this sentence had 'all the resounding opacity of such phrases at their most dense' (Hoggart 1978: 27). In the same passage, he expressed his distrust of the many other 'extraordinary assertions' found in UNESCO's Constitution, all of which were deployed ritually and unquestioningly as key elements of the institution's constitutive rhetoric, its own 'language-to-live-by'. Most staff members played it safe with the rhetoric; others reacted to it with irony, yet others with cynicism. Hoggart, on the other hand, appreciated its inspirational power, but asked that the inspiration be acted upon effectively. The first 'fine fiction' he took from the sociologist Gunnar Myrdal, for whom such organisations 'are something more than their component parts, something above the individual states' (Myrdal, cited in Hoggart 1978: 14). He also shared Dag Hammarskjöld's belief that 'anyone of integrity, not subjected to undue pressures, can, regardless of his own views, readily act in an "exclusively international" spirit and can be guide in his actions on behalf of the Organisation solely by its interests and principles...' (cited in Hoggart 1978: 44). He acknowledged the various reasons for which States would be less than enthusiastic about such a professional stance, including the position then openly expressed by the Soviet Union and like-minded States that, as Nikita Khrushchev put it, 'there are no neutral men'. In his book, however, Hoggart directs his most pungent criticism not at the Soviets, but at the hypocritical American procedure then prevailing, a carry-over from the McCarthy era that required the Secretariat to obtain, from the US Department of State, in the oxymoronic double-speak in which that country's officialdom revels, a positive 'advisory determination' before any American specialist could be hired or invited to one of its technical meetings. For Hoggart, this was nothing less than 'egregious' (Hoggart 1978: 50) and he made his own preferences for a totally independent international civil service crystal clear. 'Each year in which the concept survives and is honoured by some people is a year gained, so that it may eventually be put on an unshakeable footing' (Hoggart 1978:

[8] This text was drafted by the American poet and at the time Librarian of Congress Archibald MacLeish, apparently on the basis of words first uttered by the British politician Clement Atlee several years earlier, at the Conference of Allied Ministers of Education.

51). For those of us who could be counted among the 'some people' the subsequent years have brought a steady decline, culminating in the blatant negations of the principle of neutrality practiced by the Japanese Director-General, Koïchiro Matsuura, whose tenure in office (1999-2009) was marked by a high degree of subservience to Japanese cultural diplomacy objectives (with a number of programmes and projects bankrolled by that country's government).

The second 'fine fiction' was the idea enshrined in the UNESCO Constitution that 'the unrestricted pursuit of objective truth' and the 'free exchange of ideas and knowledge' are at the core of the organisation's mandate. Hoggart saw clearly what others in their self-deluding way preferred not to, namely that 'it is not in the nature of governments to believe in such things; they are more likely to find such ideas suspect and often embarrassing'. He consequently recognised that 'to work in UNESCO is sometimes to feel as though you live in an unprotected territory of boundless good intentions, pressed in from all sides by bodies with other, more practical, forceful and precise purposes' (Hoggart 1978: 52). For Hoggart, the 'intellectual community, would not respect UNESCO unless 'it is seen to be trying to fulfil its purposes, to be aiming at objectivity and at the free flow of knowledge' (Hoggart 1978: 56). Earning and keeping that respect was a daily challenge, which he shouldered with a 'sober idealism' rather than an 'unexpectant disillusion'. It is that positive attitude that became an inspiration to many of us; it was a constant summons to remember one of the organisation's 'own favourite public phrases, that there is "an ethical dimension to international intellectual cooperation' (1978: 19). Herein lies a central aporia that hinges on the idea that it is possible, at UNESCO, to accord primacy to intellectual independence over the cold calculus of nation-state interests or the easy accommodations of international diplomacy. Hoggart, together with many of those who joined the organisation up until the 1970s, believed firmly in this idea. We were able to do so because governments continued to elect directors-general who were not merely public officials but had recognised accomplishments in an intellectual field, for example Julian Huxley and Federico Mayor in the natural sciences. This ceased in 1999 however, with the successive election to the post of two senior diplomats. While the world's intelligentsias still see the organisation as a sort of independent brains trust for the world community, UNESCO's member states are distinctly less appreciative of the virtues of speaking truth to power.

Extrapolating to cultural policy issues

In this section, I shall briefly explore three sets of issues that have become salient in cultural policy: cultural democratisation vs. cultural democracy;

relativism and its discontents; the capaciousness of the culture concept. At UNESCO, Hoggart engaged partially with these questions and I shall extrapolate from my memories of those engagements. I shall leave it to the reader to make the connections between these opinions, to which he returned directly or indirectly in his writings, and his class background and intellectual trajectory, for I am not competent to comment further on either.

Beginning in the 1960s, governments across Europe, in the shadow of the Malrucian model policy-making in France, sought to 'democratise' access to and participation in the arts and heritage. Although this policy stance was not challenged by Hoggart, his own previous work on British popular culture and the way this led to the establishment of cultural studies, would place him more appropriately in a different camp, that of 'cultural democracy'. The democratisation of culture means giving people access to a pre-determined set of cultural goods and services while cultural democracy means giving them tools of agency, voice and representation in terms of their own cultural expressions. The first approach is inherently elitist, as it assumes that a single cultural canon determined on high can be propagated to 'the masses'. Nor has it been successful, as the unequal distribution of 'cultural capital' in society has made access to culture either problematic or unsolicited by the intended beneficiaries, while the scale of market-driven cultural industries has reduced the reach of subsidised cultural provision. Cultural democracy on the other hand, seeks to augment and diversify access to the means of cultural production and distribution, to involve people in fundamental debates about the value of cultural identity and expression, while also giving them agency as regards the means of cultural production, distribution and consumption. Today it has become important to explore the implications and challenges of cultural democracy on a Europe-wide, indeed global scale, since both European integration and globalisation make it necessary to look beyond the purely national level to identify the forces and flows that are changing the 'grammar' of national cultures. What patterns and forces in the cultural economy pre-determine certain kinds of exclusion as regards cultural expression, goods and services?

A second set of issues Hoggart grappled with at UNESCO was the fine line between openness to difference (in his case great, as we have seen) and the need to avoid the 'danger of falling into a meaningless total relativism' (Hoggart 1978: 196). Relativism has been one of his abiding concerns, revealed for example by several chapters of *The Way We Live Now*. His years at UNESCO coincided with the early unfolding of the extraordinary cultural self-consciousness of our time. These were the years following the great wave of decolonisation of the 1960s, particularly in Africa. UNESCO was the locus of many different contestations of

Western ethnocentrism and itself a leading contributor to this culturalism itself, which has inevitably cleaved to readings of 'culture' as a principally *national* phenomenon, readings that are in direct descent from the Herderian notion of culture as the national *Volksgeist*. The contrast between such a vision and the paths taken by cultural theory is nicely expressed by Paul Gilroy's view that the idea of culture 'has been abused by being simplified, instrumentalized, or trivialized, and particularly through being coupled with notions of identity and belonging that are overly fixed or too easily naturalized as exclusively national phenomena' (Gilroy 2004: 6). This was but one aspect of the 'shabbier sides of nationalism' Hoggart disliked, in his telling as much displayed by British officials as any others (Hoggart 1993: 149).

What is virtue in the intergovernmental arena is in other circles the vice of 'methodological nationalism', that is the assumption that the nation-state is the right container for culture. Today, however, now that the primacy of the nation-state appears past its heyday, the nexus of culture and nation no longer holds. 'Culture' is now appropriated by collectivities at narrower as well as broader levels. And, accompanying all these articulations of cultural self-consciousness, there is a growing popular awareness of the porosity of boundaries and the fluidity and multiplicity of 'cultural identities' that matches the unease expressed in the social sciences with respect to the fixity and stasis of the traditional concept. In 1998, the anthropologist Susan Wright denounced UNESCO's 'old' vision of culture, its 'map of a flat world', or what her colleague Thomas Hylland Eriksen called 'an archipelago vision of the world as made up of 'peoples' each with a radically different 'culture' like a string of separate islands'. Wright opined that the vision of a 'mosaic of cultures ... misses the dimension of "culture" as a process of contestation over the power to define organizing concepts — including the meaning of "culture" itself' (Wright 1998: 1).

More to the point, however, as regards the question of relativism, is the notion of incommensurability between cultures that underlies it and the concomitant challenge of transcending the universalism vs. particularism dichotomy. Distinctly different positions are taken regarding both by modernist and postmodernist reasoning. The modernist position relies upon an ethics of persuasion, that is, of persuading others of the 'betterness' of modernisation — as a Western project — as if Western scientific, political and economic ideas are other than contingent, a particular set of responses to the common problems of human existence. The postmodernist position on the other hand relies entirely upon an ethics of respect, which involves merely respecting differences between cultures without trying to overcome those differences. Both positions can be transcended, provided we adopt a critical stance towards our own respective cultures, on the one hand subjecting our beliefs, values and so on to a more genuinely objective evaluation, and on the other fostering a willingness to learn in a receptive but critical way from other traditions.

Yet the 'all cultures are equal' doctrine, which became canonical at UNESCO (but not just there) leads either to the kind of 'total relativism' decried by Hoggart or to the traps of moral relativism. The positions he took — always tactfully but firmly — on this matter during his years at UNESCO, were echoed decades later in the following passage from *Our Creative Diversity*, the report of the World Commission on Culture and Development:[9]

Liberalism, tolerance and pluralism incline us to find pleasure in the idea of a multiplicity of visions; the desire for objectivity, and universality, on the other hand, leads us to desire that truth be but one, not many. The logical and ethical difficulty about relativism is that it must also endorse absolutism and dogmatism; absolutism does not have to endorse relativism... Notoriously, there is no room for the assertion of relativism in a world in which relativism is true. Cognitive relativism is nonsense, moral relativism is tragic ... Let us rejoice in diversity, while maintaining absolute standards of judging what is right, good and true. (UNESCO 1996: 55)

A third set of conceptual difficulties connected to cultural policy arises out of the broadening of the concept of culture spawned by the culturalism alluded to earlier. The beginnings of this process can be dated to Hoggart's UNESCO years, but were not mainly of his making. While his own achievements as a scholar were grounded in culture, *pace* Raymond Williams, as 'the works and practices of intellectual, especially artistic, activity', *The Uses of Literacy* took him closer to the so-called anthropological notion invented by the German Romantics, that is 'culture' as a particular way of life. Till the late 1960s, the arts and heritage sense was the dominant reading in UNESCO. But then decolonisation together with a range of other factors specific to Western Europe and North America brought the 'culture as identity' (Eagleton 2000) notion to centre stage. The early 1970s were thus marked by a steadily accelerating shift in the organisation's terminology from the first sense to the second. This process culminated in the celebrated definition provided by the

[9] The author was the Executive Secretary of the World Commission on Culture and Development.

UNESCO's World Conference on Cultural Policies held in Mexico City in 1982:

> that in its widest sense, culture may now be said to be the whole complex of distinctive spiritual, material, intellectual and emotional features that characterize a society or social group. It includes not only the arts and letters, but also modes of life, the fundamental rights of the human being, values systems, traditions and beliefs ...

But this broad referential field, culture in the 'ways of life' sense, is too expansive for analytical and practical purposes. It literally encompasses everything and, in so doing, obscures important and useful distinctions between that which is principally cultural and that which is not first and foremost about meaning and signification. For example, it would be meaningless to talk about the relation between culture understood in this sense and the economy — or for that matter 'development' — since the economy is part of culture and the very definition of development is cultural in nature. But in the 1980s and beyond, such confusion got built deeply into much of UNESCO's discourse about 'the cultural dimension of development'. The terms were so capacious that it was difficult to disentangle causes and effects; they actually inhibited proper analysis of the relationships among the variables they packed together (Kuper 1999).

These were the sorts of conceptual dead ends Hoggart was always careful about. What would he have made of the frequent present-day conflation of the two understandings? In effect, it has become commonplace in cultural policy to justify investments in the arts as investments in 'protecting' or 'strengthening' entire, generally national, ways of life. In other words, what is at stake is not the flourishing of particular art forms, or of cultural expressions as ends in themselves, but as instruments in the affirmation of national or local distinctiveness. This is most obviously the case with the politically dominant current understandings of 'cultural diversity' at European Union level as another way of talking about 'cultural exception'. Ensuring the flourishing of European audiovisual culture, for example, is considered tantamount to safeguarding the 'ways of life' the former expresses, shapes and represents (Schlesinger 2001).

Conclusion

These reminiscences of Hoggart at UNESCO as well my exploration of certain ideas on the arts and culture with which he has engaged, have drawn widely on his 1978 book *An Idea and its Servants: UNESCO from Within*. This volume was positively reviewed in Britain, yet none of the UK-based reviewers, friendly though all of them apparently were, could possibly have had any kind of insight into the singular world he evoked in those pages. So it would be appropriate perhaps to conclude with an 'insider' judgment, albeit that of an observer rather partial to Hoggart's ways of seeing. In my perspective, his portrait of UNESCO and its analysis is as robust in terms of organisational sociology as it is free of the obfuscating jargon of that discipline. It unpacks the organisation's 'dance of protocol' (Hoggart 1978: 151) with humour that is as droll as it is revealing. The analysis is equally solid in the terrain of international cultural relations. More importantly, in an anthropological perspective, it is a very fine ethnography of the 'UNESCO village' as it was in the 1970s, of a reality that was 'so complex a tapestry of human failings and virtues' (Hoggart 1978: 200). Above all, in this post-Copenhagen moment of disappointment at what can and cannot be achieved through international cooperation — particularly when the latter fails miserably to become anything more than the sum of its discordant parts — Hoggart's 'sober idealism' about the post-Second World War international ideal and those who serve that ideal is a commitment well worth pondering. From where we are today, his portrait of UNESCO and its only partly well-served higher purposes has lost none of its acuity.

Bibliography

Bailey, M. and M. Eagleton. (2011) 'Introduction: The Life and Times of Richard Hoggart'. In Michael Bailey and Mary Eagleton (eds.), *Richard Hoggart: Culture and Critique* (Nottingham: CCC Press), pp. 13-29.

Beck, U. (2006) *The Cosmopolitan Vision* (Cambridge: Polity Press).

Benhabib, S. (2006) *Another Cosmopolitanism. Hospitality, Sovereignty, and Democratic Iterations* (New York: Oxford University Press).

Eagleton, T. (2000) *The Idea of Culture* (Oxford: Blackwell Publishing).

Gilroy, P. (2004) *After Empire* (Abingdon: Routledge).

Hadley, M. (2008) 'Promoting Intellectual Understanding and Cooperation: Richard Hoggart's UNESCO Years (1970-1975). In Sue Owen (ed.), *Re-Reading Richard Hoggart: Life, Literature, Language, Education* (Newcastle: Cambridge Scholars), pp. 153-74.

Hoggart, R. (1970) UNESCO internal memo ADG/SHC/3/556, 19 March 1970.

———— (1978) *An Idea and its Servants: UNESCO From Within* (London: Chatto and Windus).

———— (1993) *An Imagined Life* (Oxford: Oxford University Press).

———— (1995) *The Way We Live Now* (London: Chatto and Windus).

Kuper, A. (1999) *Culture, the Anthropologist's Account* (Cambridge, MA: Harvard University Press).

Radhakrishnan, R. (1996) *Diasporic Mediations. Between Home and Location* (Minneapolis: University of Minnesota Press).

Schlesinger, P. (2001) 'From Cultural Protection to Political Culture?

Media Policy and the European Union'. In Lars-Erik Cederman (ed.), *Constructing Europe's Identity. The External Dimension* (Boulder: Lynne Riener).

UNESCO (1970) document SHC/HUMFAC 1 (internal document of the Sector of Social Sciences, Humanities and Culture).

————— (1996) *Our Creative Diversity. Report of the World Commission on Culture and Development* (Paris: UNESCO Publishing).

Wright, S. (1998) 'Encaging the Wind', *International Journal of Cultural Policy*, 5 (1), pp. 1-10.

LITERATE SOCIOLOGY: RICHARD HOGGART'S DIALECTIC OF THE PARTICULAR AND THE GENERAL

Bill Hughes

Richard Hoggart has repeatedly stressed the importance of literary criticism for cultural studies. This may appear intuitionist or an anti-theoretical empiricism; it is, rather, a recognition of the concreteness of lived culture, and his work moves between the experiential data of ordinary life and the generalisation of theory — between the particularisation that literary criticism brings to the fore and the scientific, sociological attitude. It is thus not at all untheoretical and is, in addition, genuinely dialectical. This paper will show how Hoggart practices this literate sociology from *The Uses of Literacy* (1957) through later works such as *Speaking to Each Other* (1970) (a collection of essays mainly from the 1960s) whose very structure, divided as it is into one volume 'About Society' and one 'About Literature', displays this dialectic, and whose title reflects this dialogue between disciplines.[1]

It has been quite common to characterise the non-Marxist Richard Hoggart alongside Raymond Williams in his pre-Marxist phase, together with the Marxist E. P. Thompson (who was actually highly critical of Williams's use of the *Culture and Society* tradition) as naively untheoretical. They supposedly shared a typically English empiricism.[2] Hoggart's *The Uses of Literacy* emerged about the same time as Thompson's *Making of the English Working Class* (1963) and Raymond Williams's *Culture and Society 1780–1950* (1958); these three are often considered the founding texts of Cultural Studies.[3] In one version of this narrative, cultural studies only came of age when it imported the continental — mainly French — theory of Althusser, other structuralisms, and then poststructuralism. I want to suggest how, precisely through the repeated emphasis on the conjunction between literature and sociology, Hoggart's thought is at least as sophisticated as this rival strand. Raymond Williams would follow a

---

[1] In fact, there is probably as much on literature in the first volume as in the second; the two categories interpenetrate each other.

[2] However, see Thompson's (1995: 44) critique of the simplistic conflation of empirical practices and empiricism in his scathing polemic against Althusser, *The Poverty of Theory*, where 'the central fracture which runs through Althusser's thought is a confusion between empirical procedures, empirical controls, and something which he calls "empiricism"'.

[3] With these texts, *The Uses of Literacy* 'constituted what Stuart Hall later called the "caesura" out of which cultural studies in the British tradition took form' (Gibson and Hartley 1998: 11).

tortuous path towards Marxism; in his later moves, he defines cultural materialism as affirming the importance of particularity, as 'a theory of the specificities of material culture and literary production within historical materialism' (Williams 1977: 5). Hoggart eschews Marxism but I will argue that his project is nevertheless akin to that of Williams and is dialectical in just this way of situating the concrete within a larger structure (though crucially, of course, lacking the historical materialism). Even so, the vacuum left by historical materialism's absence is partially compensated for by Hoggart's need to account for 'cultural change' whereby '[t]he distinctive contribution of literary criticism to the discussion of cultural change is its attempt to define what is meant, in the fullest sense we can reach, by "changes in the quality of life" of a society' (Hoggart 1965a: 126). This does not in itself rule out a Marxist explanation; it is agnostic, and says only that literature can uncover the structures and dynamics of social change; the causality must be sought for elsewhere. Hoggart's project sees literature as more than a documentary source of experiential detail: 'literature seeks a new kind of wholeness — to trace the pattern or movement that can lie behind the apparently inchoate details of life' (Hoggart 1966: 21). Thus the 'distinctive knowledge' (Hoggart 1966: 19) that literature offers is how it integrates the particulars it has observed and displays them in flux. This will be illustrated and amplified below.

Hoggart is one of those thinkers who is dialectical without acknowledging it (and he might well repudiate such an ascription). I am not the first to remark on this 'dialectic between the particular and the general' — Sue Owen (2008: 8) uses the very phrase in the introduction to her book, *Richard Hoggart and Cultural Studies*, noting how Hoggart's literary insights became lost in later versions of cultural studies — but I have a slightly different emphasis. I am suggesting that thinkers like Sartre, who are predominantly dialectical, have much in common with what are perhaps unvoiced tendencies within Hoggart's writings. Compare Hoggart's method with Sartre's (1973) progression-regression in *Search for a Method*. Sartre describes the two moments of this process thus:

> We demand of general history that it restore to us the structures of the contemporary society, its conflicts, its profound contradictions, and the over-all movement which these determine. Thus we have at the outset a totalizing knowledge of the moment considered, but [...] this knowing remains abstract. (Sartre 1973: 134)

The social sciences can perform this sort of analysis. But for Sartre (and, as will appear, for Hoggart), this is not enough:

On the other hand, we have a certain partial acquaintance with our object; for example, we already know the biography of Robespierre insofar as it is a determination of temporality — that is, a succession of well-known facts. These facts appear concrete because they are known in detail, but they lack *reality*, since we cannot yet attach them to the totalizing movement. (Sartre 1973: 134)

In Sartre's method, 'a systematic cross-reference is established between the particular anecdotes' of the lived experience and 'the general determination of living conditions which allows us to reconstruct *progressively* [...] the material existence of the groups considered' (Sartre 1973: 145). I will show that Hoggart's attention resembles this programme in continually oscillating between the particular and the general, the empirical and the theoretical, recognising their mutual and dynamic interdependence.

There is something Sartrean, too, about Hoggart's own use of anecdote, alive in its particularity, as fleshing out and developing his theoretical generalisations. Often, each moment of analysis is introduced by personal reminiscences that take on a novelistic attention to detail; these passages are acute and vividly evocative.[4] He has given a fascinating illustration of his method more recently in exemplifying the ideal practice of Contemporary Cultural Studies:

It is not enough to label the process a form of 'impressionism'. It is more a matter of intense concentration alternating with entire relaxation, a holding together of uncounted details and a winnowing, until Conrad's 'precipitation' occurs. Then [...], the new insight comes up and lays its head in your hand; and you are surprised by what you see. (Hoggart 1996: 182-183)

Thus, he defends this active, creative summoning up of a totality out of 'uncounted details' in terms of the novelist's craft.

His reading of social facts is similarly literary. One principal analytical technique in *The Uses of Literacy* is the examination of individual utterances to infer deeper social structures of working-class life. *Uses* is dense with detail, and much of this is linguistic detail: sayings, typical epithets, and so on. Take his sympathetic analysis that:

[w]hen people feel that they cannot do much about the main elements in their situation, feel it not necessarily with despair or disappointment

---

[4] Jean-Claude Passeron, too, observed that part one of *Uses* 'is sometimes not unlike the novelistic tradition of the depiction of milieu' (Passeron 1971: 121).

or resentment but simply as a fact of life, they adopt attitudes towards that situation which allow them to have a liveable life under that shadow. (Hoggart 1958: 70)

This is illustrated with a long catalogue of proverbial stoicism; the accumulated, highly individualised data illuminate an underlying 'structure of feeling' (as Raymond Williams would put it) of working-class fatalism amidst immiseration:

'what is to be, will be'; 'if y' don't like it, y' mun lump it'; 'that's just the way things are'; 'it's no good kicking against the pricks'; 'what can't be mended must be made do with'; 'y've got to tek life as it cums — day in, day out'. (Hoggart 1958: 70)

The actual list is much longer than this but one can see the way that Hoggart does not simply sum up a world-view here; he has collected together particular speech acts in all their variety and vitality to render the lived experience of working people and to reveal, too, shades in those structures of feeling, as when he contrasts the 'really flat phrases' with those where 'the note is of cheerful patience' (Hoggart 1958: 70). Capturing particulars in this way thus reveals the dynamic flux of experience in a dialectical way rather than hypostasising working-class life as one objectified generality. It is, too, a method that clearly displays its origins in literary criticism, with its close reading of individual utterances and its concern to set forth the distinctive character of each variation on a theme.

Hoggart then extends this technique to concrete particulars such as the décor and furniture of a working-class living room. Or food, where the linguistic marker of 'something tasty' links this whole chain of discrete comestibles: 'black-puddings, pig's feet, liver, cowheel, tripe, polony, "ducks", chitterlings (and for special occasions pork-pies, which are extremely popular); and the fishmongers' savouries — shrimps, roe, kippers, and mussels' (Hoggart 1958: 24). You can hear Hoggart relishing the literary qualities of this inventory as well as the gustatory memories. And this cataloguing of minute particulars is itself literary; such enumerations are an oft-remarked feature of the novel. He is here, without formally articulating it, developing a phenomenology and a grammar of living space — one that draws firmly on the practice of literary criticism. Elsewhere, Hoggart performs semiotic analyses of stock phrases, of folk medicine, and of the new legends created around film stars to reveal what he characterises as the mythical character of much working-class culture (Hoggart 1958: 17-18).

Hoggart has never abandoned this sensitivity to the concrete. Here, in *The Way We Live Now*, he gives a minutely detailed imagined narrative of 'reading' the roles played by charity shops in British towns; of how '[a] little, whole world', a series of life stories, can be intuited from observing the clothes in such shops, and imaginatively reconstructing their biography:

> You may find yourself intrigued by the charity shops which proliferate in British towns. Their different roles are quite hard to 'read'. Then one day, in a predominantly middle-class town, yet another glance at the rack of discarded men's clothing holds your attention. You notice for the first time that much of that clothing, all freshly cleaned and pressed to go on display, is casual wear — sports jackets, blousons, fawn cavalry twill trousers, grey flannels, short leather coats, Barbour jackets — all of very good quality and all, you suddenly see, in styles adopted by elderly professional men. Then you have a vision of middle-class widows clearing out their husband's wardrobes as soon as they can bring themselves to do it and carrying it all down to Oxfam or one of its cousins. (Hoggart 1996: 183)

In this economical passage, Hoggart renders the autobiographical personal epiphany of the crystallisation of insight that lies at the heart of his literary method. Within this is an illustration of that method, particularised and evocative; precisely situated as regards class. This yields, as before, a phenomenology of objects but also their history — though the wider economic context of the dominance of charity shops in the 1980s is surprisingly absent.

Thus literature, for Hoggart, is an essential complement to the objective, verifiable, positivist — and inadequate — science of society: 'sociological and social-psychological techniques are already sophisticated [...] they are still crude by comparison with the complexity of what an unskilled labourer feels on his pulses every day of the week' (Hoggart 1966: 21-22). Literature can bring to life such 'pulses'. Hoggart suggests that the commitment to objectivity in sociological study is not unimportant: 'It is plain that social scientists as social *scientists* must act as if all knowledge about the life of human beings can be caught within their procedures'. But without the supplement of literature this is 'a form of mental colour-blindness' (Hoggart 1966: 22). It is interesting that Hoggart invokes Marcuse in a footnote here as another social critic who shares his 'double (and unified) vision' (Hoggart 1966: 22); 'dialectical' is another word for this integrated doubleness. There is much in common, too, with C. Wright Mills (whose *The Sociological Imagination* of 1959 was a near contemporary of *Uses*) and his double-pronged attack on 'grand theory' and 'abstracted empiricism' (Mills 2000).

In addition, Hoggart employs the literary critical approach not just as a way of seeing but because, unlike the physical sciences, and unlike mainstream sociology, the former does not aspire or declare itself to be value free.[5] For, Hoggart declares, 'that attitude which claims to be "value-free" [...] but is really a hard-nosed unimaginativeness [...] is finally as damaging to social science as it would be to literary criticism' (Hoggart 1967: 257). Literature embodies certain values, and thus has a *critical* perspective on society. In his essay, 'Two Ways of Looking', Hoggart measures a supposedly value-free technocratic ideology against a humanist position. He cites Marcuse again who, he says, finds that 'though a society's impetus may be basically behaviouristic, it can find room for some oddity, for a small amount of artistic roughage' (Hoggart 1965b: 107). But, again dialectically, he does not simply align himself against a malignant scientism; this is not a split between two culture: 'It is the difference between two ways of looking, and tends to cut horizontally across both the "cultures"' (Hoggart 1965b: 111). Yet, still, it is the literary perspective and its world of value that is used to mediate between these two ways of looking.

Hoggart says of his essays in *Speaking to Each Other* that, '[t]he main social themes seem to circle around how one understands, interprets and evaluates cultural change — as seen in attitudes to class and education, [...] "public voices" (who speaks to whom, about what, and in what tones of voice?)' (Hoggart 1970a: 7). Yet note that these are already *literary* questions or, at least, questions of linguistic pragmatics of the type that literature excels at dramatising. He goes on to say:

Where the literary essays are about particular authors, their special interest for someone with my kind of outlook is self-evident. The others seem as often as not to settle on such subjects as the peculiar nature of the 'subjective' literary imagination and its contribution to understanding society; or [...] they are about questions of tone and how very much a reading of tone can reveal. (Hoggart 1970a.: 7-8)

Such alertness to tone, and to speaking positions leads Hoggart to make a value distinction between 'processed' and 'living' culture. Though the organicist assumptions behind these labels needs examining, this distinction rests again on a respect for the particular: 'Processed culture never imagines an individual — only masses, typical audiences, status groups' (Hoggart 1961: 130). Particularity, then, is much more than an epistemological recommendation to flesh out abstract science, it is a humanist value, upheld by living culture, which 'recognizes the diversity, the particularity, of all experience' (Hoggart 1961: 130).

---

[5] Though there have been, of course, schools of literary criticism that embrace scientism and claim, or feign, objective neutrality.

The literary technique of close reading, inherited and transformed from Richards and Leavis, uncovers the representativeness of ideal types; Hoggart refers to Weber here, but Lukács also comes to mind in his invocation of the classic realist novel and ideal types as illustrating the particular in the universal (Hoggart 1965a: 121).[6] In 'Literature and Society', Hoggart analyses *Tess of the D'Urbervilles* and what it reveals about social relationships through its attention to the particularity of individual lives (once more, not unlike Lukács on typicality); here again he sees the novel as being representative through the way that Hardy 'keeps his eye on the particulars'. He argues here that the novel can give 'a sense of the texture of life as it is lived' (Hoggart 1966: 25).

His opening declaration in 'Why I Value Literature' emphasises the specialness of the view offered only by literature, amplifying that 'sense of life':

I value literature because of the way — the peculiar way — in which it explores, re-creates and seeks for the meanings in human experience; because it explores the diversity, complexity and strangeness of that experience (of individual men or of men in groups or of men in relation to the natural world); because it re-creates the texture of that experience; and because it pursues its explorations with a disinterested passion (not wooing nor apologizing nor bullying). I value literature because in it men look at life with all the vulnerability, honesty and penetration they can command ... and dramatize their insights by means of a unique relationship with language and form. (Hoggart 1963: 11)

'Good literature', for Hoggart, 'recreates the experiential wholeness of life' (Hoggart 1966: 20). A full evaluation of society can only be made through such 'honesty and penetration', for '[w]ithout the literary witness the student of society will be blind to the fitness of a society's life' (Hoggart 1966: 20). And it is *good* literature again that alone has the penetration to uncover the workings of society: 'good literature re-creates the immediacy of life — that life was and is all these things, all these different orders of things, *all at once*. It embodies the sense of human life developing in a historical and moral context' (Hoggart 1966: 21-22).

Note that Hoggart is not embarrassed to endorse the notion of 'good literature'. In fact, in his recent work he has attacked what he identifies as a modish relativism which, he argues, is in no way emancipating for ordinary people, despite the lip service it pays to democracy and 'anti-

---

[6] For Lukács (1972: 6), 'The central category and criterion of realist literature is the type, a peculiar synthesis which organically binds together the general and the particular both in characters and situations'.

elitism' (see Hoggart 1996). This concern with, and defence of, value is connected with the levelling and erasure of particularity by exchange value about which I have written elsewhere (Hughes 2008: 26), so I will not pursue this much further here. He claimed, in a 1998 interview, that this stance is not incompatible with a sense of the value of authentic working-class culture (Gibson and Hartley 1998: 14), and the first part of *The Uses of Literacy* is devoted to representing this authenticity, which he sums up thus:

> The more we look at working-class life, the more we try to reach the core of working-class attitudes, the more surely does it appear that the core is a sense of the personal, the concrete, the local: it is embodied in the idea of, first, the family and, second, the neighbourhood. This remains, though much works against it, and partly because so much works against it. (Hoggart 1958: 20)

There is a potentially fruitful suggestion here — unexplored like many of Hoggart's epiphanies. This is that the particular is not just important methodologically to flesh out the abstractions of sociology, though, as I have argued, it is this too. But there is something more: a hint that this attention to concreteness is especially important in illuminating specifically *working-class* culture, that the values of individuality that Hoggart endorses are those of working-class life (though this is not an atomised individualism). By implication, then, homogenising abstraction is not merely an epistemological mistake but a threat to that life, and one that is tied up with the critique of mass culture that Hoggart famously undertakes in the second part of *Uses*. See, for instance, how his phenomenology of the new public spaces contrasts with the warm clutter of home life:

> Though [this life] may seem muddled and sprawling, the design can be seen, ensured by an unsophisticated and unconscious but still strong sense of what a home is for. Compare it with the kind of public room which may be found in many a café or small hotel today — the walls in several hostile shades of distemper, clashing strips of colour along their centres; cold and ugly plastic door-handles; fussy and meaningless wall lamp-holders; metal tables which invite no one and have their over-vivid colours kicked and scratched away: all tawdry and gimcrack. (Hoggart 1958: 26)

This is more than accurate empirical description; it acutely conveys the active hostility towards sociality of *things*: the tables which, unlike those of the working-class home, 'invite no one'. It resembles Adorno's perhaps more paranoid meditation on furnishings in *Minima Moralia*, where 'gentle latches' have been replaced by 'turnable handles', whose operating movements 'have the [...] jerkiness of Fascist maltreatment' (Adorno 1978:

19). It is also reminiscent of Sartre's desire to develop 'a psychoanalysis of things' (Sartre 1958: 600).[7] Jean-Claude Passeron, in his introduction to the French translation of *Uses*, draws out Hoggart's theoreticism, seeing him a as an ethnographer, and Hoggart himself has Passeron noticing the phenomenological aspect of his approach: 'What Passeron says is: "Yes, the French have a lot of theories but one thing the British can show us is how you should look at things and feel them and smell them — they're very phenomenological"'.[8]

But literature also affects the observer (and Hoggart elsewhere stresses the importance of the *good* reader), persuading her to be an ethical as well as an effective one; literacy is a means as well as an end; social change can come out of the critical reading practices that Hoggart finds so crucial. Hoggart presses for 'a literate democracy'; his literate sociology always has this as its end (Hoggart 1964: 202). This may be reformist, and not overtly radical in itself, of course, but such critical, negative social analysis is potentially profoundly radical. The ethics and effectiveness are inseparable — the 'moral impact' is not 'a direct ethical prompting but the effect literature may have on the temper with which we face experience' (Hoggart 1963: 16). And this is consistent with the autonomy that Hoggart persistently grants human subjects, particular working people who are so often seen as pawns of ideological forces. In this, too, literature both inspires and casts light on such autonomy:

> Literature can help to bring us up short, to stop the moulds from setting firm. It habitually seeks to break the two-dimensional frame of fixed 'being' which we just as habitually try to put around others, to make us see them again as three-dimensional people in a constant state of becoming. (Hoggart 1963: 16)

The Sartrean echoes here are, I think, very strong; for Sartre, the 'dialectical totalization' must 'place the agent or the event back into the historical setting, define him in relation to the orientation of becoming' (Sartre 1973: 133). This approach is both analytically more truthful (because it frees us from essentialising reductionism) and more ethical: being 'responsive and alert' (Hoggart 1963: 16) and extending our humanity are one. Extending humanity, for Hoggart, is again about respect for the particular, for the

---

[7] Bill Brown (2001) gives a contemporary account of the life of the object in his introduction to a special edition of *Critical Inquiry*.

[8] Hoggart makes this claim in the 1998 interview (Gibson and Hartley 1998: 16), but it is actually Passeron's translator, Richard Dyer, who says that Hoggart's use of 'working class' is 'based not on occupational criteria but on a phenomenological understanding' (Passeron 1971: 130, note 1).

individual: thus he says the novels of Hardy or Turgenev deepen our knowledge of farm labourers, Russians, and so on (Hoggart 1963: 16-17).

In the essay that succinctly brings together his key ideas in this sphere, 'The Literary Imagination and the Sociological Imagination', Hoggart says that the literary imagination can point 'outside the literature to the life that literature examines, and claims to say something true about that life' (Hoggart 1967: 244). It is important to note that this claim is more than that literature reflects or provides 'symptomatic evidence' of society (Hoggart 1967: 244). Paralleling Sartre again, he is 'doubtful whether, since literature is produced by individual human beings, any work of literature can be explained wholly as a symptom' (Hoggart 1967: 244). Hoggart instead makes a larger claim. The 'imaginative power' of the writer is akin to that faculty which forms productive hypotheses in social science, yet the differences between the two perspectives, between the 'ideal type analysis' of the sociologist and the artist's 'significant detail' — in a perfectly dialectical movement to and fro — concern the particular in the general. The former 'abstracts from the detail of society so as to make a usable theoretic design; creative writing recognizes "significant detail" whilst at the same time recognizing and recreating the flux of untypical life' (Hoggart 1967: 249). This all may sound imprecise, intuitive and to the kind of social scientist castigated by Mills, unscientific. Yet Hoggart does lay out criteria to regulate the findings of the literary imagination: the text under consideration must be of a complexity adequate to mediate the complexity of human subjects in society; it must be economical, avoiding excess in its treatment of its subject matter; it must be compatible with what other disciplines have uncovered, so that 'each illuminates as well as mutually qualifies the others' (Hoggart 1967: 252-53). And again, the dialectic between the literary and the sociological is expressed in the way that, by 'submitting' — by engaging with the text as literature rather than symptom — the critic can move between the scientific and aesthetic judgment, judgement, modifying each in turn (Hoggart 1967: 253).

There is therefore an unrecognised theoretical component in Hoggart's work that situates his closely observed, empiricist particulars in more general social structures, bringing him into a surprising kinship with the more theoretical Williams, and with continental dialecticians such as Sartre, Lukács and the Frankfurt School. I do not mean to suggest a direct influence of these writers on Hoggart (though it would be unwise to underestimate either the breadth of his reading or his awareness of contemporary ideas).[9] However, as *Uses* reveals, Hoggart was ambivalently

[9] Thus both Marcuse and Adorno are cited at various points in *Speaking to Each Other*.

situated between contrasting social orders and cultures; he also made a deliberate choice to bring to social facts a particularising sensibility drawn from the study of literature. Both of these factors contributed to the dialectical cast of his thought.

Hoggart does reveal, of course, a very blunt scepticism towards *some* obscurantist uses of theory — I suspect particularly towards the Althusserian bent of later Cultural Studies. Yet in *The Way We Live Now* he defends his method of intuitive imagining by making it very clear that his approach is not simply a utilitarian anti-intellectualism:

> To say such things is to undervalue neither the place of theory nor the languages of theory — at the right times. Perhaps this needs stressing. There is no suggestion that 'brass tacks' are always better than finely tuned surgical instruments; nor is this a call on that 'commonsensical' outlook which can more often than not be a way of evading mental difficulties, the *ad hominem* cry which rallies the lazy. It is, though, a way of registering suspicion of those uses of theory which chiefly delight in belonging to a 'mystery'. (Hoggart 1996: 183)

However, I do not think we can ignore how Hoggart's conjunction of the objective generalisation of social science and the value-laden sensitivity to the particularity of literary analysis brings a very special *theoretical* perspective to the observation of how human beings live. And how this essentially humanist perspective, drawing deeply from the literary, is also a forceful critique of the one-dimensional forces of contemporary society that work to destroy what is individual in working-class culture and in human life. Hoggart says this much more elegantly than I can:

> Good literature insists on 'the mass and majesty' of the world — on its concreteness and sensuous reality [...] It insists on the importance of the inner, the distinctive and individual, life of man, while much else [...] tries to make that life generalized and typecast. (Hoggart 1963: 12)

Yet, he adds, literature 'will go beyond particular time and place and speak about our common humanity, will become — as we used to say more readily — universal' (Hoggart 1963: 14).

Richard Johnson makes the criticism of the cultural tradition that it fails 'to adequately theorize the results of concrete studies' (Johnson 1979a: 71).[10] He continues:

---

[10] For a survey and critique of this tradition, see Critcher (1979) and Johnson (1979b).

There is a tendency not to write about determinations that are external to, or do not easily show up in, 'culture' or 'experience'. There is a tendency to trust the 'authentic' experiential text as the exclusive source of accounts. [...] Social processes cannot be (wholly) understood in terms of the recorded experiences of individuals or classes [...] The object of an adequate history must, then, not merely be 'people' but the whole complex set of relations in which they stand, within which, indeed, they are first made as social beings. (Johnson 1979a: 71)

I think this is untrue of the later Williams, who draws on Gramsci, the genetic structuralism of Goldmann, and Prague School structuralism among others. Hoggart might more easily be accused of this; yet I have argued that there is an implicit theoretical counterpoint to his empiricism. Unlike accounts of working-class experience nearly contemporary with *Uses* (for example, that of Jackson and Marsden (1966), Hoggart constantly points beyond the gathering of discrete perceptions to a totalisation that is, admittedly, never quite spelt out. Nevertheless, his work stands as an important move towards theorising a literate sociology that is aware of the dialectic between the concrete data of experience and the structured whole of society that shapes that data and in turn responds to it.

Bibliography

Adorno, T. (1978) *Minima Moralia: Reflections from Damaged Life* (trans. E. F. N. Jephcott) (London: Verso).

Brown, B. (2001) 'Thing Theory'. *Critical Inquiry*, 28(1), pp. 1-22.

Clarke, J., et al. (eds.) (1979) *Working-Class Culture: Studies in History and Theory* (London: Hutchinson, in association with the Centre for Contemporary Cultural Studies, University of Birmingham).

Critcher, C. (1979) 'Sociology, Cultural Studies and the Post-war Working Class'. In John Clarke, et al. (eds.), *Working Class Culture: Studies in History and Theory* (London: Hutchinson, in association with the Centre for Contemporary Cultural Studies, University of Birmingham), pp. 13-40.

Gibson, M., and Hartley, J. (1998) 'Forty Years of Cultural Tudies: An Interview with Richard Hoggart', *International Journal of Cultural Studies*, 1(1), pp. 11-23.

Hoggart, R. (1958) *The Uses of Literacy* (Harmondsworth: Penguin).

————— (1961) 'Culture: Dead and Alive'. In Richard Hoggart, *Speaking to Each Other, Volume 1: About Society* (Harmondsworth: Penguin), pp. 129-132.

————— (1963) 'Why I Value Literature'. In Richard Hoggart, *Speaking to Each Other, Volume 2· About Literature* (Harmondsworth: Penguin), pp. 11-18.

————— (1964) 'The Guardians and the New Populism'. In Richard

Hoggart, *Speaking to Each Other, Volume 1: About Society* (Harmondsworth: Penguin), pp. 201-204.

———— (1965a) 'On Cultural Analysis'. In Richard Hoggart, *Speaking to Each Other, Volume 1: About Society* (Harmondsworth: Penguin), pp. 112-128.

———— (1965b) 'Two Ways of Looking'. In Richard Hoggart, *Speaking to Each Other, Volume 1: About Society* (Harmondsworth: Penguin), pp. 104-111.

———— (1966) 'Literature and Society'. In Richard Hoggart, *Speaking to Each Other, Volume 2: About Literature* (Harmondsworth: Penguin), pp. 19-37.

———— (1967) 'The Literary Imagination and the Sociological Imagination'. In Richard Hoggart, *Speaking to Each Other, Volume 2: About Literature* (Harmondsworth: Penguin), pp. 244-257.

———— (1970a) *Speaking to Each Other, Volume 1: About Society* (Harmondsworth: Penguin).

———— (1970b) *Speaking to Each Other, Volume 2: About Literature* (Harmondsworth: Penguin).

———— (1996) *The Way We Live Now* (London: Pimlico).

Hughes, B. (2008) 'The Uses and Values of Literacy: Richard Hoggart, Aesthetic Standards, and the Commodification of Working-Class Culture'. In Sue Owen (ed.), *Richard Hoggart and Cultural Studies* (Basingstoke: Palgrave Macmillan), pp. 213-226.

Jackson, B. and Marsden, D. (1966) *Education and the Working Class* (Harmondsworth: Penguin).

Johnson, R. (1979a) 'Culture and the Historians'. In John Clarke, et al. (eds.), *Working Class Culture: Studies in history and theory* (London: Hutchinson, in association with the Centre for Contemporary Cultural Studies, University of Birmingham), pp. 41-71.

———— (1979b) 'Three Problematics: Elements of a Theory of Working-Class Culture'. In John Clarke, et al. (eds.), *Working Class Culture: Studies in history and theory* (London: Hutchinson, in association with the Centre for Contemporary Cultural Studies, University of Birmingham), pp. 201-237.

Lukács, G. (1972) *Studies in European Realism: A Sociological survey of the Writings of Balzac, Stendhal, Zola, Tolstoy, Gorki and others* (trans. E. Bone) (London: Merlin Press).

Mills, C. Wright ([1959] 2000) *The Sociological Imagination* (with a new afterword by Todd Gitlin) (New York: Oxford University Press).

Owen, S. (2008) 'Introduction'. In Sue Owen (ed.), *Richard Hoggart and Cultural Studies* (Basingstoke: Palgrave Macmillan), pp. 1-19.

Passeron, J-C. (1971) 'Introduction to the French edition of *Uses of Literacy*'. *Working Papers on Cultural Studies* (Spring 1971), pp. 120-131.

Sartre, J-P. (1958) *Being and Nothingness: An Essay on Phenomenological Ontology* (trans. H. E. Barnes, intro M. Warnock) (London: Methuen).

———— (1973) *Search for a Method* (trans. H. E. Barnes) (New York: Vintage).

Thompson, E. P. (1968) *The Making of the English Working Class* (Harmondsworth: Penguin).

———— (1995). *The Poverty of Theory: or an Orrery of Errors.* New edn (London: Merlin Press).

Williams, R. (1963) *Culture and Society 1780–1950* (Harmondsworth: Penguin).

———— (1977) *Marxism and Literature* (Oxford: Oxford University Press).

APPENDIX
INTRODUCTION TO THE FRENCH EDITION OF *THE USES OF LITERACY**
Jean-Claude Passeron

J.P. is a member of the Centre de Sociologie Européenne in Paris and is co-author of *Le Metier de Sociologie*. The essay here translated by Richard Dyer appears as the introduction to the French edition of *The Uses of Literacy*. M. Passeron examines Richard Hoggart's work as a contribution to anthropology as well as to the debate about mass culture. He suggests the theoretical foundations and hypotheses in this apparently untheoretical book and goes on to indicate the ways in which it seems to have been misunderstood by bourgeois intellectuals.

Despite its subtitle, 'Aspects of Working-Class Life' it would not be paradoxical to treat *The Uses of Literacy* as a thoughtful contribution to the sociology of intellectuals and more especially of those who are professional sociologists. He analyses the imagery of the 'man in the street', so dear to journalists, or the contradictory and complementary myths of the 'rustic vigour' and 'feminine gentleness' of the working class, which are the delight of novelists, moralists and artists alike; and all the dreadful contributions imbued with viciousness or else with lyricism which have been made to the mass culture debate (a counterpoint to the pastoral nostalgia from which few sociologists are exempt) and, in each case, Richard Hoggart hints at the extent to which sociologists merely play among themselves when they play with an image of the working class. He suggests why the situation of this class, characterised negatively as cultural deprivation, constitutes a privileged symbolic object for groups of intellectuals, themselves defined in various ways by a privileged role in the production and popularisation of culture.

If it is true that intellectuals never reveal better their propensity to monopolise the social definition of culture than in their incapacity for seeing in other social groups anything other than an excuse to examine their own cultural contradictions (by an ethnocentrism which, even though in apparently opposed forms, bears witness to both aristocratic

* Published as a *Working Paper in Cultural Studies*, trans. by Richard Dyer, Centre for Contemporary Cultural Studies, University of Birmingham, No. 1, Spring 1971, pp. 120-31.

and populist attitudes), then Richard Hoggart's strategy of outlining, in order to go beyond them more easily, some of the intellectual illusions inherent in the sociology of the working classes, involves at the very least the makings of a sociological interpretation which would connect the ideological values of attitudes towards popular culture with the social position of various sorts of intellectual.

One might as well point out straight away that the extreme originality of the work is liable to disconcert many of its readers. Richard Hoggart calls into question the artful naivety, the class ethnocentrism or the hidden anachronisms of numerous analyses largely accepted today of 'the cultural homogenisation of consumer societies', the evil or beneficial power of the mass press, radio and television, on the 'atomisation' and 'massification' of the urban proletariat or of the destruction of the traditional way of life of the working class. Not without vehemence when taking fashionable ideas to pieces, he has put himself in the position of being labelled a vitriolic writer by all those who would find that a convenient way of dismissing tiresome analyses. Moreover the work, which doubtless owes much of its success to the fluidity of its style and descriptions, cannot be fitted into any neatly delineated tradition of anthropological literature. Although the author is aiming at a synthesis of the specialised studies on the life style of the working-class[1] in urban and industrial England and on the characteristics of the production arid diffusion of new cultural messages, *The Uses of Literacy*, deliberately stripped of the more obvious signs of sociological debate — jargon or statistics, crushing documentation or methodological emphasis — could be taken, in part one, as a study of manners, in which the treatment of the setting, the stories and the characters is sometimes not unlike the novelistic tradition of the depiction of milieu; whilst in its second part it could pass for an exercise in method: transposing the classic technique of literary analysis to the context and audience of the mass press. In addition there is a variety of other concerns which might dismay a reader too exclusively faithful to the religion of clear distinctions between disciplines. At one level a protest in the name of scientific objectivity against aristocratic, populist, apocalyptic or foolishly

---

[1] M. Passeron uses the term 'les classes populaires' in his analysis, for which the only English equivalents are the rather unpleasant 'common people', 'Proletariat' and 'lower classes'. Despite the fact that the French do have a term for 'working-class' ('les ouvriers'), I have chosen to use this term more or less throughout the translation, since it is the term favoured by Richard Hoggart himself. Readers are reminded however that Hoggart's use and definition of the term, as set out in the first chapter of *The Uses of Literacy* is particular to him, being based not on any occupational criteria but on a phenomenological understanding (RD).

optimistic pronouncements which come between the life of the working class and its necessarily intellectual or bourgeois observers, *The Uses of Literacy* also derives in large part — as the author admits several times — from autobiography, if not self analysis. Moreover, while he methodically sets about grasping the mechanics behind the failures of proportion or the optical illusion to which the majority of moral judgments commonly applied to popular culture may be reduced, Richard Hoggart has no intention of refraining from sticking his neck out and assessing the value of the cultural changes associated with the transformation of working-class life. Whilst offering elements of autobiography which allow him to situate himself in relation to the working class and thereby, as he suggests to his readers, to relativise his own judgements, the author never hesitates to formulate his likes and dislikes, his hopes and regrets concerning, say, the developments in popular song or furniture, changes of style in women's magazines or pornographic literature, or other transformations in popular resourcefulness and cynicism; and it is in this way that the work clearly touches on moral and aesthetic criticism.

One has to forget for a moment the rather overwhelming richness of the book in order to discern Richard Hoggart's more scientific contribution to our understanding of the situation and culture of the working class. Richard Hoggart certainly can't be numbered among those sociologists whom Wright Mills has attacked as 'bureaucratic empiricists': statistical information relegated to the notes, is there only to indicate questions of scale; the author uses only the conclusions of surveys and, doubtless caring little for the artificial delights of attitude ratings, did not consider it worthwhile to undertake a questionnaire survey in order to give his analysis numerical proof. This is a pity to the extent that the majority of his hypotheses concerning the changes in attitudes over a period or from one category to another are formulated in a way which could easily have been substantiated by statistical tests. But social science should not be defined, as a certain methodological imperialism would have it, by the exclusive use of a rigid method for the construction and assessment of facts. *The Uses of Literacy* can legitimately quote another tradition of research as authority, namely ethnography, whose heuristic fecundity and power of objectification are no less than those of statistical analysis when, employing the direct and continuous observation of conduct in a real situation, it operates according to methodically constructed categories and submits its instruments of investigation to a systematic control. If the description that Richard Hoggart offers of the development of daily life and leisure among the urban working-class in the industrial north-east of England cannot be immediately identified for what it is, this is surely only because the author refrains from relying on the terminological apparatus with which the professionals usually surround themselves in carrying out field work; perhaps too because a whole tradition accustoms us to associating the principles of ethnography with a particular type of society — that very type which some call with an experts naiveté 'ethnographic' — making us hesitate when we see them applied to the study of groups or socio-cultural milieux observable in our own society. If, instead of English workers, he had given us Trobriand islanders or the Kwakiutl, would we have had any difficulty in recognising this systematic picture of daily life as an example of an ethnographic report?

It is true that a personal experience does not in itself constitute a correct procedure for methodical observation, and that a body of documentary material — no matter how suggestive it may be — should not be confused with a correlated collection of ethnographic facts. But it is precisely characteristic of Richard Hoggart's work that, even if the liveliness of the description sometimes hides its underlying organisation, it is ordered according to a plan of observation in which one is bound to recognise the headings and operational concepts of the ethnographic inventory in its most classic form:

- organisation of space and habitation
- seasonal and weekly itinerary and movements
- rhythms and places of work and leisure
- ages of life and relations between the sexes
- structure of the family group and the education of children
- the articulation of economic, cultural and religious practices
- a repertoire simultaneously of material objects and goods and of models which govern their use.

Meticulously reviewing the various areas of activity in daily life, Richard Hoggart does not give in to the cultural critic's temptation of going directly to the 'values behind' a human group by a sort of divine intuition, probably because he is concerned to relate systematically the objective situation of the group to its habits and routines, these being seen as objectivations of some fundamental principles which govern the response to these conditions of existence: thus the analysis of values is clearly grounded in a concrete and methodical description of habits and norms as different at first sight as those which underlie food, funerals, clothing, furniture decoration, contraception, superstition, humour and health, or which by a similar logic order the relations of members of the working class to work, work prospects, wages, handling the budget, expenditure, credit and saving, as well as their contact with bureaucracy the institution of the monarchy, sport, adultery, suicide, bachelorhood, drink, sex, games and morality. In short, by a meticulous attention to the nuances of everyday life, to the details of decor (even the smells are not forgotten) and to the social physiognomy of people — right down to its effects on the silhouette — as well as by its hermeneutic orientation towards revealing the latent meanings of publicity and leisure or the most subtle connotations of key words and turns of speech, Richard Hoggart manages to draw from his autobiographical experience as an intellectual coming from a working-class background all that a careful ethnographer can draw from a good 'informant'.

Better still, the liberties in composition and narration that the author readily takes with the codified rules normal in the presentation of an enquiry's findings definitely have the effect of correcting any methodological weaknesses of the genre. One knows how difficult it is to work out the logic of action in a life style, an ideology or a culture from a dry ethnographic study, when it is reduced to a lexicon of models of behaviour. These models are cut off from the whole set of concrete conditions which occasion them and are abstracted from the series of actions which alone can explain their function. If he must be permanently on guard against the deceptiveness of his material, the misleading evidence of anecdotes or the dubious insights of participation in ceremonies, the ethnologist knows that the observation of real scenes and situations can at least suggest the hypothesis for correspondences, homologies or continuities which can only be made out in vast configurations of attitudes or events, such as biographies or genealogies, time tables or allocations of space learnt over a prolonged period of time, and institutionalised or recurrent scenes. When Richard Hoggart puts together certain total social totalities which the inventory of features only gives in a dispersed order, he thus reconstitutes significant wholes — they may be:

- lives like those of the housewife, the scholarship boy or the self-taught man
- family trees like his own family's
- occasions such as the 'chara trip' to the seaside, the way an evening or a Sunday is spent at home or in the working men's club, the audience at a court case or a family scene
- places where the regulars establish a rhythm of coming and going, such as the road, the pub, the local library or waste ground the system of social relations embodied for instance in the relationship between a working-class couple and salesmen at a big furniture store, or between the scholarship boy and his working-class family, the women at the house, the father, and his teachers, his books, exams and social success.

These minutely constructed reconstitutions do not show a literary penchant for the vignette or realistic decoration, but a properly sociological effort on the part of the author to hold together systematically a whole play of determinations and a whole constellation of attitudes which only completely reveal all their relations — be they interdependencies or contradictions — in sufficiently complex configurations of actions and reactions, observed in situations that are truly significant in the social life of the group. This is after all only a practical example of what Bronislaw Malinowski held to be the most irreplaceable contribution of ethnographic method:

> ... there is a series of phenomena of great importance which cannot possibly be recorded by questioning or computing documents, but have to be observed in their full actuality. Let us call them the imponderabilia of actual life. Here belongs such things as the routine of a man's working day, the details of his care of the body, of the manner of taking food and preparing for it; the tone of conversational and social life around the village fires ... All the facts can and ought to be scientifically formulated and recovered, but it is necessary that this be done, not by superficial registration of details as is usually done by untrained observers, but with an effort at penetrating the mental attitude expressed in them.[2]

Equally the use of a semi indirect style[3] through which the sociologist can with complete ease let the object of study speak for itself, is not a whim of the author. Hoggart's phraseology is designed to treat with complete objectivity the perspective that the working class has determined to adopt on the world, and is constructed according to a grammatical scheme which implies in principle the sociologist's exteriority to this perspective which are analysed by the imperceptible integration of phrases and semantic categories, themselves equally manifestations and indices of the working-class world view. In other words, Richard Hoggart gives himself, by this implicit syntax, a means of introducing systematically characteristic schemes of popular thought in a descriptive discourse which can thus be

---

[2] Bronislaw Malinowski, *Argonauts of the Western Pacific* (London: RKP, 1932), pp. 20-21.

[3] The term 'semi indirect style' is one common to French literary criticism, presumably because it is a style widely used by French novelists since Flaubert. It refers to the expression of personal feelings and experiences in the third person, or as M. Passeron is implying here, to a narrative presentation in which the participation of the narrator in the events described is clearly suggested (*RD*).

organised continually according to the proper logic of the object described, even if it remains distinctly at the level of interpretation and exposition. Clearly the use of this method expresses in the style of the writing the theoretical project of an author committed to uprooting and exposing intellectual ethnocentrism in all its forms; for in forcing his description to run, according to the structures, if not always in words, of working-class consciousness and speech, Richard Hoggart arms himself against the temptation of eliciting from the working-class answers to questions they do not ask themselves or not at any rate in the terms in which intellectuals for their own purposes like to put them.

But in the last analysis it is in its results that the richness of a method can be measured. Without wishing to treat here in detail the influence that *The Uses of Literacy* may have had on sociological research, one should note that the descriptive tenor of this work, which proposes for future research a whole body of systematically interconnected hypotheses, relates directly to the multiplicity and above all the style of works in the sixties devoted to the situation of the working class, their values and the concrete organisation of their daily life. The alerted reader of empirical research completed in this area must feel that numerous analyses which seem 'obvious' to him — and which in the end may find more 'literary' than those that he may have read in specialised monographs — have generally become classics only after the appearance of Richard Hoggart's work (1957). *The Uses of Literacy* attracts attention to a complex of attitudes and behaviour governed by the confused consciousness of the objective and collective destiny of the group; this complex expresses itself in the strongly felt sense of belonging, for better or worse, and irreversibly, to a community subject to the same limitations and the same constraints, and manifests itself concretely in for instance the sentimental value attached to the family circle and relations proper to the nuclear group, in the changeability of family relations with the neighbourhood, in the use of personal chains of solidarity and self-help, in the local and communal character of entertainments and of daily life, and, above all, in the fundamental separation of the world into 'them' and 'us'. This latter means a double standard in judgements and actions, moral inclinations and handling relationships with others, which is in inverse proportion according to whether one is 'one one's own ground' or must come into contact with the world of 'them'. All these aspects have subsequently been studied or even experimented upon in the work of H. J. Cans, M. Kerr, J. M. Mogey, M. Young and P. Willmott, D. E. Muir and E. A. Weinstein, E. Litwak or A. K. Cohen and H. M. Hodges.

Another set of themes describe a popular morality, a mixture of puritanism, ostentatious cynicism and sarcastic refusal of all idealism or the attitude towards 'them', a subtle blend of suspicion, retraction, pride, false deference, provocation, resignation and disparagement, or class conformity, which often also involves tolerance towards other members of the group and rests on a whole tradition of disaffection from the authorities and official society, or again the fatalism and resignation of the worst-off sections who entrench themselves in a consciousness deaf to their socio-economic destiny. All these themes underlying Richard Hoggart's analysis can be found again in the studies of F. L. Strodtbeck, L. Rainwater, R. P. Coleman and G. Handel and R. Endleman. Or look again at the personality of the mother in the working-class family, her relationship with the father and her role in the management and economy of domestic life, or the relations of parents and children at various points in their education - in addition to the authors already cited, M. L. Kohn, E. E. Carrot and W. B. Miller[4] have substantially taken over, not always without some watering down, these features which *The Uses of Literacy* brought to light with such vigour.

Richard Hoggart's analyses are at their most original when he is calling into question the image that other classes have of the working class and

---

[4] M. Young and P. Willmott, *Family and Kinship in East London* (London: RKP, 1957); M. Kerr, *People of Ship Street* (London: RKP, 1958); W. B. Miller, 'Lower class culture as a generating delinquency', *Journal of Social Issues* XIV, 1958; F. L. Stodtbeck, 'Family interaction, values and achievements' in D. C. McClelland et al, *Talent and Society* (New York: Van Nostrand, 1958); L. Rainwater et al, *Workman's Wife* (New York: Oceada, 1959); E. Litwak, 'The use of extended family groups in the achievement of social goals', *Social Problems* VII, 1959; M. L. Kohn and E. E. Carroll, 'Social class and the allocation of parental responsibilities' Sociometry XXIII, 1960; D. E. Muir and E. A. Weinstein, 'The social debt: an investigation of lower and middle class norms of social obligation', *American Sociological Review* XXVII, 1962; H. J. Gans, *The Urban Villagers* (New York: Free Press, 1962); A. K. Cohen and H. N. Hodges Jnr, 'Characteristics of the lower blue-collar class', *Social Problems* X, 1963; R. Endleman, 'Moral perspectives of blue-collar workers', in A. B. Shostak and W. Gornberg (eds.) *Blue Collar World* (New Jersey: Englewood Cliffs, 1964); F. M. Katz, 'The meaning of success: some differences in value systems of social classes', *Journal of Social Psychology* LXII, 1964.

At a more general level one can see in a bibliography of sociological literature in the English Language devoted to the condition and culture of the working class and the working-class family that the majority of studies appeared after 1956 and that those works which stand out as exceptions to the general trend (for example *Portrait of the Underdog* by G. Knupfer or *The Deprived and The Privileged* by B. M. Spinley) are precisely those whose ruling ideas are furthest away from those of Richard Hoggart. One should note that in the bibliography at the end of the present work Richard Hoggart lists either collections of documents or else historical studies far from systematic according to a sociological perspective.

their values. The author's past, born and brought up in a working-class family, becoming a scholarship boy and then a university teacher and researcher, undoubtedly puts him in a particularly advantageous position for grasping the class significance of judgements on the working class which often to the educated classes seem of the order of 'natural truths'. It may well be true that all intellectual personality is socially conditioned and that no class experience is capable of engendering by itself a properly scientific attitude (no gift of birth in any class, whether privileged, or even [Mannheim notwithstanding] intellectual, ever predestined someone to the attainment of the objectivity of sociological percipience). Even so it is clear that it is only after a period of work by himself on himself, the social situation of which is precisely that of scientific study, that Richard Hoggart has been able to make use of that approach consisting of both distancing and participation, which makes him able to perceive and explain by example even the very nuances of the behaviour of intellectuals with working-class backgrounds, technocrats with too much assurance, university teachers who 'sell out', or at any rate look down from their newly acquired class position — ready to draw on their own library, as he himself ironically remarks, to illustrate the incoherence of the self-taught man thirsty for cultural salvation. In every case, and although it is so intimately associated with the social situation of his early years, there can be no doubt that Richard Hoggart's particular *habit of mind* is peculiarly effective when bourgeois or petit-bourgeois ethnocentrism needs ousting. There is no need to recall the ideological fruits born among the middle class by those sententious speeches emphatically deploring the thoughtlessness and improvidence of the lower classes, their prodigal expenditure and their inability to think for the morrow or to manage their budget sensibly; pity is taken on 'these people' who buy — on the instalment plan — a television and not a sewing machine, which would be so much more useful for them 'with their hundreds of children', who 'throw away' their money playing bingo or betting, and who spoil their children against all the canons of child care, even encouraging the vices of vanity, prodigality, and indifference — not forgetting the supreme failing of not knowing their place — by buying them at Christmas the loveliest toys when they can't even afford to dress or educate then properly. It is by relating this behaviour to the most restricting aspects of working-class life that Richard Hoggart reconstitutes the logic of attitudes which seem illogical only when one is illogical enough to judge them according to values which are the products of other conditions of existence. If the purchase of a television set is more logical than that of a sewing machine and if the coal necessary for 'a good fire' from which all may benefit takes precedence over worrying about underclothes, this is because for the working-class preference is always, however slender the budget, for goods whose collective use can serve as a support to the gathering and hedonistic communion of the family community. Since leaning back on the privacy and even the promiscuity of the home is the only resort in a situation which would otherwise be intolerable. The 'weakness' of parents who let children 'have a good time', especially in adolescence, that last period of licensed frivolity before the burdens and worries which will come 'soon enough' is understandable enough when one sees that it expresses the need 'to take advantage of it when you can and while you can', a need which is peculiar to the underprivileged classes, deprived of any objective chance to better their lot. This need provides a key to the understanding of popular entertainments, 'all pals together', excursions where no expense is spared, the fantastic roundabouts of the fairground. Similarly one can grasp the transformation in meaning and value that what one might call the *paradigm of the bad worker undergoes*. In itself, this is the last and basic resort of petit-bourgeois moaning and the legitimation for the housewife's daily indignation at the plumber come to repair the bath ('One can't get service these days'), but the alternative meaning is apparent when the plumber's attitude towards repairing the tap is seen from the point of the wage earner, and his relation to wages, to the boss, to the work and to the class he serves.

In a more general way by this style of analysis which deliberately breaks with principles in their own way as racist as those of pre-scientific ethnographers limited to detailing the barbarism of the 'primitives', Richard Hoggart gives himself the means of escaping from interpretations, which are too 'obvious' and which are often only the promotion to the level of intellectual investigation of class biases all the better protected for being less explicit. The analysis of the functions of defence and reassurance served by the spontaneous suspicion the working class adopt towards grand words or morality or politics ('You can't kid me'), of civic pride, patriotism, the 'imperatives of growth', and the value of public administration gives one an insight into the apparently neutral language of economists and planners. For when these speak of 'putting things right in the absence of information about the economic agents' or throw into the anonymity of 'irrationality' and 'traditional resistances' anything which departs from a type of behaviour considered sovereign, they are hiding behind the screen of an ideology of experts, the assurance proper to members of the ruling class, certain from birth of the rightness and the universal value of their attitude to culture and of their modes of conduct. Nor is it a coincidence that so many sociological enquiries can be condemned precisely because they do not get at the specificity of popular attitudes except in terms of lack or lacking 'failures of motivation', lack of interest or absence of inspiration. More subtle still is the attempt to establish the 'baroque' norms of popular art `in narrative structure of conversations, in the over-elaborate style of the furnishing and *objets trouvés*, in the cloying form of the sentimental song, in the highly coloured composition of a marriage feast or in the fairground atmosphere and truculent appeal of entertainments. Here, *The Uses of Literacy* hints at the inadequacy the vocabulary of 'art' when applied to a 'taste' which, like popular taste, refers to principles indistinguishable from ethical norms, be it in the worth attached to the serious and to the minutiae of a work, or in the value given to sentiments and sentimentality, or else in the primacy given to moral edification and to the sensuous enjoyment of the struggle over form. Here as elsewhere, Richard Hoggart avoids the populist trap, which is particularly tempting for an intellectual who, even if of working-class background, is always given to endowing popular culture with a delegated or transferred existence, defined by implicit reference to the literary culture. For it is from this last, that (despite all his good intentions) the intellectual draws his definition of aims, when he attempts to rehabilitate certain 'authentically aesthetic' productions by reproducing, at the very heart of popular culture, the cleavage whereby literary culture by definition excludes 'popular taste'.

Most valuable of all from the point of view of social science, Richard Hoggart breaks with those images of popular behaviour determined by the observers membership of the intelligentsia. Too numerous to mention are the themes of sociology-fiction which have piled up until today; they constitute a vulgate of the ills and dramas of 'mass civilisation'. These owe what credibility they possess to the social and psychological functions which they perform for intellectuals, themselves, the producers and principle consumers of this literature. The analysis, alternatively or simultaneously pejorative or fascinated, of the 'conditioning', 'brutalisation' and 'penetration' of the masses by the mass media is a well enough known orthodoxy with its sects, schisms, and theological debates. *The Uses of Literacy* is among those rare works which, whilst not denying the magnitude of the transformations that the new type of leisure and the new means of communication have effected amongst the general public, does attempt a balanced assessment. This leads the author, without any great theoretical fanfares, to pose some questions as pertinent for theory as for the empirical analysis of the transformations in popular culture and the receptivity of the different class levels to the ideological solicitations contained in the messages of the cultural industry and directed at them. In this way Richard Hoggart can demonstrate the illusoriness of a concept the origins of which lie in the failure to understand the working-class' capacity to maintain a separation between the 'real and serious life' and the world of entertainment; he can show that numerous areas of ideology and practice, such as the relationships at the heart of the family group or the attitudes to illness, death, to the home and more generally to the emotions, are hardly affected at all by the influence of the national press, radio and publicity. The majority of analyses which have, like those of Denis de Rougemenot, popularised among the intelligentsia the notion of 'escapist literature' are founded upon the semantic ambiguity of the term 'mass', which leads to blaming on popular attitudes the thematics of a literature whose principle consumers are still the petit-bourgeoisie. It is far more in the situation of the middle class than in that of the working class that 'bovarysme'[5] finds its pride of place, and the image of the scullery maid so engrossed in reading the threepenny novel that she loses her sense of reality and lives out imaginary adventures with cardboard heroes is based not so much on observation as on the mental projections of certain sorts of intellectuals fascinated by the fantasm of absolute fascination, the ultimate form — and one in which they have a vested interest — of a belief in the absolute power of literature.

Richard Hoggart takes the schema in which so many specialists, by simplistic analysis of press messages, persuade themselves that such a voluminous mass of publications can only have a 'massive' effect upon its recipients, and turns it on its head, suggesting that the modern means of communication could well in the end have the effect of neutralising the effects the specialists are looking for by the very way in which they are diffused. The analysis of the 'pasteurization' of pin-up pictures which derives from a concentration on technical improvements in photography, shows how the repetition and intellectualisation of press messages tends to prevent them from using the direct or frankly emotive effects which the popular literature and emimagery of the last century almost certainly achieved more easily by its melodramatic and brutal style.

By drawing attention to the fact that the reception of a cultural message should not be disassociated from the social conditions in which it occurs and thus from the *ethos* which essentially characterises a social group, *The Uses of Literacy* proposes for further research a theoretical hypothesis far more to the point than the assumption which leads numerous psycho-sociologists to think they can get at the true relationship between members of the working class and their reading and entertainment by 'audience analysis', in which as a general rule they only succeed in getting their subjects to confess their own ideology of escapism or 'alienation'.

---

[5] The term refers to the character of Emma Bovary in Flaubert's *Madame Bovary*. She is the type of mindless inconstant sentimental inadequate petit-bourgeois.

By the direct observation of the real situations and spontaneous behaviour in which the dimensions of popular consumption are indicated, Richard Hoggart is led to a theory of casual consumption or, as he says 'oblique attention'. This takes on its full meaning when one connects these listening habits to the value system of the working class, traditionally inclined by the logic of their situation and by the ethos which is its product, to find their best protection against the world of 'them' with its authority and seductions, in scepticism, sarcastic cynicism and above all in the capacity for indifference, all the more effective for being hidden beneath an apparent availability. The truth of their profound attitude, made up of an acquiescence without consequence and of disabused tolerance, is expressed by the members of the working class when, speaking of the din of publicity surrounding the heroic captain of the 'Flying Enterprise' or of the political propaganda or of the emotions that the popular song and magazine exalt, they reply that one must learn how to 'take it or leave it'. The logic of the working class, more especially when they must come into contact with realities which do not belong to their daily environment, is a logic which makes them able to use alternatively and according to the needs of the moment, formally incompatible schemas, and this structure allows them to adopt towards the affirmations of the national press an attitude of elliptical adherence, very similar to that which makes them adhere, without ever being fooled completely, to superstitious beliefs of the traditional type. Here we recognise the techniques of institutionalised reticence, by means of which groups deprived of the cultural instruments of certainty and self-assurance arm themselves against the risk, experienced as omnipresent, of being 'taken for a ride': 'you'll not put one over on them'. The supreme folly, among the working class would be apparently to believe these 'stories' other than as 'stories' — witness the amused condescension working-class women show towards young mothers naive enough to give their daughters Christian names taken from the heroines of magazine stories.

At an even deeper lever, *The Uses of Literacy* is distinguishable from the semi-intellectual discussion of 'incredible transformations' in the life of 'the masses' by a theoretical principle which underlies from one end to the other the analysis of cultural change. In effect Richard Hoggart is trying to find in the structure of a set of attitudes the principles which govern the transformation of this structure. He shows for instance how popular taste is capable of reinterpreting the fashion in household furniture or the vogue in imitation fabrics for its own purposes of recreating the traditional atmosphere of home, congested and gaudy. He observes how the performance of pop style songs in a Yorkshire melodic idiom ends up making them resemble the ancient local songs, or, the other way about, he demonstrates how traditional tolerance can only have become moral indifference because it was so inclined anyway. In these demonstrations Richard Hoggart seeks to tease out the law which subordinates the efficacy of the factors of change to their relevance to the pre-existing structures. The originality of this theoretical approach allows him to exercise all the retrospective myths which are the illusionary principle behind a golden age of view of working-class culture and life. To the extent to which the analysis of cultural change is subordinated to the analysis of popular *ethos* (conceived of as a sort of *general grammar of attitudes*, or, as it is put by Richard Hoggart, as an 'attitude towards attitudes'), the interplay of reciprocal reinterpretations between a structure of reception and a structure of transmission (which is how ethnologists come to understand the logic of cultural growth) is transposed from the analysis of cultural diffusion in space to the analysis or cultural transformation over time.

Finally, all the qualities of this book derive perhaps from an initial daring, doubtless more probable, sociologically speaking, in Britain than in France, where the relationship of intellectuals to the working class, including those of them who come from this class or the lower echelons of the petit-bourgeoisie, is more controlled by the rules of good taste and good tone and thereby more 'intellectualised' and it needs to be said, all the more shameful for it. The discussion on the realities of class is certainly to the credit of numerous fractions of the French intellectual milieu, but it is not altogether wrong to suppose that its theoretical and abstract tone serves also to keep at bay a whole set of realities at once simple and scandalous — or worse than scandalous, vulgar. The whole empirical force of these realities is evident when a description at once ethnographic and autobiographical such as Richard Hoggart's brings them into focus directly, above literary artifice and scholarly exercises. If *The Uses of Literacy* impresses the reader at once as one of those books in which in all its simplicity and truth there shines out everything which by various means is obscured by university sociologists (those specialists in sublimation and displacement) and populist intellectuals, and even by dictionaries, virtuosos of counter-suggestion and projection, this is because the author has succeeded despite all the defence mechanisms which protect the intellectual of working-class origins from his own social origins, in finding through a study of himself at once sociological and auto-analytical, the difficult way by which to effect the return of the unprivileged.

Translated by Richard Dyer

RICHARD HOGGART: SELECT BIBLIOGRAPHY

Promises to Keep: Thoughts in Old Age (Continuum, 2005).

Mass Media in a Mass Society: Myth and Reality (Continuum, 2004).

Everyday Language and Everyday Life (Transaction Publishers, 2003).

Between Two Worlds: Politics, Anti-Politics, and the Unpolitical (Transaction Publishers, 2002).

Between Two Worlds: Essays, 1978-1999 (Aurum Press, 2001).

First and Last Things: The Uses of Old Age (Aurum Press, 1999).

The Tyranny of Relativism: Culture and Politics in Contemporary English Society (Transaction Publishers, 1997).

The Way We Live Now: Dilemmas in Contemporary Culture (Chatto and Windus, 1995).

A Measured Life: The Times and Places of an Orphaned Intellectual (Transaction Publishers, 1994).

Townscape with Figures: Farnham - Portrait of an English Town (Chatto and Windus, 1994).

An Imagined Life: Life and Times 1959-91 (Chatto and Windus, 1992).

A Sort of Clowning: Life and Times, 1940-59 (Chatto and Windus, 1990).

Liberty and Legislation (Frank Cass Publishers, 1989).

A Local Habitation: Life and Times, 1918-40 (Chatto and Windus, 1988).

An Idea of Europe (Chatto and Windus, 1987).

The Worst of Times: An Oral History of the Great Depression in Britain (with Nigel Gray) (Barnes and Noble Imports, 1986).

British Council and the Arts (British Council, 1986).

The Future of Broadcasting (with Janet Morgan) (Holmes and Meier, 1982).

An English Temper (Chatto and Windus, 1982).

An Idea and Its Servants: UNESCO from Within (Chatto and Windus, 1978).

After Expansion, a Time for Diversity: The Universities Into the 1990's (ACACE, 1978).

Only Connect: On Culture and Communication (Reith Lectures) (Chatto and Windus, 1972).

Speaking to Each Other, Volume 1: About Society (Chatto and Windus, 1970).

Speaking to Each Other, Volume 2: About Literature (Chatto and Windus, 1970).

Contemporary Cultural Studies: An Approach to the Study of Literature and Society (Univesity of Birmingham, Centre for Contempory Cultural Studies, 1969).

Higher Education and Cultural Change: A Teacher's View (Earl Grey Memorial Lecture) (University of Newcastle, 1966).

Teaching Literature (National Institute of Adult Education, 1963).

The Uses of Literacy: Aspects of Working-Class Life (Chatto and Windus, 1957).

Auden (Chatto and Windus, 1951).

NOTES ON CONTRIBUTORS

Michael Bailey teaches in the Sociology Department at the University of Essex. He is the author or editor of *Understanding Richard Hoggart: A Pedagogy of Hope* (with Ben Clarke and John K. Walton), *The Assault on Universities: A Manifesto for Resistance* (with Des Freedman), *Mediating Faiths: Religion and Socio-Cultural Change in the Twenty-First Century* (with Guy Redden), and *Narrating Media History*. He has held visiting fellowships at Goldsmiths, the London School of Economics, and at the University of Cambridge.

Peter Bailey is Emeritus Professor of History at the University of Manitoba and Visiting Scholar at Indiana University. He was Leverhulme Fellow at the University of Hertfordshire, 2004-5. He is widely published in the history of leisure, gender and sexuality in modern Britain, notably *Popular Culture and Performance in the Victorian City* (Cambridge, 1998) and is completing a social and cultural history of music hall and the variety stage in the nineteenth and twentieth century. A jazz pianist, Peter Bailey (a.k.a. Porridge Foot Pete) also writes on the history of jazz in Britain.

Rosalind Brunt was taught by Richard Hoggart when she was an undergraduate in the English Department, Birmingham University and later as a postgraduate student at the Centre for Contemporary Cultural Studies. She contributed the 'Postscript' essay to Richard Hoggart's article, 'Mass Communication in Britain' for the revised edition of *The Pelican Guide to English Literature*, Vol. 7, edited by Boris Ford (Penguin, 1973). She is currently Research Fellow in Media Studies at Sheffield Hallam University and co-editor of *Postcolonial Media Culture in Britain* (Palgrave, 2010).

Ben Clarke is Assistant Professor of English at the University of North Carolina at Greensboro. He has published on subjects including Richard Hoggart, George Orwell, Virginia Woolf, Englishness, and Western anthropological writing on Taiwan. His first book, *Orwell in Context*, was issued by Palgrave Macmillan in 2007, and he is co-author (with Michael Bailey and John Walton) of *Understanding Richard Hoggart*, which will be published by Wiley-Blackwell in 2011. He is currently writing a new monograph on political and aesthetic experimentation in British literature of the nineteen-thirties.

John Corner is currently Visiting Professor in the Institute for Communication Studies at the University of Leeds and an Emeritus Professor of the University of Liverpool. He has published widely in books and journals and his major works include *Television Form and Public Address* (Arnold, 1995), *The Art of Record* (Manchester, 1996) and *Critical Ideas in Television Studies* (Oxford, 1999). Recent publications include the edited collection *Media and the Restyling of Politics* (with Dick Pels, Sage, 2003) and the authored volume *Public Issue Television* (with Peter Goddard and Kay Richardson, Manchester University Press, 2007). His current research includes inquiry into documentary form and the relationship between media and political culture.

Macdonald Daly is Associate Professor in the Department of Culture, Film and Media at the University of Nottingham. He has published widely on literature, culture and media, and is the author of the books *Reading Radio 4* and *Politics and the Scottish Language*.

Mary Eagleton was formerly Professor of Contemporary Women's Writing at Leeds Metropolitan University,. She has published extensively in the fields of women's writing and feminist literary studies, including *A Concise Companion to Feminist Theory* (Blackwell, 2003) and *Figuring the Woman Author in Contemporary Fiction* (Palgrave, 2005), the third edition of her classic, *Feminist Literary Theory: A Reader* (Wiley-Blackwell, 2011) and on an essay on the construction of women's literary lives. She has wide experience in editing, in producing collections of essays and special issues of journals and on editorial boards. She is the founder of the Contemporary Women's Writing Association and founding editor of the journal, *Contemporary Women's Writing* (Oxford University Press).

Alice Ferrebe is Senior Lecturer in English at Liverpool John Moores University. She is the author of *Masculinity in Male-Authored Fiction 1950-2000* (Palgrave, 2005) and the 1950s volume in the Edinburgh History of Twentieth Century Literature in Britain series, entitled *Good, Brave Causes* (Edinburgh University Press, forthcoming 2011).

Corey Gibson is a Ph.D. candidate in the English Literature Department at the University of Edinburgh. His research is focussed on the cultural-political climate of twentieth-century Scotland, particularly with literary figures of the Left. He is a Carnegie Trust scholar, and has published book reviews in the *Scottish Literary Review*, and an article in the cultural magazine *The Drouth*. He has also contributed to a collection of essays, *Borne on the Carrying Stream: the Legacy of Hamish Henderson* (Grace Note Publications, 2010).

Michael Green was formerly Head of Cultural Studies and Sociology, University of Birmingham, and has also taught at universities in California, France, Germany, Canada and Taiwan. In association with Richard Hoggart, he edited *English and Cultural Studies: Broadening the Context* (1987), and also wrote on cultural studies in P. Widdowson (ed.), *Re-Reading English* (1982), M. Payne (ed.), *A Dictionary of Critical and Cultural Theory* (1996) and J. McGuigan (ed.), *Cultural Methodologies* (1997). He has co-directed research projects on equal opportunities in London housing associations, on social need in Sutton Coldfield, and on widening museum audiences.

Stuart Hall is Professor Emeritus at the Open University. He was Director of the Centre for Contemporary Cultural Studies at the University of Birmingham and Professor of Sociology at the Open University. He was a founding editor of *New Left Review*, and is the co-author of numerous books including *The Popular Arts* (1964); *Policing the Crisis* (1978); *The Hard Road to Renewal* (1988); *Resistance Through Rituals* (1989); *Modernity and its Future* (1992); *What is Black in Popular Culture?* (1992); *Cultural Representations and Signifying Practices* (1997); and *Visual Culture* (1999).

Tracy Hargreaves is Senior Lecturer in Modern and Contemporary Literature at the University of Leeds. She has published on a range of twentieth-century writers and adaptation and is the author of *Donna Tartt's The Secret History* (Continuum, 2002) and *Androgyny in Modern Literature* (Palgrave, 2004). She is currently working on a monograph, provisionally titled *Culture and Intimacy, 1945-1968*.

Bill Hughes recently completed his PhD on communicative rationality and the Enlightenment dialogue in relation to the formation of the English novel at the Department of English Literature, University of Sheffield. He has a chapter in *Richard Hoggart and Cultural Studies*, edited by Sue Owen (Palgrave, 2008). He has also published and is preparing articles on the dialogic aspect of eighteenth-century theories of language, the eroticism of knowledge in Fontenelle, the novelistic proto-feminism of Bernard Mandeville, and contemporary fictions of the undead.

Yudhishthir Raj Isar is Professor of Cultural Policy Studies at the American University of Paris and Maître de Conférence at the Institut d'Etudes Politiques (SciencesPo). He joined UNESCO in 1973 as Personal Assistant to Richard Hoggart and later held the posts of Director of Cultural Policies, Director of the International Fund for the Promotion of Culture, and Executive Secretary of the World Commission on Culture and Development. He was then appointed as President of *Culture Action Europe* from 2004-2008. He is co-editor of the *Cultures and Globalization Series* (SAGE) and a board member of, or advisor to various cultural organisations in Europe, North America and Asia.

James McGrath completed his Ph.D. in the School of Cultural Studies at Leeds Metropolitan University, where he teaches English Literature, Media and Popular Culture. He has published articles in *Interdisciplinary Literary Studies, Soundscapes, The Big Issue* and *The Independent.* His book reviews of poetry, fiction, memoir and cultural studies have appeared in *PN Review, Popular Music, The Journal of Literary and Cultural Disability Studies* and *Estudios Irlandeses*. He is currently writing a monograph on John Lennon and Paul McCartney's work, with particular attention to ideas of class.

Sean Nixon is Senior Lecturer in the Department of Sociology at the University of Essex. He is author of *Hard Looks: Masculinities, Spectatorship and Contemporary Consumption* (UCL Press, 1996 and St. Martin's Press, NY, 1996) and *Advertising Cultures: Gender, Commerce, Creativity* (Sage, 2003). He is currently completing a study of post-war advertising in Britain titled, *Hard Sell: Advertising, Affluence and Social Change in Post-war Britain* (Manchester University Press, forthcoming).

Sue Owen is Honorary Professor of English Literature and Cultural Analysis at the University of Sheffield, having retired in 2009. She has published books and numerous articles on a range of subjects (Restoration Drama, Aphra Behn, Andrew Marvell, drink in literature, among others) and is the editor of *A Babel of Bottles: Drink, Drinkers and Drinking Places in Literature,* (Sheffield Academic Press, 2000), *Richard Hoggart and Cultural Studies* (Palgrave, 2008) and *Re-reading Richard Hoggart* (Cambridge Scholars, 2008). She organised 'The Uses of Richard Hoggart', an international, cross-disciplinary conference on Richard Hoggart at Sheffield in April 2006 and co-edited with John Hartley the special Hoggart issue of the *International Journal of Cultural Studies* (2007). She is working on a book-length critical study of Richard Hoggart.

Jeremy Seabrook is a widely acclaimed author, playwright and journalist specialising in social, environmental and development issues. He has written over forty books including *The Unprivileged* (1967), *City Close-Up* (1971), *What Went Wrong?* (1978), *Mother and Son* (1980), *Working Class Childhood* (1982), *Unemployment* (1982), *A World Still to Win: The*

Reconstruction of the Post-War Working Class (with Trevor Blackwell, 1985), *Consuming Cultures: Globalization and Local Lives* (2004), *The Refuge and the Fortress: Britain and the Flight From Tyranny* (2008). He currently contributes to the *Guardian*, *New Statesman* and *New Internationalist*.

Nick Stevenson is a Reader in Cultural Sociology at the University of Nottingham. He is the author of *Cultural Citizenship* (2003) and *David Bowie* (2006). He is currently finishing a book on education and cultural citizenship.

INDEX

Also available from

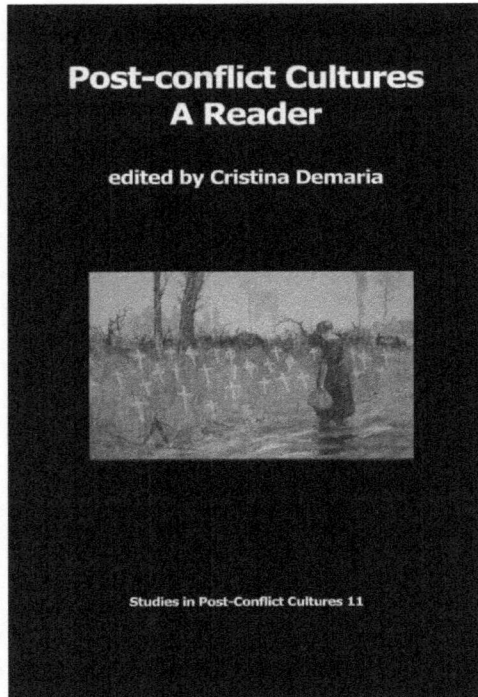

CCCP

Post-conflict Cultures
A Reader

edited by Cristina Demaria

Studies in Post-Conflict Cultures 11

Within the human sciences, as in the ever-growing field of memory and trauma studies, works on memories and post-memories of conflicts have been numerous. They have explored the ways in which the representation of individual and collective memories are closely linked to the building and rebuilding of national and transnational, local and diasporic cultures. Yet, even within such studies, rarely has the category of post-conflict been associated directly with that of culture, that is to an interpretation of conflicts, collective violence and wars, centred on the disruption of symbolic systems of cultural reproduction. This cultural dimension is what the Studies in Post-Conflict Cultures series has dedicated itself to investigating. This landmark anthology offers a generous selection from the volumes so far published in the series.

528 pp. ISBN 9781905510672
Date of Publication: 1 February 2020

Other books in the Post-Conflict Cultures series from

CCCP

Post-Conflict Cultures: Rituals of Representation

Hors de Combat: The Falklands-Malvinas Conflict in Retrospect

Diaspora(s): Movements and Cultures

Happiness and Post-Conflict

Disrespect Today, Conflict Tomorrow:
The Politics of Economic, Social and Cultural Rights

Writing Under Socialism

The Genres of Post-Conflict Testimonies

Post-Conflict Reconstructions: Re-Mappings and Reconciliations

MemoSur/ MemoSouth: Memory, Commemoration
and Trauma in Post-Dictatorship Argentina

Spanish Conquest, Protestant Prejudice: Las Casas and the Black Legend

Media Stories in the Falklands-Malvinas Conflict

Valley of the Fallen: The (N)ever Changing Face of General Franco's Monument

The Malvinas Question